A Practical Guide to Software Localization

The LANGUAGE INTERNATIONAL WORLD DIRECTORY is a series of international listings on subjects pertaining to language related practice such as language policy and planning, training, translation, modern tools for teaching, lexicography, terminology, etc.

The LANGUAGE INTERNATIONAL WORLD DIRECTORY is published under the auspices of *Language International: The magazine for language professionals.*

THE LANGUAGE INTERNATIONAL WORLD DIRECTORY

1. *Language International World Directory of Sociolinguistic and Language Planning Organizations* compiled by Francesc Domínguez and Núria López, 1995.

2. *Language International World Directory of Translation and Interpreting Schools* compiled by Brian Harris, 1997.

3. *A Practical Guide to Software Localization* by Bert Esselink, 1998.

Volume 3

Bert Esselink
A Practical Guide to Software Localization

A Practical Guide to Software Localization

JOHN BENJAMINS PUBLISHING COMPANY
AMSTERDAM/PHILADELPHIA

The paper used in this publication meets the minimum requirements of American National Standard for Information Sciences – Permanence of Paper for Printed Library Materials, ANSI Z39.48-1984.

Library of Congress Cataloging-in-Publication Data

Esselink, Bert, 1968-
    A Practical Guide to Software Localization / Bert Esselink
        p.   cm. -- (Language International World Directory, ISSN 1383-7591 ; vol. 3)
    Includes bibliographical references and index.
        1. Software localization   2. Software documentation. I. Title. II. Series.
OA76.76.D63E87   1998
005.1 -- dc 21   98-30385
ISBN 90 272 1953 2 (Eur.) / 1-55619-742-X (US) (Hb; alk. paper)   CIP
ISBN 90 272 1954 0 (Eur.) / 1-55619-743-8 (US) (Pb; alk. paper)

John Benjamins Publishing Co. • P.O. Box 75577 • 1070 AN Amsterdam • The Netherlands
John Benjamins North America • P.O. Box 27519 • Philadelphia, PA 19118-0519 • USA

Preface

Writing about software localization is like fighting against time. Just when you think you've covered the software localization process, a new localization tool is introduced. Just when you think you've explained how to translate a FrameMaker document, a new version of Frame is announced. Just when you think you've found the perfect Web site, the pages are moved.

Although the localization world is changing so rapidly, there are many issues, procedures, and tools that have been used for years and that will probably be applied for years to come. This book provides you with an overview of the most common issues in today's software localization, seen from a translator's, engineer's and project manager's view.

To keep up to date with the most recent developments, revisions in this book, or last-minute additions, visit the Language International Web site at www.language-international.com, where updates will be posted regularly.

A Practical Guide to Software Localization covers many of the things a localizer will come across. It contains chapters on translating software, translating online help and documentation, translation memory tools, project management, and terminology management. Still, numerous issues are not covered by this book, such as internationalization, double-byte localization, multimedia localization, and operating systems such as OS/2 and UNIX. Although the examples in this book are applicable to most languages, they reference a typical localization project translated from English into French, Italian, German and Spanish. The platforms discussed are Microsoft's Windows and Apple's MacOS.

Over the past few years, there have been numerous publications about software localization and internationalization. So far, most of these books were addressed to software developers, Web site designers, and international marketing managers. The daily tasks and responsibilities of project managers, localization engineers, and–most importantly– translators, has never been given much attention.

A Practical Guide to Software Localization was written to fill that gap.

I would like to thank my colleagues at International Software Products and Alpnet in Amsterdam for everything they have taught me over the past six years. Special thanks to Amancio Quant and Arjen-Sjoerd de Vries for helping me with the documentation and project management chapters, and Sue Ellen Wright for reviewing the book so thoroughly. Finally, I would like to thank Caroline for her incredible patience and support.

Bert Esselink, Haarlem 1998

Trademarks

Table Of Contents

CHAPTER 1: INTRODUCING LOCALIZATION..1

1   WHAT IS LOCALIZATION? 1
   1.1   Internationalization 1
   1.2   Localization 2
   1.3   Globalization 3
   1.4   Translation 3
2   WHAT IS LOCALIZED? 4
   2.1   Software...4
   2.2   Online Help 4
   2.3   Documentation 4
3   WHO IS INVOLVED IN LOCALIZATION?...5
4   HISTORY AND FUTURE...6
   4.1   Market Developments...6
   4.2   Localization Service Providers...7
   4.3   Technology 8

CHAPTER 2: TRANSLATING SOFTWARE 9

1   INTRODUCTION 10
   1.1   Software Components...10
   1.2   Preparation 11
2   WINDOWS...14
   2.1   Introduction 14
   2.2   Resource Files 15
   2.3   Program Files...27
   2.4   Software Localization Tools 37
3   MACINTOSH...50
   3.1   Introduction 50
   3.2   Translating Software 52
   3.3   Translating Installers 69

CHAPTER 3: TRANSLATING ONLINE HELP 71

1   WINDOWS HELP FILES...72
   1.1   Introduction 73
   1.2   Translation 75
2   HTML FILES 86
   2.1   Introduction 86
   2.2   File Format: Overview 87
   2.3   Translation 88

3   MACINTOSH APPLE GUIDE FILES 93
    3.1   *Introduction* 93
    3.2   *Translating Guide Script Files*.. 94
    3.3   *Using Guide Maker*.. 95
    3.4   *Translatable Resources*... 97
    3.5   *Image Resources* 99
4   MACINTOSH HELP FILES 100
    4.1   *QuickHelp Compiler* 100
5   README FILES 101

CHAPTER 4: TRANSLATING DOCUMENTATION **103**

1   INTRODUCTION 103
    1.1   *Preparation*.. 104
2   TRANSLATING MANUALS.. 108
    2.1   *General* 108
    2.2   *Using FrameMaker*... 109
    2.3   *Using Word* 117
    2.4   *Translating Indexes*.. 120
3   TRANSLATING COLLATERAL MATERIAL 122
    3.1   *Using QuarkXPress* 122
    3.2   *Using PageMaker* 125
4   PROOFREADING DOCUMENTATION 127
    4.1   *Accuracy and Consistency* 128
    4.2   *Examples and Screen Captures*.. 128
    4.3   *General Page Layout* 128
    4.4   *Cross-references* 129
5   CREATING ONLINE DOCUMENTATION... 129
    5.1   *Creating Adobe Acrobat PDF Documents*............................. 129
    5.2   *Testing Adobe Acrobat PDF Documents* 132

CHAPTER 5: TRANSLATION MEMORY TOOLS.. **133**

1   INTRODUCTION 134
2   TRADOS TRANSLATOR'S WORKBENCH 136
    2.1   *Software* 137
    2.2   *Help*.. 140
    2.3   *Documentation*.. 141
3   IBM TRANSLATIONMANAGER 142
    3.1   *Software* 142
    3.2   *Help*.. 146
    3.3   *Documentation*.. 146
4   ATRIL DÉJÀ VU 147
    4.1   *Software* 147
    4.2   *Help*.. 149
    4.3   *Documentation*.. 149

5	Miscellaneous		150
	5.1	Amptran	150
	5.2	STAR Transit	151
	5.3	TSS/Joust	152
	5.4	XL8 TransPro	153
	5.5	Eurolang Optimizer	153

CHAPTER 6: LOCALIZATION ENGINEERING **155**

1	Windows		156
	1.1	Software	156
	1.2	Windows Help	188
2	HTML Files		211
	2.1	Localizing Web Sites	211
	2.2	HTML Help	220
3	Macintosh		223
	3.1	Software	223
	3.2	Help	242
4	Other Environments		247
	4.1	Visual Basic	247
	4.2	Delphi	248
	4.3	Java	249

CHAPTER 7: PROJECT MANAGEMENT **251**

1	Creating Quotations		252
	1.1	Components	253
	1.2	Profile Information	257
2	The Localization Process		258
	2.1	Analysis of Received Material	260
	2.2	Scheduling and Budgeting	261
	2.3	Glossary Translation or Terminology Setup	264
	2.4	Preparation of Localization Kit	265
	2.5	Translation of Software	266
	2.6	Translation of Help and Documentation	267
	2.7	Processing Updates	270
	2.8	Testing of Software	270
	2.9	Testing of Help and DTP of Documentation	271
	2.10	Product QA and Delivery	271
	2.11	Post-mortem with Client	272
3	Communication		273
	3.1	Translators	273
	3.2	Clients	273
4	Structured Project Management		274
	4.1	Successful Project Management	274
	4.2	Why Projects Fail	275

APPENDIX A: TERMINOLOGY...**277**

  1   GLOSSARY TYPES 277
    1.1   *Operating Environment Glossary*................................277
    1.2   *Client Glossaries*..278
    1.3   *Project Glossaries*..278
    1.4   *Software Glossaries* 279
  2   CREATING SOFTWARE GLOSSARIES 279
    2.1   *Windows*...279
    2.2   *Macintosh*...281
  3   FINDING TERMINOLOGY...282
    3.1   *English Computer Terminology*................................282
    3.2   *Multilingual Glossaries* 283
  4   TERMINOLOGY MANAGEMENT 284
    4.1   *Glossary Tools* 285
  5   STANDARD TERMINOLOGY 290
    5.1   *Keyboard Key Names*..290
    5.2   *Readme File Names* 290

APPENDIX B: LOCALIZATION RESOURCES **291**

  1   WEB SITES 291
  2   NEWSGROUPS...293
  3   MAILING LISTS 294
  4   MAGAZINES AND NEWSLETTERS...295
  5   BOOKS 297
  6   COMPANIES...298
    6.1   *Localization Service Providers*................................298
    6.2   *Translation Tools Developers*...................................300

INDEX..**303**

Chapter 1:
Introducing Localization

*In this chapter, you will find general information about
localization, those who are involved in localization, and the
history and future of software localization.*

M any different definitions for and ideas about localization are used in the
software industry. In the approximately 15 years that software applications have
been localized, localization has progressed from an extra effort by some
software publishers to a huge and professional industry sector. Software internationalization
and localization has become an important issue for companies that want to sell their
products in countries where other languages are spoken.

The following sections will tell you what localization is, which products are localized, and
who are involved in localization. The chapter will end with some statistical and technical
information about the past and future of localization.

1   What is localization?

In the localization industry, several terms are used in relation to the localization of software
products. In the next section, you will find definitions for the most commonly used terms:
internationalization, localization, globalization, and translation.

1.1   Internationalization

During development, the software is designed in a way to allow for translation into other
languages without the need for re-design or re-compilation.

An important aspect of internationalization is the separation of text and source code.
Translatable, user-visible text should be moved to separate strings-only resource files that
will prevent translators from translating–or breaking–the program code.

Central in internationalization is the ability to represent the character set of a particular
language. If a software product is to be translated into Japanese, for example, it must
support double-byte characters. Besides, different foreign keyboard layouts should be
supported.

Examples of internationalization errors that should be prevented by internationalizing during software development are:

- Length restrictions. Typically, translated text is 30% longer than the English original, but the increase may be as much as 100 percent.

- Fixed date, time, number, or currency formats. Apart from the different date/time and decimal separators, the order is also important. For example, 6/10/97 means 10 June 1997 in the United States and 6 October 1997 in European countries.

- Fixed address formats. English-speaking countries generally place the house number before the street name. In most European countries, the street name is written first.

- Jargon or U.S. specific language. For a European user, the expression "stock exchange index" will be more informative than "the Dow". Especially sample files, such as forms or templates, are often not designed for international markets.

- Text in graphics. If a lot of text is included in icons or bitmaps, this will increase localization costs because the text needs to be translated by editing the graphics, which is more time consuming than regular translation work.

- U.S. specific icons. Icons may have different meanings in different countries. Apple's Trashcan icon, for example, initially looked like a postal box to British Macintosh users.

If a product has been internationalized well, it cannot only be sold worldwide, but it can also be easily localized because international issues are already considered during development of the English product.

A term that is often used in the context of internationalization is *enablement*. Enablement is the process of adjusting software to make it usable in certain countries or regions. For example, a software product can be *enabled* to process text used in Far-Eastern countries.

Internationalization is often abbreviated to "I18N", where "18" indicates the number of letters between the "I" and the "n".

1.2 Localization

The process of adapting and translating a software application into another language in order to make it linguistically and culturally appropriate for a particular local market.

> **Note**
>
> Please note that some software developers consider *localization* as a part of the development process of a software product.

A localization project might include the following activities:

- Translation of software

- Translation and desktop publishing (DTP) of help and documentation

- Linguistic and functional testing of software and help

Localization projects may also involve customizing features in the application to country-specific standards, such as date/time formats, communication protocols, currency and financial data, or default paper sizes.

Typically, products are localized from English into other languages because most software applications are still being developed in the United States.

A well-localized product enables users to interact with a software application in their own language. They will be able to read all interface components such as error messages or screen tips in their native language, and they can enter information with all accented characters of their language using the local keyboard layout.

Often "L10N" is used as an abbreviation for localization.

1.3 Globalization

A term used to cover both internationalization and localization. Software developers will "go global" when they start developing, translating and distributing their products for foreign language markets.

Globalization ("G11N") is typically used in a sales and marketing context, i.e., it is the process by which a company breaks free of the home markets to pursue business opportunities wherever their customers may be located.

1.4 Translation

Translation is the process of converting written or displayed text or spoken words to another language.

In localization, translation is not a word-for-word "global replacement" process. It requires accurately conveying the total meaning of the source material into the target language, with special attention to cultural nuance and style.

The user interface, help system, and the documentation are common components of a localization project.

2 What is localized?

Typically, localization projects involve the following components:

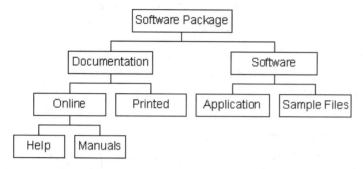

2.1 Software

Today, a software product is usually distributed on a set of disks, CD-ROM or through the Internet. Setup disks contain compressed installation files that are uncompressed and copied to the hard disk by a setup program. After installation, applications on the hard disk typically consist of several program files (EXE, DLL, DRV, etc.), help files (HLP, HTML, CHM, etc.) and readme files (WRI, TXT, etc.).

The names or extensions of these files may differ per platform. On the Macintosh platform, for example, file extensions are not used. Instead, program components are identified by their file type, creator, and icons.

More and more applications are distributed on CD-ROM. Because these disks can store a large amount of data (up to 700 MB), software manufacturers often include sample files, tutorials (CBTs), demos, and trial versions of other products with the application.

2.2 Online Help

Online help consists of hypertext documents that usually can be accessed from within the application. Typically, these documents are context-sensitive. This means that from within a particular section of the application it is possible to directly access help about that section, for example a dialog box.

2.3 Documentation

Increasingly, software developers include online documentation with their software products instead of printed documentation. This not only reduces printing costs, but also makes it easier to distribute updates or fixes to the documentation via the Internet or another online service.

2.3.1   Printed Documentation

Most software products come with one or two manuals, typically an Installation Guide and a Getting Started Guide. The Installation Guide will tell the user how to install the application. A Getting Started Guide will typically provide a short introduction to the application.

Other types of printed documents that are often included with software packages are tutorials, quick reference cards, marketing materials, and promotional material. These documents are often referred to as *collateral material.*

2.3.2   Online Documentation

Online manuals are electronic versions of the manuals that may also have been included in printed form. These files are usually in an electronic exchange format, such as Adobe Portable Document Format (PDF). Users can open these files using a helper application and print the sections or pages that they need.

Sometimes, software products are partially localized for certain target markets. For example, a software developer can decide to only translate the software and not documentation, or only parts of the documentation. More and more, Installation Guides and Getting Started Guides are translated and Administrator or Reference Manuals are included in English.

3 Who is involved in localization?

Typically, software products are localized by one of–or a combination of–the following parties:

- The software developer, with in-house translation staff

- The software developer's subsidiary in the target language country

- The distributor of the software in the target language country

- A localization vendor

Increasingly, software developers are outsourcing localization projects to specialized localization/translation vendors to avoid large in-house localization groups that only have work for limited periods of time.

In localization agencies, the people involved in a typical localization project are:

- Project Manager

- Translator

- Localization Specialist/Senior Translator

- Proofreader/QA Specialist

- Localization Engineer

- Testing Engineer

- Desktop Publisher

The project manager schedules the project, assigns resources, reports to the client, and monitors the project workflow. Localization specialists review the work that translators do and manage terminology. Localization engineers are responsible for all technical aspects of software localization projects, such as software and help engineering, compiling and testing. Often, dedicated testing engineers take care of the final, functionality testing of a translated product.

Desktop publishers take care of the layout of the printed or online material and sometimes do preparation for pre-press production. Translated software, help, and documentation files are proofread by a dedicated proofreader or editor.

4 History and Future

The localization industry is relatively young. Until approximately 15 years ago, U.S.-based software developers usually did not realize there was a need for internationalized and localized products. This has changed dramatically since the beginning of the nineties. Especially the growth of the Internet has made it much easier for American software developers to market and distribute their products overseas.

Ireland is the world center of localization. The main reasons for this development was the positive tax situation enforced by the European Union and the number of skilled people available. Most major software firms have a significant presence in the field in this country.

4.1 Market Developments

Historically, the largest markets for localized products have been France, Germany, and Japan. Medium-sized markets are Italy, Spain, Sweden, Norway, and the Netherlands. Software developers often want their products localized into FIGS (French, Italian, German, Spanish) and Japanese first. These languages may be followed by Swedish, Norwegian, Danish, Dutch or Brazilian Portuguese.

According to an OVUM report that was published in Language International , Vol 9.3 (1997), worldwide revenues from software product localization will have increased from US$ 396 million in 1994 to US$ 2,389 million in the year 2000. The total of worldwide revenues for globalization-related services will increase from US$ 2,831 million in 1997 to US$ 6,264 million in 2000.

The OVUM report forecasts that Japanese will account for 31% of all localization service revenues, with German following at 12% in 2000.

Because the localization industry grows at a yearly average of 30%, the need for localization specialists is more obvious than ever. Translators need more computer knowledge, engineers need more language skills. Many translation schools and universities are acknowledging this market potential and are starting localization courses.

4.2 Localization Service Providers

Most software developers are outsourcing translation and localization activities to localization service providers. In the 1980's, large in-house localization divisions were commonplace. Today, these divisions have either been closed or reduced to just a quality assurance department. Often, only a localization manager remains to function as a link between the development department and the localization vendor.

Around 1996, major mergers and consolidations have taken place in the localization industry, resulting in a dozen of large service providers with offices all over the world. Not only have many smaller localization companies been bought by global ones, many partnerships were also formed to create worldwide networks of offices.

Most software developers today are interested in working with *multilingual vendors* (MLV) who will take care of a range of target languages. Multilingual vendors are highly specialized firms, having expertise both in languages and in technology. The main benefit of this approach is that project management and technical activities are centralized in one location.

Another approach for localization projects is risk spreading, where software developers divide the languages between different localization agencies to spread the risk when things go wrong. Because localization agencies want to offer as many languages as possible, many of them have subsidiaries or partners in other countries.

4.3 Technology

The past years have also shown a change in international software development. Software application users are able to produce multilingual content without any special international software support or add-ons. On the other hand, software engineers are more aware of international issues and learn how to integrate international support in their products.

One important technology in localization is the Unicode standard. Unicode offers a solution to the character sets problem, i.e., it offers support for all scripts that are being used around the world today. The Unicode standard uses two bytes for each character instead of just one and it is being implemented throughout the Microsoft Windows platforms, Macintosh operating system, and other computing platforms. Unicode merged with the ISO/JEC 10646 standard in 1991 to form version 2.0 of the Unicode standard.

Another major change in international software development has been the introduction of a *single worldwide binary*. Single worldwide binary means that there is only one version of your program, which can handle all of the world's languages. This single binary is often combined with *resource-only DLLs* in which all of the application's user interface text, such as dialog boxes, menus and strings, is centralized. All program code is separated from the resources, which means that running an application in another language can be done just by replacing the resource-only DLL with a localized version.

Chapter 2:
Translating Software

This chapter contains information for translators of software files. Topics include translation of software on Windows and Macintosh platforms, as well as several examples of software localization tools that can be used.

Most localization projects start with the translation of the software. In an ideal situation, the translation of help and documentation does not start until the software is fully translated and validated. Since this does not always happen, terminology management is very important. For more information about terminology, refer to the Terminology Management section on page 284.

It is essential that translators know the meaning of every option or command they translate. For this reason, translators should always be provided with sufficient reference information, such as the English version of the online help or documentation files, even if these are not yet final.

Providing translators with sufficient reference material is important for the following reasons:

- Knowing the exact function of each option makes choosing the right translation easier.

- The first translation of the software should be as final as possible. Changing software translations later in the localization process will imply updating of the online help files and documentation that may have been (partly) translated based on the first software translations.

If previous versions of the translated product exist, glossaries should be provided to avoid terminology inconsistencies between versions.

1 Introduction

This section provides a general overview of the software translation process. It lists all elements that are being considered for localization, different resource file types, and commonly used software localization tools.

1.1 Software Components

Typically, in a software application, the following components are translated:

- Dialog boxes

- Menus

- Strings

1.1.1 Dialog boxes

Dialog boxes are the windows or screens where users can change options or settings. Most operating systems support the use of *tabbed* dialog boxes.

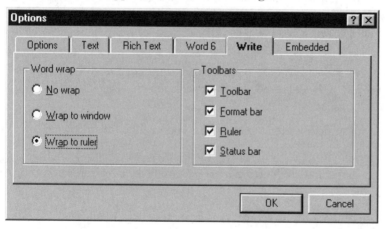

1.1.2   Menus

Menus are the drop-down lists that are used to select commands and options, or to access dialog boxes. Menu or button commands that are followed by three dots open a dialog box with options. Choosing a menu command without dots immediately executes a task.

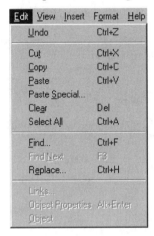

1.1.3   Strings

Strings contain the error messages, status messages, questions, and tooltips that are used in the application.

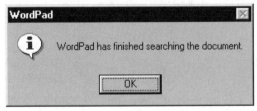

1.2 Preparation

Preparation is an essential step in software localization projects. Software translators should be provided with all the necessary reference material and tools, and it should be made clear exactly what should be translated.

1.2.1   Requirements

If possible, software translators should be provided with the following:

- All hardware and software necessary to run the application that is to be translated

- A version of the operating system (DOS, Windows, Macintosh) in the language of the application to be translated

- The English version of the application to be translated, including the online help and, if available, documentation

- In case of updates, the previously translated version of the software application

- Online glossaries of the operating system and, in case of updates, previous versions of the translated software. In addition, glossaries of competitive products or other products from the same client might be a useful source of information.

1.2.2   File Management

To structure your work and avoid loss of information, create a work directory or folder on your computer's hard drive or on the network in which all your translations are stored.

For example, create a folder called \Work with subfolders like *project_name_1* and *project_name_2* in the root of your hard drive or on the network. Next, subdivide these folders into a \Glossary, \Source and \Target folder.

Subdivide the source and target folder into project component folders, such as:

\Docs – for documentation files
\Exe – for compiled software files
\Sw – for software resource files
\Help – for help files.

Also, add an \Admin folder to your project folder, in which you can store the files you have received and sent, word counts, project status reports, and other project-related documents.

> **Tip:**
>
> If you choose a name like \Aawork or _Work for your work folder, it will always appear at the top of folder lists.

The following illustration shows an example of a work folder hierarchy:

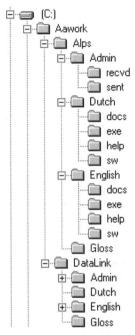

There are many advantages to storing all your project files in one central work folder with an identical folder hierarchy:

- It is easier to locate and backup all the relevant files, not just for yourself but also for colleagues working on the same project.

- If you store your work in a folder named after the project in the root of your hard drive, there is a risk of losing your work when you install the application. If, for example, you are translating an application called DataLink, do not store your work in a folder called C:\DataLink. It is possible that the DataLink Installer will delete all the files in this folder because the application is installed in the same location.

- You can use a folder synchronization tool to systematically keep the files on the network up-to-date with the files on your local hard drive, or vice versa.

- You keep a copy of the original English files for later reference.

2 Windows

2.1 Introduction

A software application for Microsoft Windows consists of a set of files, which can be subdivided into four categories: executables (EXE or COM), additional program files like drivers (DRV) or dynamic link libraries (DLL), help files (HLP, CHM and CNT), and readme files (TXT, DOC or WRI).

All of these file types may contain translatable strings or text.

The executables and program files contain the menus, dialog boxes, commands, and messages associated with the application. Increasingly, software developers include all user interface elements in a separate DLL file, called a satellite DLL or a resource-only DLL, which is the only file that requires translation. In Microsoft Windows NT 5, for example, all user interface elements are isolated from the binary code, which means that a user can switch the language of the user interface at run-time.

Software files can be translated in two ways, either in text-only *resource files* or directly in the binary *program files*:

- *Resource files* (typically files with the extension RC or DLG) are text-only files that contain all localizable application components, such as messages, menus, dialog boxes, default settings for languages, and country codes. These files can be translated using a Windows-based text editor or word processor. After translation, they need to be compiled into binary program files.

- *Program files* (typically files with the file extension DLL or EXE) need to be translated in a resource editor like Microsoft App Studio or Borland (now called Inprise) Resource Workshop. The advantage of translating already compiled DLL files is that you immediately see how your translation will be displayed in the actual dialog box or menu. Translators know immediately what impact their translations will have on the user interface layout. In addition, dialog boxes can be resized directly in these files to make translations fit. Some software localization tools also allow for direct translation of program files. Examples of these tools can be found in the Software Localization Tools section on page 37.

It is also possible to open and translate text-only resource code files directly in a resource editor, such as Microsoft Developer Studio, which has all the advantages of translating directly in binary program files. One risk of this method is that different resource editors or even different versions of the same editor may change the structure of the resource files.

The following sections discuss how resource files and program files are translated.

2.2 Resource Files

Resource files contain all user interface information for an application, such as menu items, dialog box titles and options, error messages, and strings. They are compiled into program files using a resource compiler such as Microsoft Visual C or Borland C. Because resource files are in text-only format, they contain no formatting, such as bold or italic text.

2.2.1 File Format

Windows resource files should be saved as Windows text only (ANSI). To make sure the translated files are saved in the correct format, translate them using an editor that runs in the target environment. For example, translate Windows resource files in a Windows-based text editor or word processor, such as Notepad or Word for Windows.

2.2.2 Extensions

Resource files for Windows applications usually have the extension RC or DLG. However, it is possible that files with other extensions are part of the software, such as files with the STR, TXS or TXT extension, and require translation.

A localization engineer or technical translator should identify the files that require translation. Refer to the Preparing for Translation section on page 158 for more information.

2.2.3 File Contents

In Windows resource files, only text that is placed between quotation marks is translated. Surrounding programming code should not be changed. Resource files are subdivided in the three sections that were explained in the introduction of this chapter: dialog boxes, menus, and strings.

2.2.3.1 DIALOG BOXES

In a Windows resource file, a dialog box section looks like this:

```
14 DIALOG FIXED IMPURE  0, 0, 356, 196
STYLE DS_MODALFRAME | DS_3DLOOK | DS_CONTEXTHELP | WS_POPUP |
WS_VISIBLE | WS_CAPTION | WS_SYSMENU
CAPTION "Page Setup"
FONT 8, "MS Sans Serif"
BEGIN
     GROUPBOX          "Paper",1073,8,9,224,56,WS_GROUP
     LTEXT             "Si&ze:",1089,16,24,36,8
     COMBOBOX          1137,64,23,160,160,CBS_DROPDOWNLIST | CBS_SORT |
                       WS_VSCROLL | WS_GROUP | WS_TABSTOP
     LTEXT             "&Source:",1090,16,45,36,8
     COMBOBOX          1138,64,42,160,160,CBS_DROPDOWNLIST | CBS_SORT |
                       WS_VSCROLL | WS_GROUP | WS_TABSTOP
     GROUPBOX          "Orientation",1072,8,69,64,56,WS_GROUP
     CONTROL           "P&ortrait",1056,"Button",BS_AUTORADIOBUTTON |
WS_GROUP |
                       WS_TABSTOP,16,82,52,12
 ...
     DEFPUSHBUTTON     "OK",1,190,174,50,14,WS_GROUP
     PUSHBUTTON        "Cancel",2,244,174,50,14
     PUSHBUTTON        "&Printer...",1026,298,174,50,14
     GROUPBOX          "Preview",34,240,8,108,158
     CONTROL           "",1080,"Static",SS_WHITERECT,254,46,80,80
     CONTROL           "",1081,"Static",SS_GRAYRECT,334,50,4,80
     CONTROL           "",1082,"Static",SS_GRAYRECT,262,122,80,4
END
```

After compilation, the dialog box will look like this in the running program:

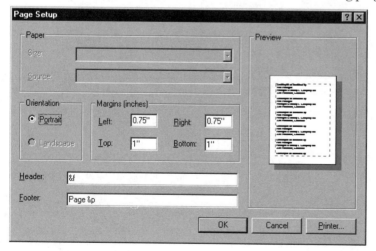

In this example, the word DIALOG in the first line indicates that the section defines a dialog box. All dialog box objects, called controls, are identified by words like PUSHBUTTON (a button), GROUPBOX (field title) or LTEXT (option).

The ampersand (&) character defines the hot keys. Refer to the Hot Keys section on page 18 for more information.

Theoretically, in software resource files all text between double quotes needs to be translated. However, this is not always true. In the dialog box example above, "MS Sans Serif" is the name of the font used in the dialog box, which should not be changed. Another example is "Button", which indicates the control type.

The numbers at the end of each line contain information about the size and position of the item. For example, in the example the numbers in the "Paper" control line indicate that the Paper field starts 8 positions from the left, and 9 positions from the top side of the dialog box. The width of the Paper field is 224 and the height is 56.

Mostly, size values need to be adjusted to make a translated string fit in a button or dialog box. This resizing work is performed in a resource editor or in the text-only resource files. Refer to the Resizing section on page 167 for more information.

2.2.3.2   MENUS

In a Windows resource file, a menu section looks like this:

```
6 MENU FIXED IMPURE
BEGIN
    POPUP "&File"
    BEGIN
        MENUITEM "&New...\tCtrl+N",              57600
        MENUITEM "&Open...\tCtrl+O",             57601
        MENUITEM "&Save\tCtrl+S",                57603
        MENUITEM "Save &As...",                  57604
        MENUITEM SEPARATOR
        MENUITEM "&Print...\tCtrl+P",            57607
        MENUITEM "Print Pre&view",               57608
        MENUITEM "Page Set&up...",               32771
        MENUITEM SEPARATOR
        MENUITEM "Recent File",                  57616, GRAYED
        MENUITEM SEPARATOR
        MENUITEM "Sen&d...",                     57611
        MENUITEM SEPARATOR
        MENUITEM "E&xit",                        57665
    END
    MENUITEM SEPARATOR
    MENUITEM SEPARATOR
END
```

After compilation, the menu text will look like this when the program is run:

In this example, the word MENU in the first line indicates that the following section is a drop-down menu. The MENUITEM lines define the commands and separation lines.

The ampersand (&) character defines the hot keys. Refer to the Hot Keys section on page 18 for more information. Some commands are followed by three dots, which indicates that they will open a dialog box. The \t variable will insert a tab in the menu command during compilation. Some of the commands are followed by Control keys. Refer to the Control Keys (Shortcut Keys) section on page 19 for more information.

2.2.3.2.1   Hot Keys

In menu commands and dialog box options, one of the letters is marked, i.e., underlined. This is the hot key (accelerator or mnemonic key), which is used to activate a certain command by pressing it in combination with the Alt key. Hot keys provide an alternative way to access menu commands or dialog box options.

2.2.3.2.1.1   *Hot Key Symbol*

In Windows resource files, hot keys are preceded by the ampersand (&) symbol. The menu string "&Open..." in a resource file, for example, will appear as *Open...* in the running application. Files written in Visual Basic use the tilde (~) instead of the ampersand.

2.2.3.2.1.2   *Uniqueness*

A hot key may only be used once in a menu or dialog box. Usually, localization engineers will ensure that each menu or dialog box is using unique hot keys. Refer to the Checking Hot Keys section on page 169 for more information.

Submenus are treated as separate menus. This means that a hot key that is already used in a menu may be re-used in a submenu of that menu.

2.2.3.2.1.3   Operating Environment

Consistency with the hot keys used in the target operating environment is important. Especially for the standard commands, such as Open, Save, Print, Copy, and Paste, consistent hot keys should be used.

For example, in Windows applications the hot keys for the menu options *Open...* and *Save...* are always the letters O and S. In German, the translations are consistently *Öffnen* and *Speichern*, with the hot keys on *f* and S.

Try to stay consistent with other Windows applications in your language.

For Windows 3.1, you will find the translations and hot keys for common commands in the Microsoft GUI Guide. Terminology extracted from Windows 95/98/NT and other Microsoft software can be found on the Microsoft Developer Network CD-ROMs or Microsoft's FTP server at ftp.microsoft.com/developr/msdn/newup/glossary.

2.2.3.2.1.4   Accented Characters

Preferably, hot keys should not be used on accented characters because not all keyboards contain keys that support the accented characters.

For example, if the German translation for the Open command, *Öffnen*, had a hot key on the first letter, users with a non-German keyboard would not be able to type the hot key letter in combination with the Alt key.

Accented characters should only be used as accelerators when there really are no other letters or characters available.

2.2.3.2.2   Control Keys (Shortcut Keys)

In most applications, it is also possible to activate commands by pressing the Ctrl key in combination with a function key or letter. For example, in most Windows-based applications, pressing Ctrl+S will save the current file, and pressing Ctrl+P will print the file.

2.2.3.2.2.1   Function Keys

Ctrl keys that are used in combination with function keys (such as Ctrl+F12 for the Preferences command) should never be changed.

2.2.3.2.2.2   Letters or Symbols

Combinations of the Ctrl key with a letter, such as Ctrl+C for Copy, or a number or symbol, such as Ctrl+= or Ctrl+9, may be changed by the translator or localization engineer. However, it is preferable to keep them identical to the original version. Check the Windows version in your language to see if the Control keys have been translated, for example in Wordpad or any Microsoft Office application.

Changing Control key combinations might be necessary when a certain key combination cannot be used on a particular local keyboard. Especially the @ $ { } [ ] \ ~ | ^ ' < > characters can cause problems on non-English keyboards.

In addition, on a French keyboard, Ctrl key combinations with numbers cannot be used because the numbers are always entered using the Shift key. Please discuss with the localization engineers which key combination should be used.

2.2.3.2.2.3   *Uniqueness*

A Control key may only be used once in an application. When Ctrl+P is assigned to the Print command, it cannot be used for another command.

2.2.3.2.2.4   *Key Names*

In many European languages, the key names are also localized. For example, the Shift key is called *Umschalt* in German and *Maj* in French. Refer to the Keyboard Key Names section on page 290 for a complete listing of key name translations.

2.2.3.2.2.5   *Operating Environment*

Many hot key combinations are standard in a certain operating environment, such as Ctrl+B for Bold in Microsoft Windows applications. It is very likely that your language will also have standard combinations. Refer to the operating system glossaries or a Windows version in your language.

If you decide to change a Control key, change it not only in the menu resource item, but also in the Accelerator section of the resource file. For example, if the menu item is `MENUITEM "&Paste\tCtrl+V",` 57637, and you want to change the Control key to Ctrl+U, the Accelerator section of the resource file will have one or more items with the same menu ID number 57637 and a "V" key definition. These items should be changed accordingly.

2.2.3.2.3   **Length Restrictions**

The localized main menu bar must fit on the screen in any resolution, especially standard VGA. When the menu bar does not fit, a common solution is to change the Help menu name to a question mark.

2.2.3.3 STRINGS

In a Windows resource file, a string section looks like this:

```
STRINGTABLE FIXED IMPURE
BEGIN
    100     "OLE initialization failed.  WordPad can not continue."
    102     "Failed to create object. "
    103     "Can't find record %s."
    104     "%d%% complete  Formatting ... please wait"
    105     "%d%% complete"
    106     "Do you wish to save this file in a different format?"
    107     "Do you want to save changes to %1"
    108     "%1 already exists.\nDo you want to replace it?"
    109     "Changes page layout settings\nPage Setup"
    110     "Sets Options\nOptions"
    111     "Inserts a bullet on this line\nBullets"
    112     "EXT"
    113     "CAP"
    114     "NUM"
    115     "Rich Text"
    116     "Word 6"
    117     "The measurement must be between %1 and %2."
    118     "%1 already exists.\nDo you want to replace it?"
    119     "Do you want to save changes to %1?"
    120     "%s to %s"
END
```

In this example, the word STRINGTABLE indicates that the section contains strings. Strings may contain error messages (item 100-103), status messages (104-105), questions (106-108), tooltips/status bar messages (109-111), or keyboard modes (112-114).

String sections are most complex and most time-consuming to translate. Often, messages are cryptic or require in-depth programming, product or context knowledge. A good example are the so-called *single word messages*, such as "None". In many languages, this word can have several translations or grammatical versions, depending on its context.

The following section discusses some of the most common problems that translators experience when translating strings in software resource files.

2.2.3.3.1   Variables

Programmers use many variable parameters in strings. Examples of variables can be seen in strings 104, 105, 107, 108, 117-120 in the example shown above.

Variables are characters that are preceded by a percentage (%) sign and that are replaced by another word, value or string at run-time. For example, string 105 in the example will show up as *65% complete* in the application, and string 119 will be displayed as *Do you want to save changes to SAMPLE.DOC?*

2.2.3.3.1.1   Variable Order

If one string contains two identical variables, the order in the translated string should stay the same. For example, a string such as *Choose %s to copy %s* should not be translated like *To copy %s, choose %s*, because this might result in a screen message like *To copy Continue, choose SAMPLE.DOC.*

2.2.3.3.1.2   Plurals

Programmers often include plurals that are constructed at run-time. A string section like:

```
1.      "Copying %d file%s."
2.      "Copying %d folder%s."
3.      "s"
```

will insert the letter *s* when the variable %d is two or more. In translation, this causes a problem in many languages. For example, if *file* were translated with the German word *Datei*, and *folder* with *Ordner*, this would cause a problem. The plural of *Datei* is *Dateien*, the plural of *Ordner* is *Ordner*. A possible solution for this problem would be to delete the %s variable (not the entire string resource!) and to create a translation that handles both singular and plural, such as *Datei(en)*.

2.2.3.3.1.3   Common Variables

The following table contains common variables, along with the parameters that they will be replaced with.

Variable	Parameter
%s	string
%d	decimal integer
%ld	decimal long integer
%x	integer in hexadecimal form
%g	floating point value
%u	Unicode character
%p	page number

2.2.3.3.2   Control Codes

Control codes provide formatting information within strings. If required, these formatting codes can be moved to enhance the visual display of the string.

In the example, the string `"%1 already exists.\nDo you want to replace it?"` will be displayed on two separate lines in the message box, because \n is the line break control code.

The \n control code is also used to separate status bar text from tooltips. In string 109, for example, the "Changes page layout settings" string will be displayed in the status bar of the application window when the command is selected. The "Page Setup" string is the help balloon string that will be displayed when the cursor is positioned on the command icon.

The following table shows the most common control codes:

\012 or \r	line feed
\015 or \n	line break
\011 or \t	tab character

2.2.3.3.3   Fixed Names

String sections may contain entries that should not be translated and that might corrupt the program when they are.

Usually, untranslatable items are written as one word, e.g., ConnCount, which is short for *Connection Count*. However, it can also happen that a string that looks translatable, such as "Copy", has to stay in English.

Preparation and marking of translatable strings by a localization engineer or technical project manager should prevent errors. If you are in doubt about a certain string or group of strings, consult an engineer or the developer of the application.

2.2.3.3.4   Length Restrictions

Strings in the Windows environment typically have a length restriction of 251 characters, including spaces. Always keep this restriction in mind when you are translating software strings. For 32-bit Windows environments, this restriction is 4000 characters.

As a general rule, keep your translations as short as possible. Try to adopt a concise and clear translation style for software strings. This will also reduce engineering time!

2.2.3.3.5   Hot Keys

Strings often contain menu or dialog box items that are dynamically used in the application at run-time. For example, when a menu contains an item that toggles, such as the *Show/Hide Toolbar* command, the standard menu resource will contain *Show Toolbar*, and the *Hide Toolbar* string will be taken from the string section.

You need to verify in the application where these strings will show up, and whether they cause hot key conflicts with other menu or dialog box items.

2.2.3.3.6   Concatenated Strings

Programmers often concatenate strings. Concatenation is the process of adding text elements or strings together to form a larger string. A good example is the Undo command, to which the last executed command is usually added at run-time.

Many applications concatenate "Undo " and a command name such as *Copy* to obtain a more specific *Undo Copy* menu item. If the application is then localized to German, the concatenation reads *Widerrufen Ausschneiden,* which does not make sense. The reverse order, *Ausschneiden Widerrufen,* would be correct.

> **Important**
>
> Be careful not to delete leading or trailing spaces! For example, if you delete the space following the string "Installing ", a status message might show up at run-time saying *InstallingApplication.*

If reversing the order of this concatenation is impossible, a solution would be to add a colon after the translation of "Undo".

2.2.3.4   VERSION INFO

Windows resource files usually contain a Version–or version stamp–section, in which the company name, application name, copyright, version number, and language edition of a program are specified.

This is an example of a version stamp:

```
/////////////////////////////////////////////////////////////////////
/////////
//
// Version
//

1 VERSIONINFO
 FILEVERSION 4,0,950,0
 PRODUCTVERSION 4,0,0,0
 FILEFLAGSMASK 0x3fL
#ifdef _DEBUG
 FILEFLAGS 0x1L
#else
 FILEFLAGS 0x0L
#endif
 FILEOS 0x4L
 FILETYPE 0x1L
 FILESUBTYPE 0x0L
BEGIN
  BLOCK "StringFileInfo"
  BEGIN
    BLOCK "040904e4"
    BEGIN
      VALUE "CompanyName", "Microsoft Corporation\0"
      VALUE "FileDescription", "WordPad MFC Application\0"
      VALUE "FileVersion", "4.00.950\0"
      VALUE "InternalName", "wordpad\0"
      VALUE "LegalCopyright", "Copyright © Microsoft Corp. 1995\0"
      VALUE "OriginalFilename", "WORDPAD.EXE\0"
      VALUE "ProductName", "Microsoft Windows (TM) Operating
System\0"
      VALUE "ProductVersion", "4.0\0"
    END
  END
  BLOCK "VarFileInfo"
  BEGIN
      VALUE "Translation", 0x409, 1252
  END
END
```

In the above example, only the value text following the FileDescription, LegalCopyright, and ProductName value names would be translated. Never translate the value names!

The version stamp also defines the language of the RC file. Refer to the Language Settings section on page 163 for more information about setting the language in a resource file.

2.2.3.5 COMMENT

Most software resource files contain strings that are enclosed or preceded by comment delimiters. These strings are comment text that has been added manually by the programmer or that is automatically inserted by the compiler.

Following are examples of comment delimiters for some programming languages:

Java, C or C++ files:

```
// commentcommentcommentcomment.
or
/*commentcommentcommentcomment.*/
```

Pascal or Delphi files:

```
{ commentcommentcommentcomment.. }
or
{*commentcommentcommentcomment..*}
```

Assembly files:

```
; commentcommentcommentcomment.. ;
```

Java property files:

```
! commentcommentcommentcomment..
or
# commentcommentcommentcomment..
```

Because these strings are *commented out*, they are not included in the compilation and will never show up in the program. Unless instructed otherwise, these comments are not translated.

Often, programmers include information for software localizers in comments. For example, if a set of strings should not be translated, it might be marked by a `//Do not translate` comment line.

> ### Note
>
> Sample files, batch files, INI files, or other non-compiled configuration files *may* contain comment text that needs to be translated. Consult with your client to make sure.

2.2.3.6 SPACE RESTRICTIONS

One of the most common problems in software translation is space restriction. Most European languages are longer than English, often up to 30 percent. In a dialog box, for example, part of an option or button text may be truncated, i.e., not be visible on the screen, when localized software is compiled.

Usually, items in dialog boxes can be resized to make translations fit in the control boxes. This work is mostly performed by localization engineers, but more and more translators are resizing dialog boxes while they are translating. In some development environments, forms with fixed sizes are used. In these cases, translators need to pick shorter translations or to abbreviate words.

Sometimes, only a limited number of characters can be used for options, error messages, or other strings. In many cases localization engineers can make more space available, but it is advisable to keep menu names, commands, and other software text as short as possible.

2.3 Program Files

Increasingly, translation is performed directly in program files. The DLL files or EXE files are edited by the translator without the need for compilation.

For 16-bit applications, DLL and EXE files can be edited using the Microsoft App Studio (Visual C++ 1.x) or Borland Resource Workshop resource editor. Translating 32-bit program files can be performed in Microsoft Developer Studio (Visual C++ 4.x) or Microsoft Visual Studio (Visual C++ 5.x), or Borland Resource Workshop.

Note

It is impossible to edit and save 32-bit program files using Microsoft Visual C++ in a Windows 9x environment. You need to run your resource editor under Windows NT.

2.3.1 Microsoft App Studio

Microsoft App Studio can be used to open and edit resource scripts (RC), executables (EXE), dynamic link libraries (DLL), resource files (RES), bitmaps (BMP), icons (ICO), and cursors (CUR).

App Studio can only be used to edit 16-bit executable or DLL files, i.e., applications that also run on Windows 3.1. If you open a 32-bit program file in App Studio, the following warning message will be displayed:

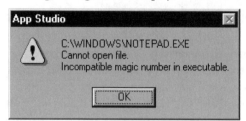

When you open a 16-bit executable or dynamic link library, a screen with resource types and resources is displayed:

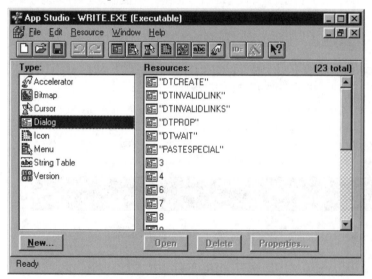

2.3.1.1 DIALOG BOXES

To translate dialog boxes, follow these steps:

1. Click on the Dialog resource type, and double-click on the first item in the Resources list.

2. In the dialog box that is displayed, double-click on each text item, and translate the text in the Caption field of the property window.

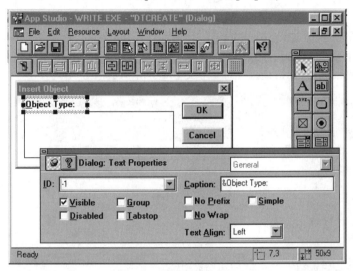

3. When all text is translated, close the dialog box resource by pressing Ctrl+F4 and open the next item in the Resources list.

Tip

Click on the pushpin button in the property window to keep it open. Clicking on a text item in the dialog box will automatically display the text in the Caption field.

Please note that the ampersand (&) symbol defines the hot key that is used for the option. Refer to the Hot Keys section on page 18 for more information.

When you have translated a dialog box, you can test it by choosing Test from the Resource menu, or pressing Ctrl+T. This test mode enables you to type in text, select options, choose commands, and test hot keys.

The numbers in the lower right corner of the window show the item's position and dimensions. Refer to the Dialog Boxes section on page 16 for more information about translating dialog boxes. Refer to the Resizing section on page 167 for more information about resizing dialog box controls.

2.3.1.2   MENUS

To translate menus, follow these steps:

1. Click on the Menu resource type, and double-click on the first item in the Resources list.

2. In the screen that is displayed, double-click on each menu and submenu item, and translate the text in the Caption field of the property window.

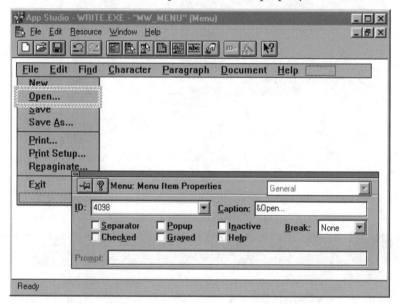

3. When all text is translated, close the menu resource by pressing Ctrl+F4 and open the next item in the Resources list.

Be careful not to delete the three dots that follow some of the commands. They indicate that the command will open a dialog box.

If a menu item contains a Control key definition that you want to change, such as Ctrl+C for the Copy command, follow these steps:

1. Open the Accelerator resources.

2.   Locate the menu ID of the menu item you want to change.

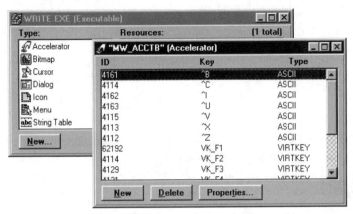

3.   Change the Control key letter accordingly.

Refer to the Menus section on page 17 for more information about translating menu resources. Refer to the Checking Hot Keys section on page 169 for more information about checking hot keys in menu resources.

2.3.1.3   STRINGS

To translate strings, follow these steps:

1.   Click on the String Table resource type, and double-click on the first item in the Resources list.

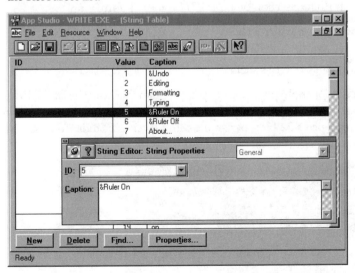

2. In the screen that is displayed, double-click on each string item, and translate the text in the Caption field of the property window.

3. When all text is translated, close the menu resource by pressing Ctrl+F4 and open the next item in the Resources list.

Refer to the Strings section on page 21 for more information about translating string resources.

2.3.1.4   OTHER RESOURCE TYPES

Resource types such as bitmaps, cursors, and icons might also contain translatable text or letters. To browse through a list of bitmap resources, click on the first item, choose the Properties button, click on the pushpin button, and browse down the list using the arrow keys. This is the quickest way to search for translatable text.

If a bitmap contains text, you can translate it in the integrated bitmap editor, or export the bitmap, edit it in a graphics editor, such as Adobe Photoshop or JASC Paint Shop Pro, and import it again.

An example of bitmaps that might be translated are the buttons for Bold, Italic, and Underline.

In some languages, these buttons are translated. Check the Wordpad application in your localized Windows version to check if they are translated in your language.

Refer to the Bitmap Editing section on page 170 for more information.

2.3.2   Microsoft Developer Studio

Microsoft Developer Studio is a shell for Microsoft Visual C++ 4.x and higher. The 32-bit resource editor is integrated in this shell.

With Microsoft Developer Studio, you can open program files for translation. Editing and saving 32-bit program files is only possible when you run Developer Studio on a Windows NT platform. If you open a 32-bit program file with Developer Studio running under Windows 9x, a message like this will be displayed:

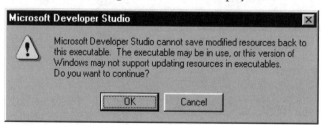

Opening a program file will display a screen containing a list of all resource types.

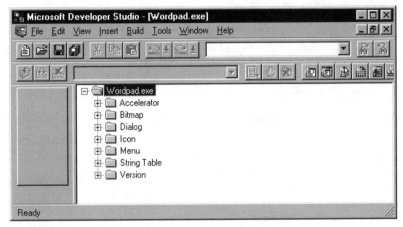

Clicking on the plus sign next to a resource type will open a list of resources. For more information about translating the different resource types in Microsoft Developer Studio, follow the steps in the Microsoft App Studio section on page 27.

Tip

Please note that in Visual C++ 5, you need to select Resource in the Open as field of the Open dialog box. If you don't, the file you selected will open as a project workspace.

There are a few differences between translating resources in Developer Studio, and working in App Studio:

- In Microsoft Developer Studio, you can specify the language of each resource. Refer to the Language Settings section on page 163 for more information.

- Developer Studio can check if there are no duplicate hot keys in a dialog box or menu. Refer to the Checking Hot Keys section on page 169 for more information.

- The menu resource property window contains an additional field, called Prompt. This field may contain the status bar text and tooltip for the selected menu command. This prompt text is stored in the String Table resources. You can translate it in the Menu Item Properties window or in the string section.

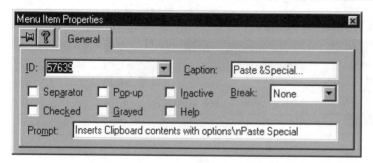

When you have the entire build environment of a program file on your machine, including RC or DLG files, you can also open a RC file for editing. Translating RC or DLG files in Microsoft Developer Studio is done in the same way as translating program files, except that included files such as icons and bitmaps can be found in a separate resource folder.

2.3.3   Borland Resource Workshop

Borland Resource Workshop is available as part of the Borland C++ and Turbo C compiler packages or as a separate package up to version 4.5.

Unlike Microsoft Developer Studio, Resource Workshop allows you to edit and save 32-bit program files under Windows 9x. If you are translating RC files, make sure you use the compiler and resource editor that was used to create the project file.

To translate resources in Borland Resource Workshop, follow these steps:

1.   Start Borland Resource Workshop.

2.   Choose the Open Project command from the File menu, and select the program file (EXE, DLL) or resource file (RC, DLG) that you want to edit.

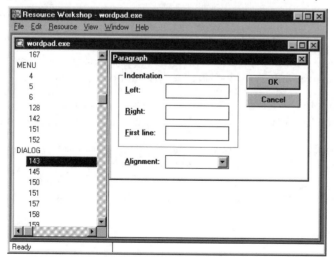

3. In the Resource Workshop window, scroll down the resource types (bitmaps, menus, dialog boxes, etc.) and double-click on a resource to open it.

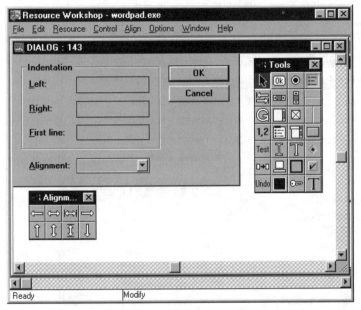

4. Double-click on the item that you want to translate, and type your translation in the Caption field.

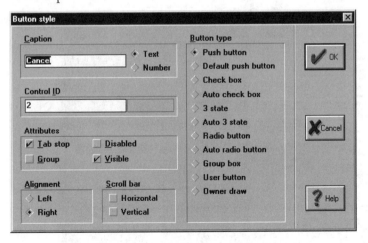

5. Alternatively, to translate controls by changing their properties, choose Show
    Properties from the Options menu. Click on an item, select the Caption
    property, and type your translation in the text box.

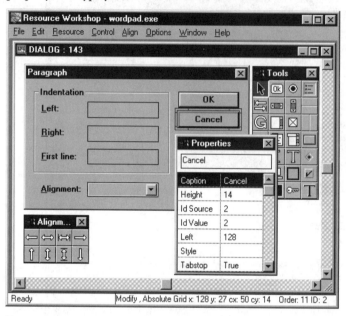

6. For menu resources, translate the menu item in the Item Text field and the
    status bar text in the Item Help field.

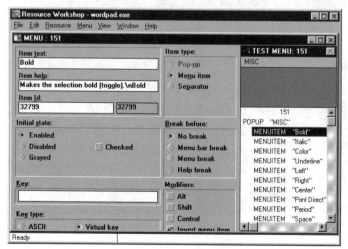

7. To save your translations, choose the Save Project command from the File
    menu.

2.4 Software Localization Tools

2.4.1 Resource Localization Tools

Resource localization tools are designed to help you localize software resource files. Most of these tools contain translation memory, leveraging (re-using), validating, and spell checking functionality.

Often, these tools contain pseudo-translation features, which allow you to "translate" the string using specified (accented) characters or string lengths. The purpose of pseudo-translation is to find problems that may occur when the translation is actually produced.

The following pages contain brief descriptions of the most commonly used software localization tools that are currently on the market.

2.4.1.1   COREL CATALYST

Corel Catalyst is a software localization application that can be used to translate binary, 32-bit Windows-based files, such as DLL, EXE, and OCX files, and software resource files, such as RC and DLG files. It can also be used to update translated files, to create glossaries from previously translated files, and to check resource files for common localization errors.

Corel Catalyst's interactive localization environment allows you to translate and review all objects in your resource files using editing capabilities in a protected WYSIWYG environment. Depending on the object type you select in the Navigator window, Catalyst automatically opens the appropriate object editor in the Project window. You can use Catalyst to translate and review text strings, menus, dialog boxes, and various custom resources supported by Windows 9x and Windows NT.

Because Windows 9x does not allow changed resources to be saved back to EXE or DLL files, Catalyst provides it's own TNT format. Working under Windows NT does allow you to save changes directly to binary files.

To translate software resource files using Corel Catalyst, follow these steps:

1. Start Corel Catalyst.

2. Create a new project using the Document Selection dialog box.

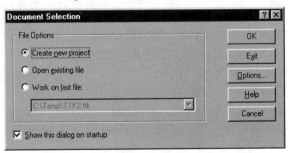

3. Choose the Insert Files command from the File menu to import the files that you want to translate.

4. Next, in WYSIWYG mode or non-WYSIWYG mode, translate the resources in the file.

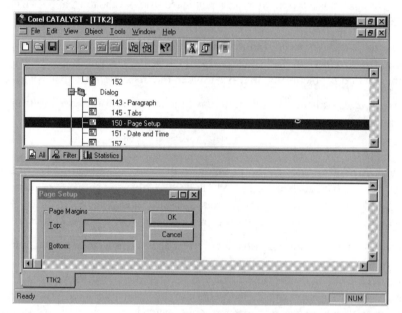

Corel Catalyst provides functions for leveraging (re-using) existing translations, validating localized strings, creating software glossaries, pseudo-translations, filtering, and spell checking.

Recent versions of Corel Catalyst also include support for Windows Help project files, such as HPJ, RTF and CNT files.

For more information about Corel Catalyst, visit the Catalyst Web site at catalyst.corel.ie.

2.4.1.2 APPLOCALIZE

AppLocalize is the 32-bit version of the AppTranslator utility, which has been developed by Software Builders. It is used to translate binary resource (RES) or executable (EXE) files. Resource changes in executable files can be saved under Windows NT only.

To translate RES or EXE files using AppLocalize, follow these steps:

1. Choose the New command from the File menu to create a new AppLocalize project.

2. Choose the Languages command from the Description menu to enter the source and target language(s).

3. Choose the Add/Merge from Base Resources File command from the Actions menu.

4. In the Add/Merge from Base Resources File dialog box, select the RES or EXE files that you wish to import.

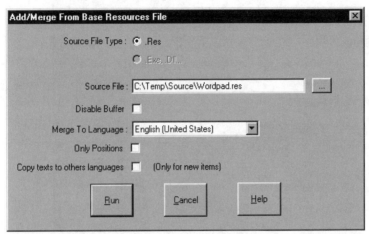

5. In the main translation window, translate dialog boxes, menus, and strings.

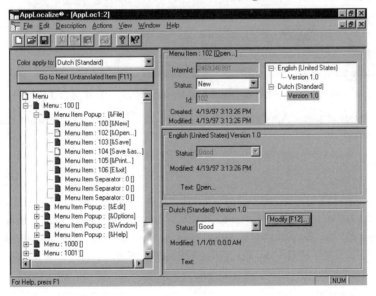

6. Export your translations to a new RES file using the Generate translated
    Resources File command from the Actions menu.

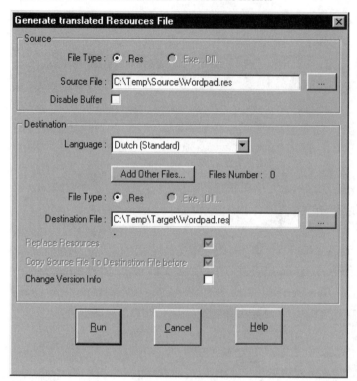

7. Use the translated RES file to build a program file, for example a DLL.

For more information about AppLocalize and a demo version, visit the Software Builders
Web site at www.sbuilders.com.

2.4.1.3   ACCENT GLOBAL DEVELOPMENT KIT

The Accent Global Development Kit consists of programming tools and translation tools.
The programming tools can be used to develop multilingual applications or to add
multilingual support to existing 16-bit and 32-bit Windows applications. The translation
tools are included in the Accent Globalization Suite, a set of Windows applications that
help you automate and manage the task of translating an application's user interface into
your choice of target languages.

The Accent Globalization Suite consists of the Developer's, Administrator's, and
Translator's tool. These tools can be used to translate RC and DLG files in a WYSIWYG
interface.

An advanced, stand-alone version of the Administrator's and Translator's tool has been released under the name Loc@le. This tool provides an easy and efficient system for translating your application's user interface. Loc@le extracts user interface strings from your resource files, provides an interface and tools for translating the strings, and generates new resource files containing the translated strings.

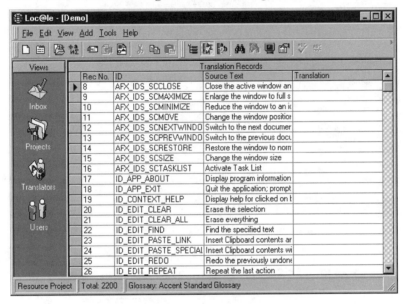

To translate software resource files using Accent GDK, follow these steps:

1. Start the Developer's Tool, and create a new project with the resource file that you want to translate.

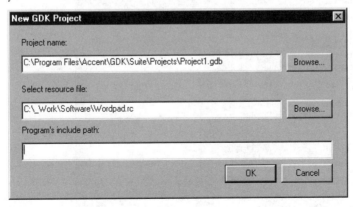

2. When the RC file is parsed, you will see a list of dialog, menu, and string resources in the project window. Clicking on a resource will display a list of

records on the right. To view the resource in WYSIWYG mode, choose the Resource Context command from the View menu.

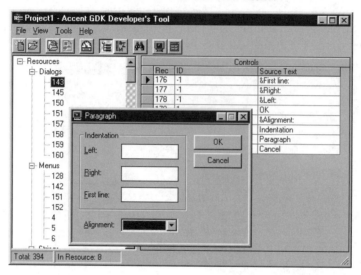

3. Exit the Developer's Tool, and start the Administrator's Tool.

4. Open the project file that you have just created. You can use the Administrator's Tool to add notes to records, or to mark them as "do not translate".

5. Choose the Add Language command from the Tools menu to select the target language(s) for the RC file.

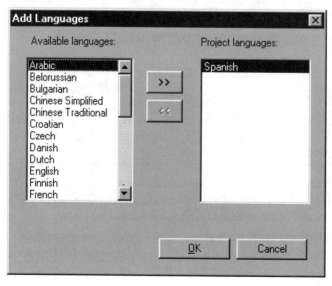

6. Choose the Create SLMs command from the File menu to create a file that can be translated. SLM stands for Single Language Module. You can select one or more target languages.

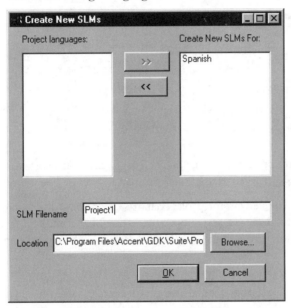

7. Exit the Administrator's Tool, and start the Translator's Tool.

8. Open the project SLM that you have just created.

9. Enter your translations in the Translation field.

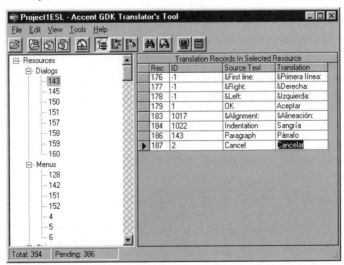

10. Choose the Resource Context command from the View menu to display the translated resource next to the English resource. In context view, you can also resize the controls in the translated dialog box.

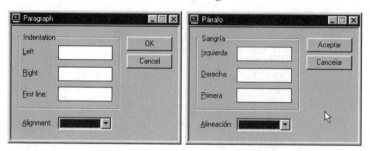

11. When all records have been translated, you need to export your translations. Choose the Create SLE for All translations command from the File menu.

12. To merge your translations with the project database, start the Administrator's Tool, open the project database, and choose the Merge SLE command from the File menu. You can now edit the translations or change the record status of each record.

13. To generate the translated RC file, start the Developer's Tool, open the project database and choose the Generate Resource Files command from the File menu.

The Translator's Tool allows you to enter a translation once, which is then inserted throughout the resource file. For example, the first time you translate the Cancel button, the translation will be automatically inserted in all dialogs or strings where Cancel is used.

The tool will also provide you with detailed word counts and progress information. It alerts the user when a special character, such as an ampersand for hot keys, is not present in the translation, or when a hot key is used more than once in a dialog or menu resource.

For more information about the Accent Global Development kit or Loc@le, visit the Accent Software International Ltd. Web site at www.accentsoft.com.

2.4.1.4 MISCELLANEOUS

2.4.1.4.1 Microsoft RLToolset

The Resource Localization Toolset was designed to automate localization of products that make use of the Windows resource model. It allows the localizer to extract localizable resources directly from the applications that use them, modify the resources, and use the modified resources to create localized versions of the original applications.

In the RLToolset, localizable resources are extracted from a source resource file and put into special text file called a token file. Each token is contained on a single line of text and consists of a unique identifier followed by the localizable data associated with that particular resource. These tokens can then be localized either by using the tools provide by the RLToolset or by using a standard text editor.

There is a command line tool called RLMan, a one-pass tool called RLQuiked, and a long-term project set of tools: RLAdmin and RLEdit. For 32-bit applications, RLToolset only runs on Windows NT.

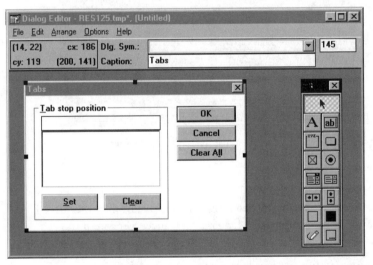

The RLToolset is not maintained or supported by Microsoft anymore, but can still be downloaded from Microsoft's FTP server at ftp.microsoft.com/Softlib/mslfiles.

Microsoft Espresso is the follow-up to RLToolset. It has been used for years as an internal localization tool by Microsoft.

2.4.1.4.2   RC-WinTrans

RC-WinTrans is a tool that can be used to translate Windows resource script (RC) files. You can create, translate and maintain multiple language versions of the resource file from your projects. RC-WinTrans can also be used to leverage (re-use) existing translations, and to resize dialog box items using its built-in dialog layout editor.

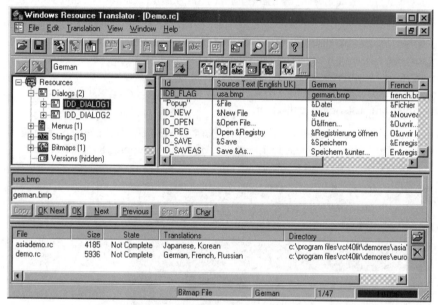

For more information about RC-WinTrans, visit the RC-WinTrans Web site at members.aol.com/ibsdevelop/rct/default.htm.

2.4.1.4.3   Proprietary Tools

Many large software developers have developed tools for localizers of their products. For example, Microsoft has developed Espresso, which is an advanced version of the RLToolset.

Other examples of proprietary software localization tools are Oracle's TTT, Lotus' Red, and Symantec's Pebbles.

2.4.1.4.4   CAT Tools

Most computer aided translation tools also support translation of text-only resource files. For example, Trados Translator's Workbench, IBM TranslationManager, and Atril Déjà Vu offer import filters for software resource (RC) files. More information about these tools can be found in Chapter 5, Translation Memory Tools.

2.4.1.5 COMPARISON TABLE

The following table lists the file formats supported by the translation tools described in the previous sections.

	.RC .DLG	.DLL .EXE	.RES	.OCX	C/C++	16-bit .DLL
Accent GDK	√					
Amptran	√					
AppLocalize		√	√			√
Catalyst	√	√		√		
Déjà Vu	√				√	
RC-WinTrans	√					
RLToolset		√	√			√

2.4.2 Dynamic Localization Tools

A dynamic localization tool is a software program that translates the user interface of an application while it is running. Translations are entered in dictionaries that are used to dynamically translate the interface components of specified applications, such as dialog boxes, menus, and strings.

2.4.2.1 JARGON

Jargon is a dynamic localization utility that has been developed by Alda Technologies Ltd. Jargon works by referencing text used in your applications user interface controls (menus, buttons, list boxes, etc) with that found in its Phrasebooks. The Phrasebooks contain foreign language translations of the text used by your applications and system buttons or menus such as the Cancel, Apply, and OK buttons.

The source code of the application remains unchanged. You can use the Phrasebook
Editor to customize Phrasebooks for your application, and to add translations. If the phrase
is not found in one of the Phrasebooks, it is left unchanged.

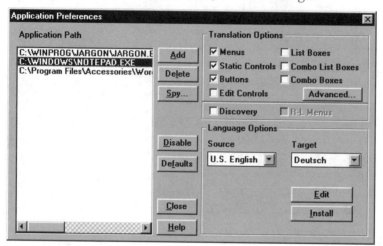

In the Application Preferences dialog box, you can set which applications you want to be
dynamically translated, which elements of the user interface you want translated, and source
and target languages. During Setup of the application, you can choose which language
modules you want to install.

If you use Jargon's Discovery Mode, all user interface strings that are not found in one of
the Phrasebooks are automatically entered in a Phrasebook for you to translate.

To manually add translations to a phrasebook, click the Edit button in the Application
Preferences dialog box, and add source and target term in the Phrasebook Editor.

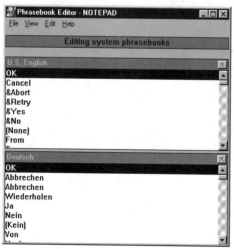

For more information about Jargon, ordering information, and a demo version, visit the MDR Telemanagement Limited Web site at www.alda.com.

2.4.2.2 SUPERLINGUIST

The SuperLinguist package was developed by KT International Inc. It consists of four software products: SuperLinguist, SuperLinguist Terminal Manager, SuperLinguist Resource Editor, and SuperLinguist Resource Manager.

SuperLinguist is used to dynamically translate the user interface of a Windows application to another language while the application is running. The SuperLinguist Manager captures the source user interface strings and builds an application dictionary. The application dictionary can be translated using the Manager. After translation of the dictionary, the SuperLinguist Engine performs the real-time translation.

SuperLinguist Terminal Manager can dynamically translate the display of an application using a 5250/3270 terminal emulator. It can also adjust screen items such as date, time, or currency fields to local conventions. SuperLinguist Resource Editor is used for adjusting dialog templates to make translations fit. SuperLinguist Resource Manager is used for extracting translatable strings from resource files and adding them to a custom dictionary.

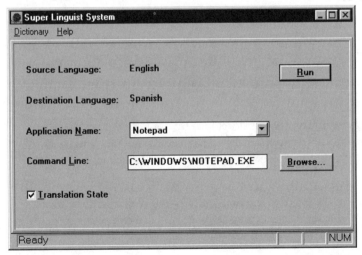

The SuperLinguist interface is very basic. You can open a language dictionary and select which application you want translated.

For more information about SuperLinguist, visit the KT International Web site at www.ktintl.com.

3 Macintosh

3.1 Introduction

On Macintosh computers, most software is translated directly in the program file resources. Usually, the translator does not edit text-only resource files that need to be compiled, but works directly in the executable of a Macintosh application.

This section discusses some of the most commonly used tools for translating Macintosh applications.

3.1.1 Localization Tools

The program that is used mostly for translation of Macintosh applications is called ResEdit. ResEdit is a powerful resource editor from Apple Computer, Inc. Refer to the Using ResEdit section on page 52 for more information.

Other localization tools for Macintosh applications include MPW, Resorcerer, Icepick, ViewEdit, AppleGlot, and PowerGlot.

- MPW (Macintosh Programmer's Workshop) is a text-based Macintosh resource editor and compiler.

- Resorcerer is comparable to ResEdit, but is often considered faster and easier to use. Refer to the Using Resorcerer section on page 59 for more information.

- Icepick and ViewEdit are small tools that are only used to translate coded MacApp VIEW resources.

- AppleGlot is a localization utility that was developed by Apple Computer. It contains advanced functions for automatically updating and translating extracted resource files. Refer to the Using AppleGlot section on page 230 for more information.

- PowerGlot is a commercially available resource translation tool that extracts, sorts, and presents all translatable text contained in an application in a comprehensive way.

The Apple International Developer Resources site at www.apple.com/developer contains more information about localization tools from Apple.

3.1.2 Resource Types

Every Macintosh application consists of a number of resources. All resource type names are four characters long. In every resource, a specific component of the application is coded. Examples of resource types are menus (MENU), dialog boxes (DITL), and strings (STR#).

The following table shows common localizable application components and their resource types:

Resource Type	Description
aedt	AppleEvents
ALRT	Alert window definition
cicn	Color icon
CMNU	Command menus (MacApp)
CNTL	Control definitions (buttons)
crsr	Color cursor or mouse pointer
CURS	Cursor or mouse pointer
DITL	Dialog box
DLOG	Dialog box definition
hdlg	Balloon help for dialog boxes
hfdr	Balloon help for Finder icon
hmnu	Balloon help for menus
hwin	Balloon help for windows
icl4	4-bit icon
icl8	8-bit icon
ICN#	1-bit icon
ICON	Icon used in dialogs or menus
MENU	Application menus
PICT	Picture (bitmap)
STR	Strings
STR#	List of strings
TEXT	Text
Vers	Finder version info
View	Dialog box definition
WIND	Document window definition

3.1.3   Preparation

Make sure you always work on copies of the original file. If your Macintosh crashes while you're editing a program file in ResEdit or Resorcerer, it is very likely that the file will be corrupted. Therefore, it is very important to make copies of the file you are working on frequently, preferably every 15 minutes. To make a copy of a program file, click on the file in the Finder and press Command-D. The file is duplicated and the word *copy* is added to the name. Replacing the word *copy* with a number makes it easy to keep control of the version of the file you're editing.

Do not open a copy of the file in the same folder as the original file. ResEdit might save changes to the wrong file or to both files.

Important

If your computer crashes when you're editing a file in ResEdit, do not continue to work on this file! Delete it and continue working with the last copy you made of the file.

You might find it easy to run the application you are translating while you are working on a copy of it in ResEdit. This enables you to view every dialog box you are translating at run-time.

Before you start translating a Macintosh application, check if a previously translated version is available. If this is the case, you can automatically update the new version using the existing translations. Refer to the Using MPW section on page 229 or Using AppleGlot section on page 230 for more information.

3.2 Translating Software

3.2.1   Using ResEdit

ResEdit is the most commonly used tool in Macintosh software localization and translation. Although there are newer versions available, version 2.1.1 is the most stable one.

ResEdit can be downloaded from Apple's FTP server at ftp.apple.com/devworld/Tool_Chest/Developer_Utilities.

More information on how to use ResEdit and resource types can be found in the ResEdit reference guide, which can be downloaded from the Apple Developer FTP site: dev.apple.com/devworld/Technical_Documentation/Inside_Macintosh/ResEdit

Note

Detailed information about the use of ResEdit can be found in the ResEdit Complete manual by P. Alley and C. Strange.

It is recommended to start by translating the menus, dialog boxes, and then translate the strings and other resources.

When you open a Macintosh program file with ResEdit, a window similar to the one below will be displayed:

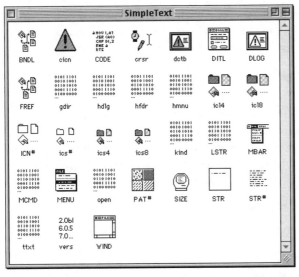

Double-clicking on a resource type opens a window with numbered resources. The next section contains information about the specific resource types and ways to translate them.

3.2.1.1   MENUS

The MENU and CMENU resource types contain all menus and drop-down list boxes. To edit a menu, open it, select the title or menu item and type the translation in the Title or Text box. Do not delete the three dots or the shortcuts following some commands.

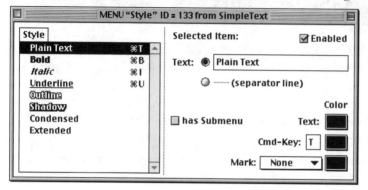

You might choose to change the Command key for a menu item by typing another letter in the Cmd-Key field. However, typically these key combinations should stay identical to the source. Refer to the Control Keys (Shortcut Keys) section on page 19 for more information.

3.2.1.2   DIALOG BOXES

The DITL, DLOG, ALRT, and WIND resource types contain all windows and dialog boxes. The contents of most dialog boxes can be found in the DITL (Dialog ITem List) resources. The DLOG and WIND resources are used to define the size of the dialog boxes or windows, and to translate the titles. ALRT resources are a subset of the DITL resources that report errors or alerts. They usually contain only buttons and icons.

To translate DITL resources, follow these steps:

1.   Double-click on the DITL icon to open a list of dialog boxes. Each dialog box has an ID number.

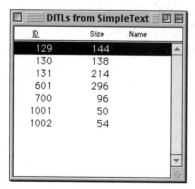

2. Double-click on the first item to open the dialog box. Press Option to display the borders and ID numbers of all items in the dialog box. Select the Show Item Numbers option in the DITL menu if you prefer to make the borders and numbers display by default.

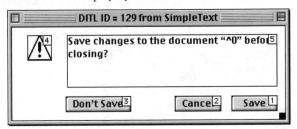

3. To open an item in the dialog box, double-click on it. It is also possible to choose Select Item Number in the DITL menu and type the number of the desired item. Opening items this way is recommended when items overlap other items.

Tip

To open all items in a dialog box, press Command-A to select, and Command-O to open them. To close items one by one, press Command-W.

4. In the window that is displayed, the translation can be entered. In this window, you can also change the size of the item box. Never resize by dragging with the mouse button because this will not give you accurate and consistent sizes. For example, if you resize the Cancel button, its new size should be consistent in all dialog boxes of the applications.

Note

When resizing items, make sure the Show Item Numbers option in the DITL menu is selected to prevent overlapping other–hidden–items!

After you have translated and resized all items within a certain DITL, you can either continue with the next DITL, or translate the title of the DITL you have just translated. To change the size or title of a dialog box, open the DLOG, ALRT or WIND resource with the ID number that corresponds with the DITL number.

Double-clicking on a DLOG resource displays a window containing an image of your desktop with the associated dialog box in it. You can use the Left, Right, Top and Bottom fields to change the size of the dialog box.

One thing you must remember when increasing the size of a dialog box is that it must fit on all possible screen sizes. To test if your dialog still fits on all Mac screens, you can select several screen types from the MiniScreen menu when you have opened a DLOG resource.

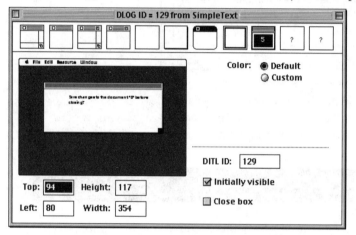

To translate the title of the dialog box, choose the Set DLOG Characteristics command in the DLOG menu and type your translation in the Window Title box.

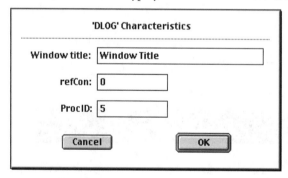

After all DITLs and DLOGs have been translated, open the ALRT resources. Translation and resizing of the ALRTs and the WIND is done in a similar fashion as the DLOGs.

Note

Dialog boxes are sometimes included in MacApp View resources. To translate View resources, use a tool like IcePick or ViewEdit.

3.2.1.3 STRINGS

Open the STR, STR# and TEXT resource types to see if they contain translatable text. The STR# resources usually contain error messages, but they may also include menu items or dialog options. Refer to the Strings section on page 21 for more information on translating strings.

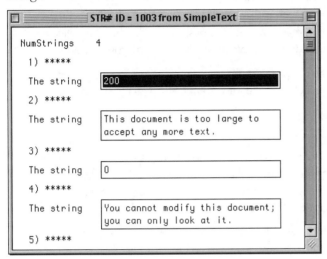

3.2.1.4 CONTROLS

Controls are button definitions or labels. To translate controls, double-click on a Control resource and translate the text in the Title field.

3.2.1.5 IMAGES

The PICT resources contain the images that are used in the application, such as splash screens. To edit the text in a bitmap, open the resource, press Command-C and paste the image in an image editor like Adobe Photoshop. Color PICTs should be edited in indexed color mode, monochrome PICTs in bitmap mode.

Tip

When you choose the New command in Adobe Photoshop after you have copied a bitmap from a resource to the clipboard, the new image will have the same dimensions as the resource bitmap that is on the clipboard. Press Command-V in Photoshop to paste the bitmap in the new image.

After editing, paste the bitmap back in the resource, and close and save the resource. Refer to the Bitmap Editing section on page 223 for more information on editing bitmaps from Macintosh resources.

The ICN# and ICON resource types contain the icons for all program files. Double-click on an icon resource to open an icon editor in which you can edit the icon text. An example of translatable icon text is *PREFS*, which is displayed on preferences files. To activate translated icons, restart the Macintosh and rebuild the desktop. You rebuild the desktop by holding down the Option-Command key combination when starting your Macintosh.

The CURS resource type contains cursors and mouse pointers that sometimes contain localizable text or letters. Double-click on a cursor resource to open a cursor editor in which you can edit the cursor text.

3.2.1.6   BALLOON HELP

The hfdr, hdlg, hmnu, and hwin resource types contain balloon help text. Balloon help text will be displayed when you choose the Show Balloons command in the Finder's help menu. These strings are hard-coded and need to be translated using a ResEdit template. Resorcerer supports Balloon Help templates by default.

Often, balloon help hmnu resources contain links to text in STR# resources. In this case, the hmnu resource will then contain references to these STR# resources.

Please note that each balloon help string is limited to 255 characters.

3.2.1.7   VERSION

Vers resources contain the language version and the copyright information that will show up when you select Get Info from the Finder's File menu with the application's icon selected. Double-click on a vers resource item to open the version info window. Change the Country Code to your language and translate the text in the Long Version String box.

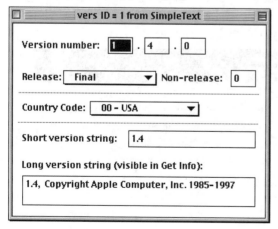

3.2.1.8   USING TEMPLATES

ResEdit's template editor lets you edit some sorts of resources in a dialog box format, with fields where you can replace the source text with your translation. ResEdit contains predefined templates for several resource types, and customized templates can also be created.

3.2.2   Using Resorcerer

When you open a Macintosh program file with Resorcerer, a window simlar to this one will be displayed:

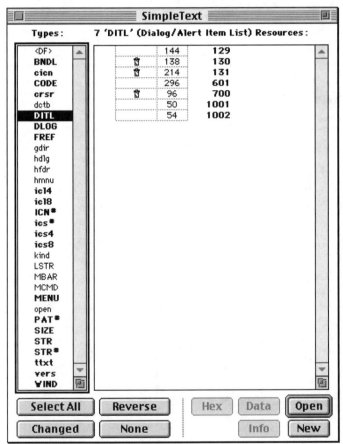

Double-clicking on a resource type in the Types list will display a list of numbered resources. The next section contains information about the specific resource types and ways to translate them.

3.2.2.1   MENUS

The MENU and CMENU resource types contain all menus and drop-down list boxes. To edit a menu, open it, select the title or menu item and type the translation in the text box. Do not delete the three dots or the shortcuts following some commands.

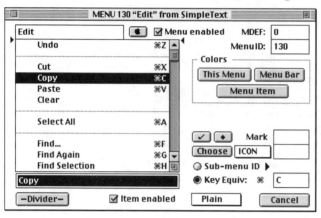

3.2.2.2   DIALOG BOXES

The DITL, DLOG, ALRT, and WIND resource types contain all windows and dialog boxes. The contents of most dialog boxes can be found in the DITL (Dialog ITem List) resources. The DLOG and WIND resources are used to define the size of the dialog boxes or windows, and to translate the titles. ALRT resources are a subset of the DITL resources that report errors or alerts. They usually contain only buttons, icons, and empty text fields where messages from the string section are inserted at run-time.

To translate DITL resources, follow these steps:

1.   Click on the DITL resource type to display a list of dialog boxes. Each dialog box has an ID number.

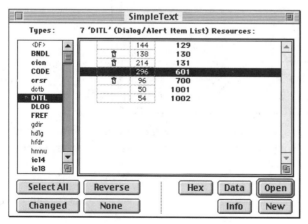

2. Double-click on the first item to open the dialog box. Click Open Related to Continue.

3. Press Command-2 to display all items in the dialog with ID numbers. Press Command-3 to display all items in the dialog with boxes. To make the borders and numbers display by default, select Preferences from the Dialog menu. In the Dialog Editor Preferences dialog box, enable the Initially Show Item Numbers option.

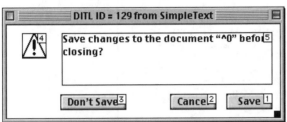

4. To open an item in the dialog box, double-click on it. It is also possible to choose the Select Range command from the Resource menu and type the number of the desired item. Opening items in this way is recommended when items overlap other items.

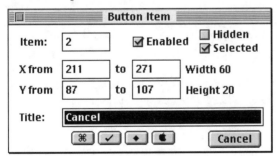

5. The translation can be entered in the window that is displayed. In this window, you can also change the size of the item box. Never resize by dragging with the mouse button because this will not give you accurate and consistent sizes. For example, if you resize the Cancel button, its new size should be consistent in all dialog boxes of the applications.

6.   To translate the title of the dialog box, choose the Set Dialog Info command
     from the Dialog menu. Type your translation in the Title box. In this window,
     you can also change the size of the dialog box.

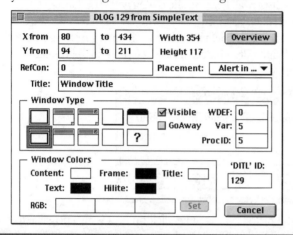

Note

When resizing items, make sure the Show Item Numbers option in the Item
menu is selected to prevent overlapping other–hidden–items!

After all DITLs and DLOGs have been translated, open the ALRT resources. Translation
and resizing of the ALRTs and the WIND is done in a similar fashion as the DLOGs.

3.2.2.3   STRINGS

Open the STR, STR# and TEXT resource types to see if they contain translatable text. The
STR# resources usually contain error messages, but they may also include menu items or
dialog options. Refer to the Strings section on page 21 for more information on translating
strings.

3.2.2.4 CONTROLS

Controls are button definitions or labels. To translate controls, double-click on a Control resource and translate the text in the Title field.

3.2.2.5 IMAGES

The PICT resources contain the images that are used in the application, such as splash screens. To edit the text in a bitmap, open the resource, press Command-C and paste the image in an image editor like Adobe Photoshop. Color PICTs should be edited in indexed color mode, monochrome PICTs in bitmap mode.

> **Tip**
>
> When you choose the New command in Adobe Photoshop after you have copied a bitmap from a resource to the clipboard, the new image will have the same dimensions as the resource bitmap that is on the clipboard. Press Command-V in Photoshop to paste the bitmap in the new image.

After editing, paste the bitmap back in the resource, and close and save the resource. Refer to the Bitmap Editing section on page 223 for more information on editing bitmaps from Macintosh resources.

The ICN# and ICON resource types contain the icons of all program files. Double-click on an icon resource to open an icon editor in which you can edit the icon text. An example of translatable icon text is "PREFS", which is displayed on preferences files. To activate translated icons, restart the Macintosh and rebuild the desktop. You rebuild the desktop by holding down the Option-Command key combination when starting your Macintosh.

The CURS resource type contains cursors and mouse pointers that sometimes contain localizable text or letters. Double-click on a cursor resource to open a cursor editor in which you can edit the cursor text.

3.2.2.6 BALLOON HELP

The hfdr, hdlg, hmnu, and hwin resource types contain balloon help text. Balloon help text will be displayed when you choose the Show Balloons command in the Finder's help menu.

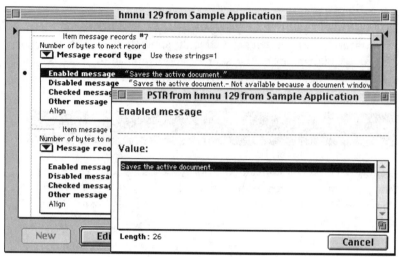

To translate help balloon text, open the balloon help resource, select the Help Message line and click on the Edit button. You can type your translation in the window that is displayed.

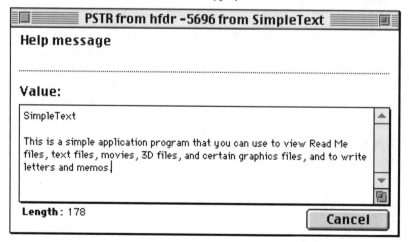

Please note that each balloon help string is limited to 255 characters. The length of the string you are translating is displayed in the Length field of the hfdr resource window.

3.2.2.7 VERSION

Vers resources contain the language version and the copyright information that will show up when you select Get Info in the Finder with the application's icon selected. Double-click on a vers resource item to open the version info. Change the Country Code to your language and translate the text in the Long String box. This text will be displayed in the Version line of the Info window. To open the Info window, select the application icon in the Finder and choose the Get Info command (Command-I) from the File menu.

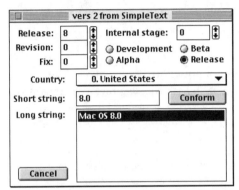

For more information on Resorcerer and a demo version, visit the Mathemaesthetics, Inc. Web site at www.mathemaesthetics.com.

3.2.3 Using AppleGlot

AppleGlot can be used to extract text resources from Macintosh program files, or to update previously localized versions of an application. Refer to the Using AppleGlot section on page 230 for more information about extracting resources or updating software.

An AppleGlot work glossary contains the text from the resources in the following format:

```
Resource type, ID and item number [item information]
        <Source text>
        <Translation>
```

Typically, a work glossary file looks like this:

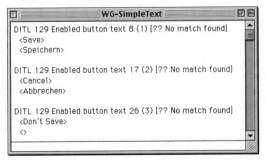

Work glossaries can be created in the following format: MPW, MS Word, MacWrite, TeachText or Microsoft Excel. The file format is specified in AppleGlot's Preferences dialog box. Typically, TeachText format is used, which can be handled by most word processors and text editors.

If the work glossary is too big to be opened in TeachText or SimpleText, an alternative text editor you can use is BBEdit. For more information about BBEdit and a Lite version, visit the Bare Bones Web site at www.barebones.com.

When you translate a work glossary, it is very important to look at the resource information line that indicates the resource and item type. Refer to the Resource Types section on page 50 for a complete list of resource types.

The [item information] tag also contains important information when you are translating a work glossary. This section will tell you if an item is new, previously translated, or a guess. The following table shows [item information] tags and their meanings:

Tag	Meaning
[?? Exact match – Internal Glossary]	The item was found in the previous source and translated versions, with the same resource and position as in the new version.
[?? Multiple Text Guesses]	Different translations were found for the same source text. The translator needs to pick the correct translation.
[?? No Match Found]	No match was found. The item is new and needs to be translated. In this case, the <Translation> section is empty.
[?? Text Match – Application Database Match]	The translation was found within in the application database. This translation needs to be verified.
[?? Text Match – Internal Guess]	A match that was found in AppleGlot's internal database. This is the database that's automatically created when AppleGlot reads the old source and old localized files. This translation needs to be verified.
[?? Text Match – Language Glossary Match]	The translation was found in one of the language glossaries that were used. This translation needs to be verified.
[??:•• Wild Guess by position]	No match was found and the item that was in the same position in the previous version is inserted in the <Translation> section. Wild guesses need to be verified carefully.

If a string marked with the [?? No Match Found] tag does not need to be translated, just skip it. For example, when the source text is <Apple> leave the target line blank (< >).

3.2.4 Using PowerGlot

PowerGlot is a MacOS localization tool that extracts, sorts, and presents all translatable text contained in an application in a comprehensive way. It was developed by Florent Pillet, a French Macintosh developer.

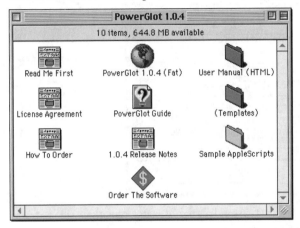

PowerGlot has advanced features for creating word counts from your Macintosh applications, leveraging (re-using) previously translated versions, and creating error reports.

To translate a Macintosh application using PowerGlot, follow these steps:

1. Make a copy of the program file that you want to translate.

2. Start PowerGlot, and select Add Work Files from the Database menu.

3. PowerGlot reads the resources of the application and displays the resources in the database window.

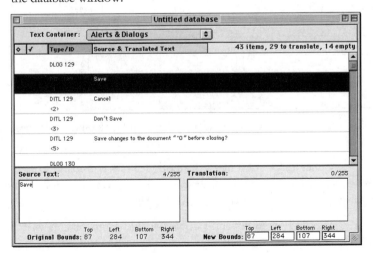

4. Specify the project settings, such as source and target language. Choose the Database Settings command from the Edit menu.

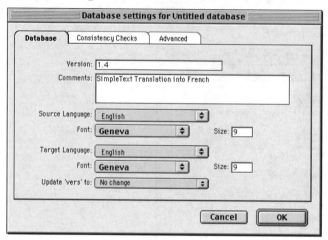

5. From the Text container drop down list, select the resource type that you want to translate, for example Menus.

6. Click on a menu item and type your translation in the Translation field.

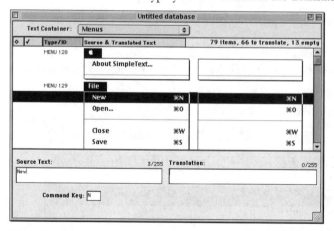

7. Translate the other resource types, such as alerts and dialog boxes, strings, and window titles.

8. Choose the Generate localized files - from original files command from the Database menu to build a localized version of your application. You will be asked to specify a location for your localized application.

For more information about PowerGlot and a downloadable demo version, visit the PowerGlot Web site at www.powerglot.com.

3.3 Translating Installers

Most Macintosh installers can be translated in translator applications that are created using the Installer VISE application. Refer to the Using Installer VISE section on page 225 for more information about Installer VISE.

A translator application allows you to translate all disk names, file information, file descriptions, package information, and easy install text that will be included in the localized installer. Most of the standard interface components will be already localized in the localized installer files that are included with Installer VISE.

To translate a translator application, follow these steps:

1. Double-click on the English to *language* file to launch the translator application.

2. Click on the Disk Information window and enter your translation in the right column. The left column contains the folder names of the original application archive.

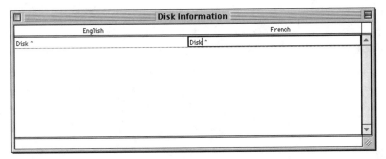

3. Click on the File Information window to translate the names of the files and folders that will be installed. You can also choose the File List option from the Windows menu.

4. Click on the Package Information window, or select Package List from the Windows menu to translate the names and descriptions of the packages. Typically, the packages are Easy Install and Custom Install.

5. Next, click on the Easy Install Text window, or select Easy Install Text from the Windows menu to translate the text that will be displayed in the installer when the user selects the easy install option.

6. To save your translations, choose the Save command from the File menu.

If you have a previously translated version of the translator application, you can select the Import Translator command from the File menu. The target column in the new file will be filled with any information from the old translator application that matches the text in the left column.

Chapter 3:
Translating Online Help

This chapter contains information for translators of online help documents. Topics include Windows Help, HTML Help, and Apple Guide.

For most localization projects, online help is the largest component. Help files and online manuals have taken over the role of printed manuals. Over the past years, help files have gained functionality. For example, movie files, animations or sound can be embedded.

Advantages of online help compared to printed manuals include:

- Context-sensitive help gives users direct access to the information that is needed. For example, pressing the Help button in a dialog box will open a help window that explains all options in that specific dialog box.

- Users can quickly navigate to the required information with hypertext jumps and index keywords.

- Printing costs decrease substantially for software manufacturers.

There are many types and formats of online help. In this chapter, the most common types will be discussed:

- Windows help

- HTML files

- HTML Help files

- Macintosh Help files

- Macintosh Apple Guide files.

1 Windows Help Files

Help files for Windows applications are files with an HLP file extension. They are called hypertext documents, which means they contain links (*jumps*) to other topics, pop-up definition windows, and graphics. Help files can be opened from the Help menu in the application, directly from the File Manager (Windows 3.1) or Explorer (Windows 9x), or from within a dialog box in the application.

Windows 3.1 and Windows NT 3.x help files were based on WinHelp 3.x. Windows 9x and Windows NT 4 introduced a new help system, WinHelp 4.x. HTML Help was introduced with Windows 98 and Windows NT version 5.

A typical help file for Windows 3.1 with WinHelp 3.x looks like this:

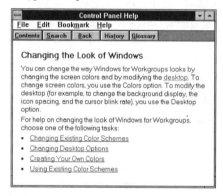

A typical help file for Windows 9x with WinHelp 4.x looks like this:

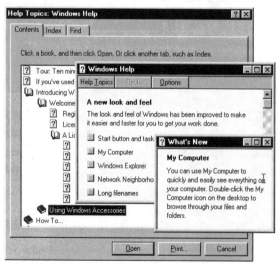

1.1 Introduction

In a WinHelp 4.x environment (Win32s, Windows 9x or Windows NT), help files often have a contents file. This file, with the extension CNT, contains a table of contents for the entire help file or a set of linked help files.

1.1.1 Navigation

You can navigate through a help file in several ways:

- The Contents button will display the table of contents of the help file. Click on a topic title to jump to that topic.

- Click the Search or Index button or tab to display an index of keywords that will help you find information. You can either select an entry from the list or type (part of) a word and press Enter.

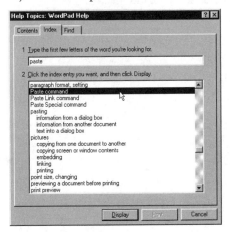

- Click the Find button for a full text search index of all words in the help file (WinHelp 4.x help only).

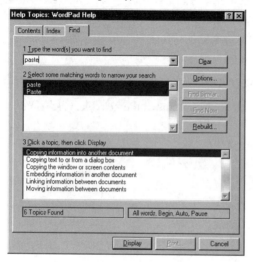

- In a help topic, click a jump, in WinHelp 3.x help a green item with solid underline, to open the help information for that topic. Jumps can be text, graphics or parts of a graphic. Jumps in graphics are called hotspots. The Back button on the help navigation bar will return you to the page where the jump was located.

- Click a definition pop-up, a green item with dotted underline, to display a window with the definition or explanation of the word, string, or graphic.

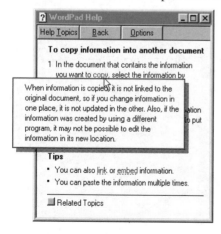

- Use the browse buttons (>> and <<) on the help navigation bar to browse through the help file page-by-page.

- Press the Help button or F1 key in a dialog box or screen to display help information about that dialog box. This function is called context-sensitive help. In WinHelp 4.x help, click the small question mark symbol at the top of a dialog box, and then click the item about which you want information. This help type is called "What's This" help.

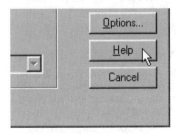 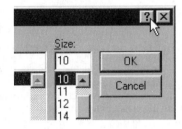

The mouse pointer changes shape when it is over a jump or hotspot. The Back and History buttons are additional navigation tools. Refer to How to Use Help in the Help menu of Program Manager (Windows 3.1) or Start - Help - How to - Use Help (Windows 9x/NT) for more information on navigating through help files.

1.1.2 Compilation

A Windows help project is based on a project file with the extension HPJ. This file contains all help file settings. The HPJ file is an ASCII text file that is used by the help compiler to compile one or more RTF (Rich Text Format) files into a HLP file.

Typically, the Microsoft Help Compiler is used in combination with a Word macro shell like Robohelp, Doc-To-Help, Help Magician or ForeHelp.

Refer to the Windows Help Engineering section on page 188 for more information about compiling and testing Windows help files.

1.2 Translation

The actual help file text is translated in RTF files. Other files that require translation are the CNT (Contents), and HPJ (Project) files.

Before you start translating a help file, make sure you are using the right word processor. The RTF output of different–versions of–word processors might differ, which could cause problems when the help files are compiled. For example, some older versions of the Microsoft Help Compiler do not accept RTF files that have been saved with Microsoft Word 8. If you're not sure which word processor to use, ask your client.

Tip

When a help shell like Robohelp is used, translation is usually performed in Word files (DOC). These Word files will be automatically saved as RTF before they are compiled into a help file.

1.2.1   RTF Files

RTF files can be translated in any Windows-based word processor that supports the RTF format. Most of the time, Microsoft Word is used. A page in a RTF file looks like this:

$ k + Changing the Look of Windows

You can change the way Windows for Workgroups looks by changing the screen colors and by modifying the desktopdesktop@glossary.hlp. To change screen colors, you use the Colors option. To modify the desktop (for example, to change the background display, the icon spacing, and the cursor blink rate), you use the Desktop option.

For help on changing the look of Windows for Workgroups, choose one of the following tasks:

{bmc Cont0000.BMP}   Changing Existing Color SchemesChanging_Existing_Color_Schemes
{bmc Cont0000.BMP}   Changing Desktop OptionsChanging_Desktop_Options
{bmc Cont0000.BMP}   Creating Your Own ColorsCreating_Your_Own_Colors
{bmc Cont0000.BMP}   Using Existing Color SchemesUsing_Existing_Color_Schemes
---Page Break---

Changing_the_Look_of_Windows

$ Changing the Look of Windows

κ look, changing; changing the look of Windows

+ Main:000

When you are using Microsoft Word, the following tips might help you work effectively with RTF files:

- Set your page view to display hidden text. To enable this option in Microsoft Word, choose Options in the Tools menu and select Hidden Text in the View tab. You can also activate the ¶ button on the toolbar.

- Make sure you disable the Replace Straight Quote with Smart Quotes option of the AutoCorrect feature from the Tools menu.

- Never use the Autoformat command from the Format menu. This will overwrite the styles in the template that is attached.

- Do not save the file in any other format than RTF.

- Do not insert or delete manual page breaks, paragraph marks, or hyphens in the text, because all lines in a help file are wrapped by the help system. Wrapping of the text is adjusted automatically to the size of the help window in which the information is displayed.

- Pay special attention to periods and commas that precede or follow a link. Periods and commas should not be part of the green underlined jump text or hidden text.

1.2.1.1 JUMPS AND POPUPS

In RTF files, items with single green underlines (desktopdesktop@glossary.hlp) will become definition popups in the compiled help file. Items with double green underlines (Changing Existing Color SchemesChanging_Existing_Color_Schemes) will become jumps. The text with dotted underline following these items is hidden text containing the ID code of the topic that the link will jump to. Topic IDs are defined by the footnotes, which are linked to every topic title. Refer to the Pound '#' character section on page 78 for more information about topic IDs.

This hidden code text is only visible when you enable the View Hidden Text option in your word processor.

Never translate or change hidden jump text in help source files! When you change or delete these codes, the jump will not work anymore in the compiled help file.

1.2.1.1.1   Consistency

Because help files contain many jumps and references to other topics in the help file, consistency in translation is very important. If, for example, the help file contains the sentence "See also: Using Jumps and Popups for more information", the translation of "Using Jumps and Popups for more information" should exactly match the actual topic title that is referred to.

When a computer aided translation tool, such as IBM TranslationManager or Trados Translator's Workbench is used, the translation memory will automatically suggest the correct translation after it has been entered for the first time. Because most help files are very repetitive, it is recommended to use a translation memory tool for these files. Refer to Chapter 5, Translation Memory Tools, for more information.

If you are not using translation memory, you might save some time by searching and globally replacing topic titles in (a collection of) RTF files.

1.2.1.1.2   Topic Titles

Translate topic titles in a consistent and systematic manner. Especially for help topics describing menu items or dialog box titles, it is recommended to translate topic titles like index entries, i.e., keyword first. Refer to the Translating Indexes section on page 120 for more information.

1.2.1.2   FOOTNOTES

Topic titles are usually preceded by the #, $, K and + symbols, which are linked to footnotes in the RTF document. Footnotes tell the help compiler how to access and link individual topics.

In Microsoft Word, choose the Footnotes command from the View menu to display the footnotes.

> **Tip**
>
> Double-click on a footnote symbol, such as the $ symbol, to jump directly to the footnote that is linked to the symbol.

Typically, pages in RTF files contain these footnotes:

```
# IDH_CONTENTS
$ Contents
K Contents;Index
+ main:000
```

1.2.1.2.1   Pound '#' character

The string following the pound (#) character is the context string that uniquely identifies the topic among all topics in the help system. It is like the address of the topic, which is required. All items in CNT files and all links in a help file refer to this topic ID.

This footnote text **should not** be translated.

1.2.1.2.2   Dollar sign '$' character

The string following the dollar sign ($) character is the title string which is displayed when the reader uses the search feature of Windows Help. It is displayed in the Go To box (WinHelp 3.x) or Topics Found box (WinHelp 4.x), the Bookmark dialog box, and the History window.

Usually, this string is identical to the subject title. Copying the topic title and pasting it in this footnotes field is the fastest way to translate this footnote, and to retain consistency. When you browse down in the footnote field using the arrow key, the document window automatically displays the subject that belongs to the footnote.

This footnote text **should** be translated.

1.2.1.2.3   Letter 'K' character

The string following the letter 'K' character contains search keywords for the topic, separated by semi-colons (without spaces). The keywords are displayed in the index list of the Search dialog box or Index tab of a Windows help file. First and second level entries are separated by commas or colons.

The following ᴷ keyword text will result in the index entries listed below it:

ᴷ first;second, third;fourth

first
second
    third
fourth

Help keywords are comparable to index entries in a printed manual, and should be translated as such. Refer to the Translating Indexes section on page 120 for more information.

Please note that no more than 255 characters may be used per keyword. This footnote text **should** be translated.

1.2.1.2.4   Plus '+' character

The string following the plus (+) character is the browse sequence string which is used by Windows Help to provide a browsing order accessed by the left and right browse buttons on the button bar of Windows Help.

This footnote text **should not** be translated. However, help engineers might want to change the browse sequence for alphabetized help topics, such as glossaries. Refer to the Browse Sequence section on page 196 for more information.

1.2.1.2.5   Letter 'A' character

This type of footnote functions like the 'K' character except that it is never seen by the user and is not included in the Index. The items in this footnote are hidden search phrases that are mainly used to activate Alink macros.

This footnote text **should not** be translated.

It is possible that the document contains other footnote types, but these are not of interest for translators. Refer to your help compiler documentation for more information about other footnote types.

1.2.1.2.6   The @ sign

This footnote is used to add comments to a footnote section. The author of the help file may have included comments for the localizer.

This footnote text **should not** be translated.

1.2.1.3   GRAPHICS

Most Windows help files contain graphic images, such as screen captures. These images are not embedded in the RTF files, but linked.

A string like {bmc GFXFILE.BMP} indicates that a bitmap with the name GFXFILE.BMP will be inserted when the help file is compiled. The compiler will check for this file in the path that is specified in the BMROOT= option in the HPJ file.

Bitmap names and links to the bitmaps should never be changed. In bitmap links, *bmc* indicates that the bitmap will be aligned as a text character, i.e., treated as regular paragraph text. If *bml* or *bmr* is used, the bitmap will be aligned along the left, respectively right margin of the help topic.

Apart from bitmaps with the extension BMP, it is also possible to include graphics of the following types in help files: Windows metafiles (WMF), Windows Help multiple-hotspot (SHED) bitmaps (SHG), and Windows Help multi-resolution bitmaps (MRB). Refer to the Graphics section on page 194 for more information about these graphic types.

1.2.2   HPJ Files

HPJ files contain all settings that are used to compile the help file. A HPJ file is a text-only file that can be edited in an ASCII editor or Microsoft Help Workshop (WinHelp 4.x only).

The following pages list the sections in a HPJ file that might require translation.

1.2.2.1   TITLES

The title of a help file, which is displayed in the title bar of the help file, needs to be translated in the HPJ file. For WinHelp 3.x projects, open the HPJ file as ASCII text and translate the words following the TITLE= line in the [OPTIONS] section.

If you use Microsoft Help Workshop, open the HPJ file, click on the Options button, click on the General tab and translate the title in the Help title field.

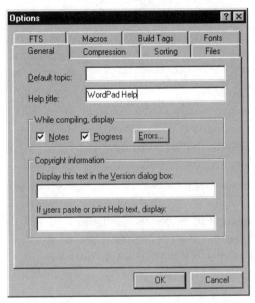

A help file can also contain secondary windows. Secondary windows often contain systematic instructions for tasks that are mentioned in the main help window. Titles for these windows can be translated in the [WINDOWS] section.

In Microsoft Help Workshop, click on the Windows button, choose the General tab and translate the Title bar text for each window type.

1.2.2.2 BUTTON NAMES

The [CONFIG] section in a HPJ file contains entries that will activate macros that insert buttons in the button bar of the help file, or customized menus in the menu bar. Commonly used buttons are the Glossary and Close buttons that respectively display a list of terms and close the help file.

Apart from these custom buttons, the button bar will also contain a set of standard help buttons, i.e., Contents, Index, Find, Help Topics, Back, Options, and Print. These buttons will be displayed in the language of the operating system–or rather, of the WinHelp viewer– you are running.

The custom buttons are defined by the CreateButton macro. If the [CONFIG] section contains a macro line like:

```
CreateButton("Glossary_Btn","&Glossary","JI
(`bubble.hlp>Gloss',`IDH_Glossary')")
```

A button titled *Glossary* will be created on the button bar. In this statement, the word &*Glossary* should be translated, with the ampersand (&) character followed by the letter that will be the accelerator key. This accelerator key should be unique on the button bar.

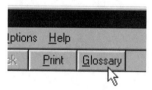

In Microsoft Help Workshop, click on the Config button, select the line with the button macro, click on Edit and translate the button title.

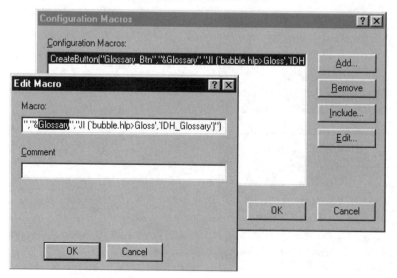

If the [CONFIG] section contains a statement like:

```
ExtInsertItem(mnu_file,itm_wpad,&Launch Wordpad, ExecFile(wordpad.exe),3)
```

a menu item labeled *Launch Wordpad* will be inserted on WinHelp's File menu.

1.2.2.3   COPYRIGHT INFO

If a HPJ file contains a COPYRIGHT= option, the text following the equal symbol will be displayed if a user selects the Version command in the Help menu. To translate copyright info in Microsoft Help Workshop, click the Options button, select the General tab, and translate the text in the Display this text in the Version dialog box field.

The CITATION= option defines text that will be appended if users copy and paste or print text from the help file. To translate citation text in Microsoft Help Workshop, click the Options button, select the General tab, and translate the text in the If users paste or print Help text, display: field.

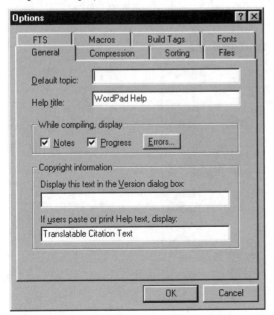

1.2.3   CNT Files

The contents (CNT) file is an ANSI text file that provides all information that is displayed when you click the Contents tab in the Help Topics dialog box. The CNT file also determines from which help files the keywords are displayed on the Index and Find tabs. Only WinHelp 4.x help files support CNT files.

A CNT file can be translated in a Windows-based text editor or in Microsoft Help Workshop. However, be careful using Microsoft Help Workshop to translate CNT files. Some versions of the Help Workshop corrupt CNT files by deleting @*help_file_name.hlp* references.

1.2.3.1   TITLES

The string following the `:Title` marker in the beginning of the CNT file can be translated. The title will show up in the title bar of the Help Topics window. Text that is preceded by a semi-colon is comment text and does not need to be translated.

> **Important**
>
> The first lines of a .CNT file might contain markers that should not be translated, for example `:Base`, `:Index`, and `:Link`.

In Microsoft Help Workshop, open the CNT file and translate the title in the Default Title box.

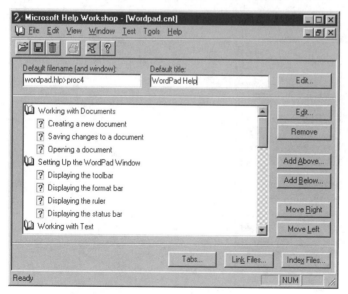

1.2.3.2 CONTENTS

Each line in a CNT file starts with the level number. If you translate the CNT file in a text editor, only the text preceding the equal symbol (=) should be translated. Be careful not to delete any codes. The codes following the equal symbol are help topic IDs.

```
1 Working with Documents
2 Creating a new document=WRIPAD_CREATE_DOCUMENT
2 Saving changes to a document=WRIPAD_SAVE_FILE
2 Opening a document=WRIPAD_OPEN_DOC
1 Setting Up the WordPad Window
2 Displaying the toolbar=COMMON_TOOLBAR_ON_OFF@common.hlp>proc4
2 Displaying the format bar=WRIPAD_FORMAT_BAR
```

To translate a CNT file in Microsoft Help Workshop, open the file and activate the Translation option in the File menu. This option will ensure you only translate visible text. You cannot modify topic IDs, help file names, or window names.

To translate an entry in a CNT file, double-click on the entry and type your translation in the Title field of the Edit Contents Tab Entry dialog box.

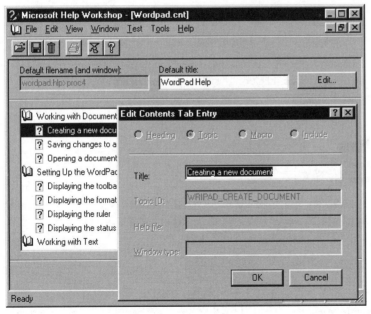

When the entire CNT file has been translated, you can automatically test it using Microsoft Help Workshop. Refer to the Contents File (WinHelp 4.x only) section on page 206 for more information.

If the HLP file has already been translated, and the CNT is the last thing that needs to be translated, follow these steps to make sure the translations in your CNT file correspond to the actual help topic titles:

1.   Open the folder containing the HLP and corresponding CNT file.

2.   Make a copy of the CNT file, and add the TXT extension to the copy.

3.   Double-click on the HLP file to display the Contents window with the contents of the CNT file.

4.   Open the TXT file using Notepad or any other Windows-based text editor.

5.   Open the first topic in the Contents window, and double-click on the first topic (with a question mark).

6.   In the topic window, which is translated, select the title and press Ctrl+C to copy the title.

7.   Switch to Notepad and replace the original topic title before the equals symbol (=) with the translated title that you just copied.

8.   Switch to the help window, and click the Help Topics button to display the Contents window and copy the next topic title.

When all titles in the TXT file have been translated, delete the original CNT file. Change the TXT extension to CNT and double-click on the HLP file to open the translated Contents window.

2 HTML Files

2.1 Introduction

HTML, short for HyperText Markup Language, is the file format that is used on the World Wide Web. In the future, most online help will be published in HTML or HTML Help formats.

HTML is a simplified version of SGML, Standard Generalized Markup Language, which is an international standard for information exchange that was adopted as a standard of the International Organization for Standardization (ISO 8879) in 1986. An SGML document has an associated document type definition (DTD) that specifies the rules for the structure of the document. HTML files do not use a DTD. A new standard is the XML (eXtended Markup Language), which is an initiative proposed by the W3C as an alternative to HTML. XML is a language that allows you to create your own markup, optimized for use on the Internet.

All markup language files are text-only files with tags that enable formatting of the pages, inserting pictures, forms, etc. These tags are typically enclosed between < and > characters. HTML files can be viewed using a browser, such as Microsoft Internet Explorer or Netscape Navigator.

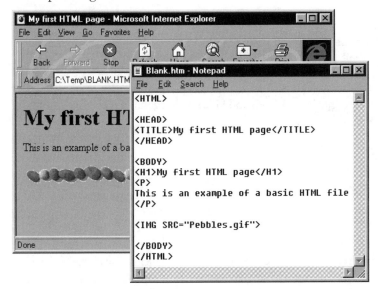

There are thousands of HTML tags, and each new HTML version comes with new tags. HTML tags are defined by the World Wide Web Consortium (   ). Because there are only few tags of interest for translators, I will concentrate on a general outline of the HTML format and language-dependent tags. Typically, tags should not be changed. However, sometimes it is necessary to change text *within* a tag.

2.2 File Format: Overview

2.2.1 Sections

Each HTML file starts with the <HTML> tag and ends with </HTML>. An HTML file consists of two sections, the HEAD and the BODY sections. Typically, the HEAD section contains the title of the page, the application that was used to create the HTML file, and the name or e-mail address of the creator. The BODY section contains everything that appears on the page, including text, images, or embedded Java applets.

2.2.2 Paragraphs

Paragraphs within the BODY section can have styles, such as <H1> for Heading 1 or <OL> for ordered lists. Paragraphs are enclosed between <P> and </P> tags. Within a paragraph, tags can be used to change the character settings of a word or string. For example, if a word is enclosed between <B> and </B> tags, it will be displayed in boldface type.

2.2.3   Images

Images are inserted into an HTML document using the `<IMG>` tag.
For example: `<IMG SRC="Pebbles.gif">`.

2.2.4   Comments

Comment text is enclosed between **`<!--`** and **`-->`** tags.
For example: `<!-- This is comment text -->`.

2.2.5   Java Applets

Many HTML pages on the Internet contain Java applets, which are Java applications that don't run standalone but can only be run from an HTML page within a Java-compatible browser. Java applets are marked with the `<APPLET>` tag.

2.3   Translation

2.3.1   How to Translate

HTML files can be translated in three ways: using an HTML editor, using a text editor (directly in the HTML source code), or using a translation memory tool.

2.3.1.1   USING AN HTML EDITOR

There are numerous commercial and non-commercial HTML editors available and most modern word processors or desktop publishing applications are capable of editing HTML files. Examples of commonly used HTML editors are Microsoft FrontPage, Claris Home Page, and the HTML editors that come with the Internet Explorer and Netscape Navigator browsers.

The main advantage of translating files in an HTML editor is that the translator will view and edit the HTML file in WYSIWYG mode, with all layout and graphical information present. In addition, it is more difficult to corrupt or delete tags from the HTML code.

Preferably, HTML files should be translated in the same version of the editor that was used to create the files. To find out which editor was used to create an HTML file, view the HTML source and check if the HEAD section contains a line like:

`<META NAME=GENERATOR CONTENT="Claris Home Page 2.0">`.

Translating or editing HTML files in another HTML editor than the one that the files were created with might change the HTML tags or scripted code considerably, or even corrupt them. Therefore, this method is not advisable! If you are not sure which editor you should use to translate the files, ask your client.

2.3.1.2   USING A TEXT EDITOR

Since the HTML language changes on a regular basis, some HTML files might contain elements or tags that are not yet supported by the HTML editor that is used to translate the files. In these cases, the translator needs to open the HTML file as source text in a text editor and locate the translatable text between the HTML tags.

For example, if you choose the Source command from the View menu in Microsoft Internet Explorer, the HTML source code will be displayed in a Notepad window. You can also right-click on the HTML page or frame and select the View Source command.

There are some disadvantages to translating HTML files directly in the source:

- The layout of the HTML file is not visible, except when the file is loaded into the browser.

- Special and accented characters and tabs are often represented by *ampersand tags*, or escape sequences. For example, the © character will be displayed as © and the é character will be displayed as é. Some HTML editors, such as HomeSite, contain features for automatically searching and replacing extended characters with their HTML equivalents.

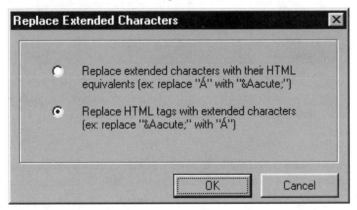

- It is easy to corrupt the HTML code, for example by accidentally deleting < markers.

- There is a risk that translatable text will be overlooked.

Important

The use of ampersand tags in HTML will assure correct display of extended characters on all platforms and browsers. Therefore, it is essential to always use these ampersand tags in HTML files.

A good alternative to translating HTML files in a text editor is using a text-based HTML editor. These editors will allow you to edit the HTML code in text-mode with all tags and HTML information displayed in different colors. An example of a text-based HTML editor is Allaire's HomeSite.

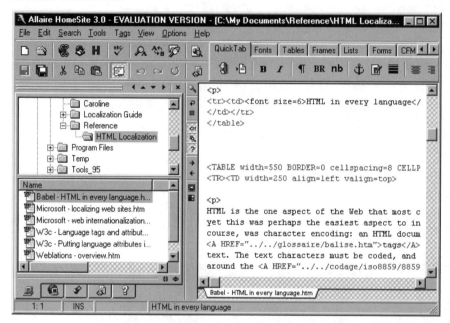

HomeSite allows you to edit HTML pages, view pages in an external or internal browser, check the spelling of pages, search and replace strins, and verify links. For more information about HomeSite and a demo version, visit the Allaire Web site at www.allaire.com.

2.3.1.3 USING TRANSLATION MEMORY TOOLS

Apart from translating HTML files in an HTML editor or directly in the text source, most translation memory tools have filters for HTML files. Because HTML file collections on the Internet usually contain very repetitive text, using translation memory will lower translation time and costs considerably. Also translating updates of Web sites will be a lot easier and quicker when a translation memory of the previous version exists.

Examples of translation memory tools that support the HTML formatare Trados Translator's Workbench, IBM TranslationManager, and Atril Déjà Vu.

Of course, the filters used to import the HTML files in these translation memory tools need to support all the HTML tags that are present in the files that you are translating. Make sure you run some tests with the HTML files before you start translating.

Refer to Chapter 5, Translation Memory Tools, for more information about translating HTML files using translation memory tools.

2.3.2 What to Translate

In the following section, we will assume that you will be translating the HTML file in the source code. If you are using an HTML editor or translation memory tool, these procedures do not apply. In either case, it is useful to have a basic knowledge of HTML coding before you start translating an HTML-based project.

2.3.2.1 TITLE

In the head section of each HTML file, the title is defined. The text between `<TITLE>` and `</TITLE>` will show up in the title bar of your browser.

The head section of the HTML file might also contain META tags. A META tag is used to convey information about the document or to specify headers for the document. In the following examples, the text to be translated is bold:

- `<META NAME="keywords" CONTENT="`**`keyword keyword keyword`**`">`. This tag provides keywords for search engines such as Excite, Yahoo, or AltaVista. The keywords that are defined here are added to the keywords found in the document itself.

- `<META NAME="description" CONTENT="`**`This is a site`**`">`. Search engines which support the above tag will display the text you specify here, rather than the first few lines of text from the actual document when the document shows up in a search results window.

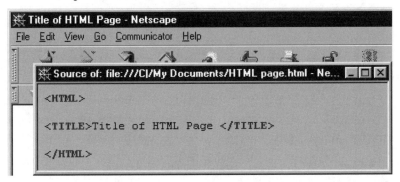

2.3.2.2 BODY TEXT

Apart from the text that is visible in the browser, HTML files may contain other translatable text. The following sections contain the most common examples.

2.3.2.2.1 Image Placeholders

`<IMG SRC="Header.gif" ALT="`**`Header Image`**`">`
This line will insert the Header.gif image on the HTML page. The ALT attribute defines the text that will be shown when the image is loading, or when the image is not available.

2.3.2.2.2   Scripts

```
<input Type="button" Value="Welcome to..." onClick="alert('My
First Home Page')">
```

This line will insert a button with the name *Welcome to* on the HTML page. Clicking on this button will open a window with the text *My First Home Page*. Obviously, this needs to be translated.

2.3.2.2.3   Comment Text

Comment text, which is enclosed in **<!--** and **--!>** tags will usually not be translated.

2.3.2.2.4   Status Bar Text

One tag which may be easily overlooked is the onmouseover=window.status tag. The text following this tag is displayed in the browser status bar when the mouse pointer is positioned over a link.

```
<a href="edit.htm" onmouseover="window.status='Copying and pasting
text';   return true">Copy and Paste</a>
```

This line will display *Copying and pasting text* in the status bar when the mouse is on the link "Copy and Paste".

2.3.2.2.5   Java Applets

Java applets are marked with the <APPLET> tag. This is an example of a Java applet section in an HTML file:

```
<APPLET codebase="../Home" code="SATextOverlay.class" width=534
height=49>
<param name=image value="./images/AdminBanner.gif">
<param name=text value="Text Overlay Applet Example">
<param name=font value="SansSerif-plain-28">
<param name=posx value="68">
<param name=posy value="center">
</APPLET>
```

This example contains a so-called *text overlay* applet, where text is placed on top of an image. Only the text following *text value* would require translation. The applet box can be resized using the coordinates in the first line, which should match the sizes of the AdminBanner.gif image used.

Text used in applets can also be stored in *resource bundles*. For more information about resource bundles, refer to the Java section on page 249.

The best way to ensure that you translated everything is to open the HTML file in a browser while you are translating it in a text editor. If you save the HTML source, and click the Refresh button in the browser, your changes are displayed.

2.3.2.3   GRAPHICS

Most HTML pages contain links to graphics. Graphics linked to HTML pages are in GIF or JPG format and may contain banners, buttons, and titled photographs.

Because graphics are often used to create banners with special fonts, colors and backgrounds, they are most complex to translate. Ask your client for font information, layered graphic files with a separate text layer, or blank background images. For more information about graphics editing, refer to the Bitmap Editing section on page 170 and the Graphics Editing section on page 186.

3   Macintosh Apple Guide Files

Apple Guide is an online help system for Macintosh computers that can be accessed using the Help command in an application. Apple Guide files typically function as general help, tutorial, or shortcut overview.

3.1   Introduction

The Apple Guide help system was introduced with System 7.5 in 1994. An Apple Guide help system consists of one or more guide file databases, which are created using a word processor or text editor in combination with a help authoring tool, such as Guide Maker.

Apple Guide files can contain text, sound, graphics and movies. A typical Apple Guide help file contains an access window with Topics overview, an index, and search screen.

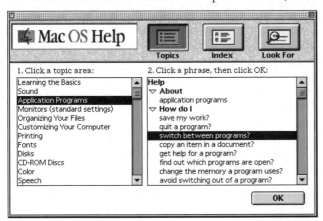

Apple Guide files can be translated in two ways: either directly in the Guide Script text files, or by exporting and importing localizable text from a Guide database using Guide Maker. When you export text from a Guide database using Guide Maker's Localize utility, all character style information is lost, including the blue color and underlining from links. Therefore, translating directly in the Apple Script resources is recommended if your Apple

Guide file contains font and style information that is embedded in the source file. If the source file contains style information that is defined using the `<Define Format>` commands, it is safe to use Guide Maker's Localize feature.

3.2 Translating Guide Script Files

A Guide Script file typically contains information that is structured like this:

```
<Define Panel> "How do I localize Apple Guide files?"
<Format> "Tag"
<PICT> 9457, RIGHT
<Format> "Body"
<End Panel>
```

After this panel definition is compiled using Guide Maker, it will look like this:

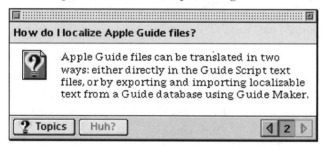

Follow these instructions when you are translating a Guide Script file:

1. In Guide Script, tags are surrounded by angled brackets (< and >). These tags should not be changed or translated.

2. Comments (or remarks) are preceded with a # character. They usually only document the code. The comments should not be translated.

In Apple Guide, all sections are related to each other, so consistent translation of topics, panel and sequence names is very important. Often, Apple Guide files contain coach marks, which are indicators that point a user to a specific element. Usually a coach mark draws a red circle around a software menu or dialog box option. Coach marks require special attention during translation because the translation needs to exactly match the software option in order to work.

If you are not completely sure if a string needs to be translated, try to locate the screen in the running Apple Guide file, and compare it against your Guide Script document.

3.3 Using Guide Maker

Guide Maker provides a Localize utility to help you translate all elements of an Apple Guide file, such as topic areas, topics, panel titles, text in panels, coach marks, button labels, index terms, and other content.

To localize an Apple Guide file using Guide Maker, follow these steps:

1. Start Guide Maker. Select the Localize command from the Utilities menu.

2. Click in the Script Source File area of the Localize window to select the source Guide Script file that you want to extract text strings from.

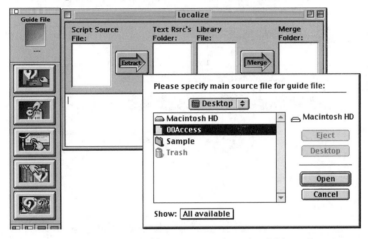

3. Click in the Text Rsrc's Folder area to select the folder where you want to place the files containing the extracted strings.

4. Click in the Library File area of the Localize window to create a localization library file. The localization library file contains information about the position of the extracted text strings in the source files.

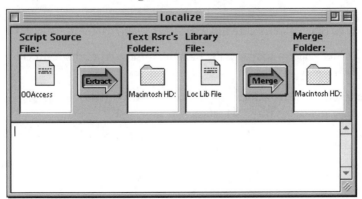

5. Click the Extract arrow in the Localize window to extract the text strings. A text file is created for each source file, with the RSRC extension added to the file name.

6. Use a resource editor such as ResEdit or Resorcerer to translate the extracted strings. All translatable text can be found in the TEXT resource. Guide Maker stores the extracted text strings as TEXT resources with resource names that give information about the text string. By looking at a resource name, you can determine the Guide Script command associated with the text string, and from that information you can induce the structure of the text string. Refer to the Translatable Resources table section on page 97 for a description of these resources.

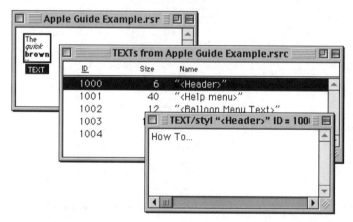

7. Apart from translating the TEXT resources in the extracted Guide Script files, there is also a Standard Resource file included with the build environment. This resource file contains image (PICT) resources. For more information on translating these resources, refer to the Image Resources section on page 99. Also, check if there are other localizable art resource files included in the file.

8. Click the Merge Folder area of the Localize window to select the folder where you want to place your localized files.

9. Click the Merge arrow to merge the translated strings from the RSRC files and localization library.

10. Build a guide file with the localized source files. Refer to the Compiling Apple Guide Files section on page 244 section for more information.

3.4 Translatable Resources

The following table lists the typical TEXT resource names (Apple Script tags). The information is an extract from the Apple Guide Complete Web site at developer.apple.com/techpubs/mac/AppleGuide/AppleGuide-2.html.

Text Resource Name	Description of Associated Text String
<Balloon Menu Text>	Specifies the text for the help balloon associated with your guide file's menu item name in your application's Help menu.
<Checkbox>	Specifies a label for a checkbox.
<Define Context Check>	Specifies an additional parameter in a context check and indicates a text string type LPSTRING.
<Define Item Coach>	Specifies the item that is highlighted by a coachmark.
<Define Menu Coach>	Specifies the menu name or menu item that is highlighted by a coachmark.
<Define Prompt Set>	Specifies a navigation prompt that appears on the bottom of a panel.
<Define Sequence>	Specifies a sequence display title.
<Define Window Coach>	Specifies a window in which a coachmark is drawn.
<Exception>	Specifies a word that should not be stemmed when Apple Guide parses a search phrase.
<Header>	Specifies a header associated with a particular topic area or index term.
<Help Menu>	Specifies the name of a guide file or the Command key shortcut.
<Hot Text>	Specifies hot text in a panel.
<If>	Specifies text (with data type LPSTRING) that is part of a condition.
<Ignore>	Specifies a word or phrase that Apple Guide ignores when parsing a search phrase.
<Index>	Specifies an index term.
<Look For Instruction>	Specifies an instruction that appears above the search phrase entry box in the Full Access window when Look For is the active list.

Text Resource Name	Description of Associated Text String
<Look For Results Instruction>	Specifies an instruction that appears above the list of topics in the Full Access window when Look For is the active list and the user has performed a successful search.
<Look For Search Btn Instruction>	Specifies an instruction that appears above the Search button in the Full Access window when Look For is the active list.
<Look For String>	Specifies text that appears in the search phrase entry box in the Full Access window when Look For is the active list.
<Make Sure>	Specifies text (with data type LPSTRING) that is part of a condition.
Panel: *panel name*	Specifies the body text to be displayed in the panel specified by the panel name the text in the panel is divided into multiple pieces.
<Radio Button>	Specifies a label for a radio button.
<Skip If>	Specifies text (with data type LPSTRING) that is part of a condition.
<Standard Button>	Specifies a label for a standard button.
<Synonym> *index term, synonymous term*	Specifies a synonymous term for the index term specified in the text resource name.
<Define Text Block> *text block name*	Specifies a block of text. This block of text typically appears in the body text of howdy window.
<Topic>	Specifies a topic. This text string appears in the right column of the access window.
<Topic Area>	Specifies a topic area. This text appears in the left column of the Topics screen the access window. Note that you are limited to 31 one-byte characters.
<Topic Areas Instruction>	Specifies an instruction or a label.
<Topics Instructions>	Specifies an instruction that appears above the list of topics in the Full Access window when Topics or Index is the active list.
<Version>	Specifies version information for the guide file.

3.5 Image Resources

Images that are used in the Apple Guide file, such as the common Oops and Huh? buttons, are stored as individual PICT resources in the Standard Resources file that are compiled into the Apple Guide file. To edit an interface button, you'll need to copy it from the resource file and edit it in Photoshop (or another image editing program). For more information about translating PICT resources, refer to the Images section on page 57.

These are common translations of Apple Guide terms:

English	Oops	Huh?	Tip	Do This
French	Attention	Infos	Conseil	Action
German	Hinweis	Noch Fragen?	Tip	Aktion
Italian	Ops	Come?	Consigli	Fai così
Spanish	¡Ojo!	?Qué?	Consejo	Haga esto

Translations for other languages can be found in Chapter 2 of the online version of the Apple Guide Complete manual at developer.apple.com/techpubs/mac/AppleGuide/AppleGuide-2.html.

If you have localized versions of the Apple Guide extension, or the Macintosh Guide file, you can copy most of these standard buttons from these files to your Standard Resources file. The PICT resources contain four versions of each button: Color active, Color inactive, Black & White active, and Black & White inactive.

For more information about localizing Apple Guide files, visit the Apple Guide Web site at www.apple.com/macos/apple-guide.

4 Macintosh Help Files

Many Macintosh applications include a help system that is comparable to the Windows help file system. This help system is called QuickHelp and is developed by Altura Software, Inc.

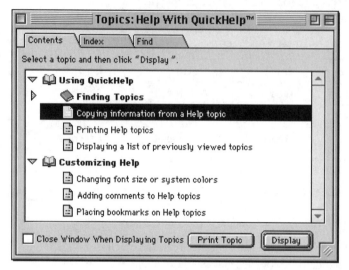

Like Windows Help, a QuickHelp project is based on RTF files containing hypertext links and bitmap references, which are compiled using a project file that can be edited and compiled on a Macintosh with the QuickHelp compiler. QuickHelp files are fully compatible with Windows Help 4.x, which means that it is possible to do full-text searches, use CNT contents files, and include secondary windows. For more information about Windows help and translating RTF files, refer to the Windows Help Files section on page 72.

Because of Windows help compatibility, the QuickHelp system is often used for cross-platform products. The QuickHelp Viewer is available in most European languages. For more information about QuickHelp, visit the Altura Web site at www.altura.com.

4.1 QuickHelp Compiler

The QuickHelp Compiler is very similar to the Windows help compiler. However, it contains additional options that must be set to resolve platform differences between Windows and Macintosh.

To compile a QuickHelp file using the QuickHelp Compiler, follow these steps:

1. Launch the compiler and open your help project HPJ file. The compiler will create a settings file that will have the same name as the project file plus the qh extension.

2. Set the desired options using the commands in the Project menu. In general, the only settings you might need to change are the paths.

3. Select the Compile command from the Project menu.

You will be asked where and under which name you wish to store the compiled help file.

5 Readme Files

Readme files are added to the setup disks of an application to provide the user with last-minute information that was not available when the manuals were printed. In addition, corrections or additions to the manual or online help, platform-specific compatibility information, and additional setup instructions can be included in a readme file.

5.1.1 Translation

Because the English readme file is often finalized before the localization of a project is finished, it is possible that much of the information contained in it can still be fixed in the localized documentation or help. For example, if corrections to the English user guide are described in the readme file, there might still be time to implement these changes in the localized user guide. This can reduce the size of the readme file considerably. Consult your client if they prefer a complete translation of the readme file or implementation of the corrections in the translated material.

Usually, the file name of the readme file is translated. For a complete listing of standard translations for these files names, refer to the Readme File Names section on page 290.

5.1.2 File Format

Readme files usually are text-only files, with the TXT extension. This means that they do not contain any character or paragraph formatting. Translation can be performed in a text editor that runs on the target platform.

For example, readme files for the Windows platform can be edited using Notepad or any other Windows-based text editor or word processor. Macintosh readme files can be translated using SimpleText or other Macintosh text editor or word processor.

On the Windows platform, readme files might also be in Windows 3.1 Write (WRI), Windows 9x Wordpad (DOC) or Windows Help (HLP) format. Wordpad files, with the DOC extension, are in fact Word 6 documents. You can translate them using Word, just make sure you do the final layout in Wordpad.

Sometimes, the English original of the readme file contains carriage returns at the end of each line. In this case, use regular paragraphs for your translation and, after proofreading and QA, save the file as text only with line breaks.

Chapter 4:
Translating Documentation

This chapter contains information about the preparation and translation of manuals, collateral materials, and creation of online documents.

A s mentioned in the introduction, most localization projects include one or more printed documents. Apart from the manuals, such as Installation or Getting Started guides, software packages usually also contain collateral material to translate, such as quick reference cards, marketing pieces, and the box that the product will be shipped in.

Please note that this chapter does not contain in-depth desktop publishing information; just issues important for translators and some general layout instructions are provided.

1 Introduction

Originally, documentation was translated by overwriting the English text in a document that is created in a word processor, such as Word, or in a document processing application, such as FrameMaker or PageMaker.

Nowadays text is usually imported into a translation memory tool, and exported back into its original format after translation. For more information about translation memory tools, refer to Chapter 5. Collateral material, such as marketing material or quick reference cards is typically translated in a desktop publishing application, such as QuarkXPress.

The original documents contain layout settings which are defined in style sheets. These style sheets define paragraph formatting, such as page setup, header styles, list numbers, bullets, notes, and spacing. These documents also contain character formatting such as bold and italic, index markers, graphics, and screen captures.

It is recommended to always use English versions of the applications mentioned in this chapter to do your translations. Files edited in translated application versions often contain field codes that don't translate back correctly when the file is opened in the English version.

1.1 Preparation

When you start translating a document that has been created in an application like Word, WordPerfect, or FrameMaker, there are several things you should keep in mind to avoid problems in the localized versions. Some of these issues are listed in the following sections.

1.1.1 Product Information

Before you start translating a manual, ask your client for a hard copy of the English document.

It is also recommended to ask for file specifications, such as deliverables, platform and version of the editor, style sheet, fonts, and printer driver.

1.1.1.1 DELIVERABLES

If you did not get specific instructions, ask about the deliverables for the "paper" or online documentation.

Usually, only translated versions of the source files need to be delivered in their original formats, such as FrameMaker files, along with a hard copy of the translated manuals. However, more and more localization agencies also deliver PostScript files, film, or online versions of the documents. For more information about creating online manuals, refer to the Creating Online Documentation section on page 129.

1.1.1.2 PLATFORM AND VERSION

If you have not been provided with specific instructions about the platform, application and application version that you should use to translate the document, don't hesitate to ask. Editing and saving documents in an application version different from the one that they were created with can change the file layout drastically.

Also, avoid converting documents into another format for translation purposes. For example, do not import a WordPerfect document in Word, unless your client approves of this.

1.1.1.3 STYLE SHEET

Check which style sheet, or template, is attached to the document. A style-sheet is a blueprint for the text, graphics, and formatting that are the same in every document of a particular type. Pre-formatted documents usually have customized attached or embedded style sheets that define the layout of the document.

If you did not receive this style sheet with the original documents, ask your client for it. Without the correct style sheet attached or embedded, the document layout will display differently in the translated versions.

Also, ask your client if the page size needs to be changed for the localized versions of the documentation files. Sometimes, special templates for localized documents are provided.

These templates would typically have a smaller font size or line spacing to allow for text expansion.

In Word, you can check the style sheet by choosing the Templates command from the File menu (Word 7), or Templates and Add-ins from the Tools menu (Word 8). In FrameMaker, template information is stored within the FrameMaker file. You can use the Import Formats command from the File menu to import the template information from another document or template.

1.1.1.4   FONTS

Make sure you have all required fonts installed on your computer, in the right type and version.

Most applications display a warning dialog box when fonts are missing. Sometimes, missing fonts are automatically substituted by other, similar fonts. When these substituted fonts are saved into the document, the layout will change compared to the original document.

Even if you have the required fonts, it is advisable to ask for the fonts that were used to create the original documents. For example, standard fonts like Arial and Garamond exist in many versions and variations.

1.1.1.5   PRINTER DRIVER

If you are planning to deliver print-ready or PostScript documents, i.e., if you are doing all page formatting, check if you are using the printer driver that will be used to print the document.

Changing printer drivers changes layout, fonts, and page flow. To make sure you do not have to re-do any desktop publishing work, use the correct printer driver from the beginning.

For high-end printing purposes, often image writer drivers are used, such as Linotronic drivers. Check with your client which settings need to be used, such as PostScript level, resolution, and crop marks.

It is always advisable to do a print test in the very beginning of the project, for example using the first translated chapter that is available.

1.1.1.6   SCREEN CAPTURES

Make sure you know which specifications and software should be used to create the screen captures and other graphics in the document. More information about creating screen captures can be found on page 183 and 239.

1.1.1.7   CONTENT

Scan the manual for language-specific information, such as part numbers, print locations and telephone numbers. Asking for this information before translation starts will prevent delays in the end of the project.

A good example is the license agreement, which is included with many printed documents. If an extensive license agreement is included, ask your client if a local version is already available. Simply translating legal texts is usually not sufficient and can cause legal problems for both you and your client!

1.1.2   Testing Source Files

To ensure that the source files that you have received are correct, there some things you should do before you start translating.

1.1.2.1   TABLE OF CONTENTS AND INDEX

First, if the source document contains generated table of contents and index files, make a copy of these files and re-generate the TOC and index.

Next, compare the files that you generated with the files that were included with the source files. If there are differences, the index markers do not match the index file that has been generated by your client. In this case, the authors of the book have manually changed the index file after it was generated.

Generating the index in the source document will allow you to spot index problems before translation starts. Fixing translated indexes is a time-consuming and tedious job. If there are differences between the index markers and index file, verify with your client which one is correct.

1.1.2.2   ONE-TO-ONE PAGE TRANSLATION

Another question that you might consider asking is if your client expects you to maintain a one-to-one page correspondence between the original and the translated version of the document.

Instructing translators before translation starts that the target text should not be much longer than the source text can prevent a great deal of post-editing later in the localization process.

1.1.2.3   GRAPHICS

Graphics and screen captures in pre-formatted documents can be embedded or linked. If graphics are linked, most word processors will ask you to specify the location of the picture files when you open a document.

When you select the folder containing the graphics, and the application continues to request the location of some graphics, follow these steps:

1. Do a file search to check if the file is located in another folder.

2. Check if there is a file with an almost identical name, and verify if this is the missing file.

3. Notify your client of the missing files and request the files.

Also, create a list of texts that requires translation in the graphics. Sometimes graphics contain examples or captions. To ensure consistency, have this text translated by the same person who is translating the body text of the document.

The best way to get correct translations is to paste the graphic in a word processor or spreadsheet document and add the source text to be translated in a table underneath the image.

1.1.2.4 GENERAL INSTRUCTIONS

The following sections contain some general instructions that should be kept in mind when translating and working with documentation.

Always work in Page Layout view, i.e., not in Draft view. Also, make sure that hidden characters, hidden text, tabs, picture placeholders, headers, footers, and markers are visible on the screen. This will prevent you from accidentally deleting any codes.

- Do not translate, change or move hidden text.

- Do not insert manual page breaks and do not change footers that contain automatic page number fields.

- Do not manually hyphenate words or justify lines.

- Do not change any of the document settings, e.g., tabs, margins, page size, line spacing, or paragraph spacing.

- Do not rename files, unless your client specifically asks you to. Renaming files might cause problems generating book files or indexes.

1.1.2.4.1 Translation Memory Tools

If the documentation files will be translated in a translation memory tool, it is recommended to scan the source files for formatting that might cause problems in the tool.

For example, hard returns within paragraphs, multiple spaces, or incorrect use of tabs might cause incorrect segmentation of the source text when imported in the translation memory tool. For more information about translation memory tools, refer to Chapter 5.

2 Translating Manuals

Manuals are mostly created and translated in an application like Word, WordPerfect, or FrameMaker. Usually, there is one file per chapter and a book or master file, which is used to automatically generate a table of contents, index, and internal cross references.

In manuals, the following components need to be translated:

- Body text

- Index markers

- Callout text (text describing graphic images)

- Screen captures and other graphics

The following sections contain information about these elements.

Generally, software manuals are different from regular documentation in many ways, i.e., there are several things that you need to keep in mind when translating a software manual.

2.1 General

2.1.1 Style

It is very unlikely that users will read software manuals from a to z. Therefore, the style is not the most important thing in the translation of documentation.

Factors that are more important are consistency, technical accuracy, correct references to the software user interface, and punctuality.

2.1.2 Software References

Most user manuals contain many references to the menu options, prompts, and error messages found in the running software.

To avoid time-consuming correction work later in the process, keep these software references correct and consistent from the very beginning. If the software that is translated is not yet final, it might be better to leave all software references in English until you have a localized version of the software.

Sometimes a manual is translated before the software is translated. In that case, translate the software references in the manual and create a separate glossary of these references. This will make the translation of the software much easier, and software translations are probably more accurate because you have also translated the descriptive text for all options. However, make sure you *do* use glossaries from the target operating environment or from other products by the same client.

2.2 Using FrameMaker

2.2.1 File Setup

A typical FrameMaker manual setup consists of a book file that is linked to a table of contents file, several chapter files, appendices, and an index file. The book file typically has a *bk* extension and can be recognized by the book icon.

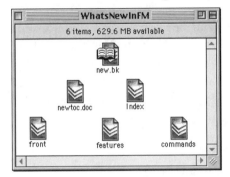

The book file is used to generate the table of contents, index and all internal and external cross-references. It is advisable to always work from within the book file, and not open the chapter or appendix files separately.

If you open a book file, a window is displayed with all the names of the files that are included. Double-click on a name in the list to open that chapter. Remember not to change the order of the files contained in a book file because this might change page numbering.

2.2.2 Opening a FrameMaker File

When you open a file, FrameMaker might ask you for the location of missing screen captures or other graphic files. A Missing File screen will be displayed:

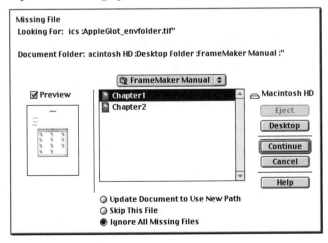

Always select the Ignore All Missing Files option and confirm this option by clicking on the Continue button. If you select the Update Document to Use New Path option, you will lose all links to the images, and missing images need to be re-imported.

If a message is displayed that your document uses unavailable fonts, install the missing fonts before continuing. Otherwise, FrameMaker substitutes fonts you do have for the missing ones.

In FrameMaker 5.5 and higher, choose Preferences from the File menu and activate the Remember Missing Font Names option. When this setting is on, FrameMaker does not permanently substitute fonts. When you reopen the file after the missing fonts have been installed, all the missing fonts will reappear.

2.2.3   Counting Words

To count words in a FrameMaker document, follow these steps:

1. From the File menu, select the Utilities command.

2. In the Document Reports dialog box, select Word Count.

3. Click the Run button to count the words in the FrameMaker document.

Please note that the word count does not include the index markers, so you also need to run the word count report on the generated index file.

2.2.4   Translating a File

Make sure you have the Text Symbols option in the View menu selected to avoid deleting index or other markers.

It is recommended to use the Delete or Backspace keys to delete English text after translation. Overtyping highlighted text will delete the index markers in the text block!

2.2.4.1   HEADERS AND FOOTERS

To translate headers or footers, choose Master Pages in the View menu. In the master pages, you will be able to edit the header or footer that is displayed on every page.

After translating the header text, choose Body Pages in the View menu and select the Keep Overrides option and the Continue button.

Sometimes headers or chapter titles are included in markers. To translate these, press Ctrl+Home (Windows) or Command-Home (Macintosh) to jump to the beginning of the text, choose the Find/Change command in the Edit menu and select Any Marker in the Find drop down list. The first marker that is found is selected. To open and edit this marker, choose Marker in the Special menu. If the marker belongs to the header, the type box will say Header/Footer.

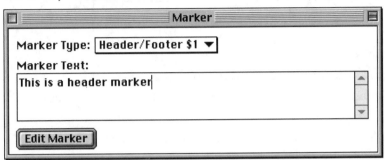

2.2.4.2   INDEX MARKERS

In FrameMaker, index entries are inserted in the main text with markers, not fields. These markers need to be opened in order to access and edit the text of an index entry.

Index markers are indicated with **T** symbols, that are only visible when the Text Symbols option in the View menu is enabled.

To translate index markers, follow these steps:

1. Open the first chapter of the document, press Ctrl+Home (Windows) or Command-Home (Macintosh) to jump to the beginning of the text, and search for the first index entry. You do this by choosing the Find/Change command from the Edit menu or pressing Ctrl+F or Command-F.

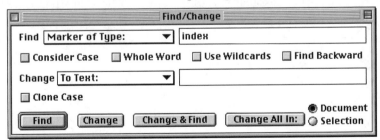

2. In the Find list menu, select Marker of Type. In the Find text box, type *index*.

3. Click on the Find button to jump to the first index marker in the chapter.

4. When the first index marker is found and selected, press Ctrl+J or Command-J or choose Marker from the Special menu.

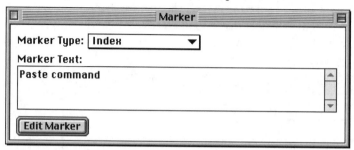

5. Translate the index marker, and press Return or click the Edit Marker button. Do not close the Marker window.

6. Press Ctrl+G or Command-G to automatically open the next index marker.

Within the marker window, a colon separates levels in an entry, a semi-colon separates entries in a marker, brackets ([and]) specify a special sort order for the entry, <$startrange> and <$endrange> indicate a page range, and <$nopage> suppresses the page number.

When all index markers have been translated, generate the index. For information about generating an index, refer to the Generating a Book File section on page 116.

Check the generated index for consistency or other errors. If you find an index marker that you wish to correct, hold Ctrl+Alt or Ctrl+Option and click on the index entry. The chapter containing the index marker will automatically be opened, with the index marker selected. To edit the marker, press Ctrl+J or Command-J. This is also an alternative way to translate an index.

For more information about translating indexes, refer to the Translating Indexes section on page 120.

2.2.4.3   CROSS-REFERENCES

Cross-references are references to other parts of the manual. An example of a cross-reference is "For more information refer to Copying Files on page 3". The section "Copying Files on page 3" is a cross-reference. The title of the paragraph that the cross-reference refers to is "Copying Files", the page where that paragraph is located is page 3.

When you click on a cross-reference, a block of text is selected. It is impossible to directly edit the text within a cross-reference.

For more information please refer to Copying Files on page 3.

If you select the cross-reference and start typing, the cross-reference will be deleted! When the paragraph title "Copying Files" on page 3 is translated, the cross-reference will automatically reflect the translated text and page number when the book file is generated. For more information about generating book files, refer to the Generating a Book File section on page 116.

Although the cross-references are automatically updated, the text between the paragraph title and the page number is part of the cross-reference format, and must be translated. In the above example, the words "on page" need to be translated. Cross-reference format text only needs to be translated once.

To translate the cross-reference format, follow these steps:

1. Double-click on a cross-reference to open the Cross-Reference dialog box.

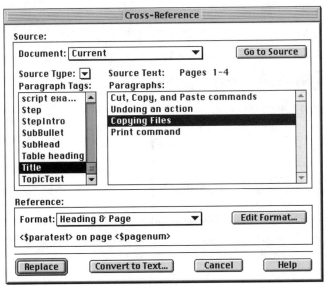

2. In the Cross-Reference dialog box, click the Edit Format button to open the Edit Cross-Reference Format dialog box.

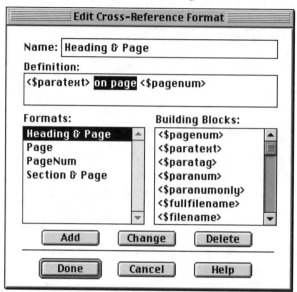

3. In the Definition field, translate the words "on page". Make sure not to change the other items in the Definition field.

4. Click on the items in the Formats box to display other format definitions that might require translation.

5. Click the Change button to store the new cross-reference format definitions.

6. Click the Done button to close the dialog box.

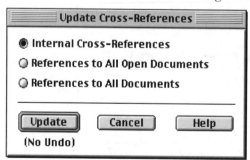

7. In the Update Cross-References dialog box, select to which files you want to apply the new format definition.

2.2.5   Spell Checking Your Translations

If you want to run the spelling checker, you first need to apply a language to your document. You also need to apply the language in order to use the hyphenation rules for your language.

To apply a language to your document, follow these steps:

1. Select all text in the document by pressing Ctrl+A or Command-A.

2. Open the Paragraph Designer (Ctrl+M or Command-M) and choose Advanced from the Properties menu. In FrameMaker 5.5 and later, the Language property can be found in the Default Font property section.

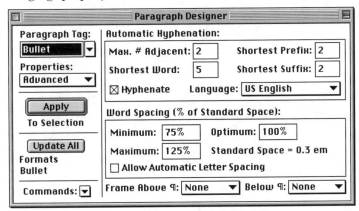

3. Change the language in the Language pop-up menu (leave the hyphenation settings as they are) and confirm the new setting by clicking the Update All button.

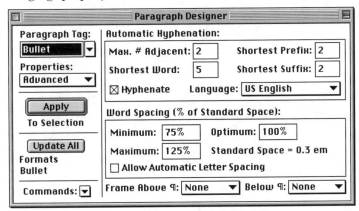

4. Select Advanced Properties Only and All Paragraphs and Catalog Entries and confirm this by clicking on the Update button.

If FrameMaker is done processing, close the window (Ctrl+W or Command-W) and start the Spelling Checker by choosing Spelling Checker from the Edit menu or pressing Ctrl+L or Command-L.

If the dictionary for your language is not installed, you can either copy it from the FrameMaker CD-ROM, or re-install the application with your language dictionaries selected. All dictionary files need to be copied to the Dictionaries folder within the FrameMaker application folder.

2.2.6   Generating a Book File

To re-generate the table of contents and index, and to update cross-references, you need to re-generate the book file that includes all your translated documents.

To generate a book file, follow these steps:

1. Open the book file and choose the Generate/Update command from the File menu.

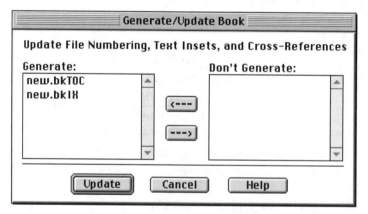

2. In the Generate/Update Book dialog box, select whether you want to generate the table of contents, index, or both. Please note that any manual changes that you've entered in the text or layout of the table of contents or index, will be lost after generating.

3. Click the Update button to update the book file.

The sort order of the index is determined on the reference page by changing the building blocks. For more information about changing the building blocks, refer to your FrameMaker documentation.

For more information about translating indexes, refer to the Translating Indexes section on page 120.

For more information about Adobe FrameMaker, visit the Adobe Web site at www.adobe.com.

2.3 Using Word

2.3.1 File Setup

Large documents that have been written using Microsoft Word usually consist of one master document and several subdocuments. A master document is comparable to a book file in FrameMaker, and can be used to generate a table of contents, index, and cross-references of a set of subdocuments, for example chapters.

Microsoft Word 8 and later provides a master document view that allows you to view an outline of the document and its subdocuments.

2.3.2 Opening a Word File

When opening a file, Word will not notify you of missing screen captures or other graphic files. Instead, a replacement box for missing linked graphic files will be displayed:

Browse through the Word document to see if any linked files are missing.

2.3.3 Counting Words

To count words in a Word document, select the Word Counts command from the Tools menu.

Please note that the word count does not include the index markers, so you also need to run the word count on the generated index.

2.3.4 Translating a File

Make sure you have the View All option selected in the Options dialog box to avoid deleting index or other markers. To open this dialog box, select Options from the Tools menu.

2.3.4.1 HEADERS AND FOOTERS

Switch to Page Layout view or Print Preview mode to see if your document contains a header of footer. Headers and footers are repeated throughout the entire document or document section.

To translate headers or footers, choose Header and Footer in the View menu. Headers and footers will not display in Normal view. To view headers or footers, switch to Page Layout.

2.3.4.2 INDEX MARKERS

To translate index entries in Microsoft Word, set your Page View to show hidden text. To enable this option in Microsoft Word, choose Options in the Tools menu and select Hidden Text in the View tab. You can also click on the ¶ button on the toolbar.

Index entries in Word are fields with the XE (Index Entry) field code. An index entry in Word is displayed like { XE "Print to File" } or { XE "Printing":"Print to File" } or { XE "Print to File"\t "*See* Printing" }.

In index fields, a colon (:) separates main entries from sub entries. If the \t instruction is used, the text following \t will be inserted in place of a page number. In the above example, the field displays the entry "Print to File, *See* Printing" in the index.

To translate index entries using Microsoft Word, follow these steps:

1. Open the first chapter of the document and search for the first index entry. You can do this by choosing the Find command from the Edit menu and typing ^d XE in the Find what: box. Another way is to select Field from the Special drop down list.

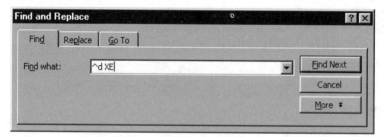

2. When the first index entry is found, leave the Find and Replace dialog box open and click in the index entry field.

3. To translate an index entry, simply replace the text between quotation marks.

Click on the Find Next button to jump to the next index entry.

For more information about generating or updating indexes, refer to the Generating a TOC and Index section on page 120.

2.3.4.3 CROSS-REFERENCES

In Word documents, cross-references are updated automatically when the index or table of contents is generated. Cross-references in Word only contain the actual heading text of the paragraph that is referred to, and the page number. All text in-between, such as "on page", needs to be translated manually.

A cross-reference can be displayed as a field code {REF_Ref401222306 \h}. To display the actual text of the cross-reference, right-click on the field code and select the Toggle Field Codes command.

2.3.5   Spell Checking Your Translations

If you want to use the spelling checker on your document, you first need to apply a language to your document. You need to have the spelling and grammar files installed for the selected language in order to do this.

Tip

Setting the correct language for a document is always useful because some text features, such as quotation mark styles, are language-dependent.

To apply a language to your document, follow these steps:

1.   Select the text that you want to apply a language to.

2.   Choose Language and Set Language from the Tools menu.

3.   Select a language.

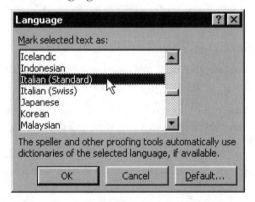

4.   Click OK to close the Language dialog box.

Now you can start the Spelling Checker by choosing Spelling and Grammar from the Tools menu or pressing F7.

2.3.6   Generating a TOC and Index

When the entire document has been translated, including all chapter and heading titles, you can automatically update the table of contents with the translated titles. To update a table of contents, right-click on the table and choose the Update Field command. You can also click on the TOC and press F9.

After all index entries have been translated, you can also generate the index by right-clicking on the index page and choosing the Update Field command.

To update the table of contents, index and cross-references, select all text within the document using the Select All command from the Edit menu, right-click on the table of contents, and select the Update Fields command. The table of contents and index can be found in the master document or in the document that you have translated.

The sort order of the index is determined by the language setting of the document.

For more information about translating indexes, refer to the Translating Indexes section on page 120.

For more information about Microsoft Word, visit Microsoft's Web site at www.microsoft.com.

2.4 Translating Indexes

Usually, indexes are generated from index entries that are inserted in the running text of a manual.

2.4.1   When to Translate an Index

You can either translate the index entries *while* you are translating the running text, or leave all index entries to be translated after the entire manual has been translated.

The best time to translate the index is when all body text of the manual already has been translated and reviewed. These are some of the advantages to translating the index *after* the rest of the manual has been translated:

- Terminology will be final; changing index entries later in the process is very time-consuming and likely to introduce errors.

- Doing the index in one go will make it more consistent because you will use the same hierarchy and terminology for index entries.

Many translators prefer to translate the index entries of a chapter after they have finished translating each chapter. This will however make it more difficult to remain consistency in index markers that are used throughout the entire manual.

2.4.2 How to Translate an Index

Indexes are always difficult to translate, especially when the index is very large or when the original is poorly written or constructed.

The most important issues to keep in mind when translating indexes are:

1. Index entries should start with the keyword. Always keep in mind what the user will search for in the index. If the English index is correct, stay as close to the original word order as possible.

2. Try to avoid similar or duplicate entries. Often, English synonyms translate into one word. When an entry appears in both the singular and the plural form, combine the two, and add an "s" in parentheses.

2.4.2.1 EXAMPLE

If the index entry "File menu" is translated into German as "Menü Datei", the German entry will be alphabetized under the "M" section. When the index also contains entries for all other menus used in the application, they will all be sorted under "M". This is not efficient because the reader will most likely be looking in the "D" section for "Datei".

A way to avoid this is to use a comma, or another separator. In this case, a translation like "Datei, Menü" would be preferable.

Other examples of commonly used index entries that need to be re-ordered in the translation are entries such as "CONFIG.SYS file" and "COPY command". Readers will search for the words CONFIG.SYS and COPY, not *file* or *command*.

Translated indexes often have entries for both the singular and the plural, or both the noun and the adjective. When starting the translation of an index, make a rule to follow one form for all entries. Then stick to this rule as much as possible. For example, the entries for "Printers" and "Printer" can be merged into one entry, unless they are specific options or commands in the software.

2.4.3 Where to Translate an Index

If a manual contains a book file with which a table of contents and index can be generated, do not translate the generated index file! If you translate the index file, it will be overwritten with the English index entries when the index is generated.

Instead, locate the index entries in the running text and translate the index entries in a consistent way.

For more information on how to translate index entries, refer to the Index Markers sections on page 111 (FrameMaker), and page 118 (Word). If you are using another word processor or application, consult the online help or documentation for more information.

3 Translating Collateral Material

Collateral material, such as quick reference cards, packaging, CD labels, promotional materials, and registration cards, require special attention. First, they are usually printed with high-quality graphics and with professional page layout. Because they need more time to be printed, they are probably translated early in the localization process.

It is important that the translator of collateral material has a good understanding of the entire product. In addition, because of the marketing purposes of most collateral material, it might be a good idea to ask your client for a review by their local marketing or sales staff.

3.1 Using QuarkXPress

3.1.1 File Setup

QuarkXPress Passport is the multilingual version of QuarkXPress 4, which allows you to run the interface of QuarkXPress in different languages. It also enables you to hyphenate and spell check documents in different languages, and run the program under any of the language-specific operating systems. If you are translating a QuarkXPress 4 document, it is recommended to use the Passport version.

Since version 4 of QuarkXPress, it is also possible to include chapters in book files. A book is a collection of documents that share the same style sheets, colors, lists, and other settings. Refer to the QuarkXPress documentation and help for more information. Version 4 and higher also allows you to save files in multilingual format, which means that the document contains sections with different language and hyphenation settings. This format is only compatible with QuarkXPress Passport.

3.1.2 Opening a QuarkXPress File

In QuarkXPress files it is possible to save a preview of an image when you save a document. This will display the image in the document even when the original image file is not present. You will need the original image when you print the document, though.

3.1.3 Counting Words

To count words in a QuarkXPress document, follow these steps:

1. From the Utilities menu, select the Check Spelling command.

2. Select the Document or Story option.

3. A word count window will be displayed. Clicking OK will start the spell check.

Please note that the word count does not include the index markers, so you also need to run the word count report on the generated index.

3.1.4 Translating a File

Make sure you have the Show Invisibles option selected in the View menu to avoid deleting layout markers.

In QuarkXPress, all text and images are contained in boxes. Because translated text usually is longer than the original, the text will move down in the box, often making it invisible on the screen. When a box contains text that is not visible, a check mark is displayed in the lower right corner of the text box.

```
In·QuarkXPress,·all·text·and·images·
are·contained·within·boxes.··Because·
translated·text·usually·is·longer·than·
the·original,·the·text·will·move·down·
in·the·box,·often·making·it·invisible·⊠
```

To avoid skipping text while you are translating, overwrite the original text instead of inserting it. Ask your client if you are allowed to resize text boxes to allow for text expansion. If boxes cannot be resized, adjust your translations.

It is also possible that text flows into the next text box. Check the following boxes in a text flow to see if it will allow text expansion.

QuarkXPress documents are usually created when complex layouts are combined with text. Therefore, be very careful when translating Quark documents. For example, do not move boxes, change color information or paragraph and character settings.

In QuarkXPress version 4 and higher, it is possible to save text as outlines by choosing the Text to box command. This outline text is not editable. You will need to recreate the text block or ask your client for a version of the document that still contains the outline text as regular editable text.

3.1.4.1 INDEX MARKERS

Indexing was introduced in QuarkXPress 4. Index entries are enclosed in red brackets and can be located by opening the Index palette and clicking on the Find Next button.

To translate the index entry, click the Edit button, and edit the text in the Text box of the Entry field. Then, click Next to locate the next index entry. It is also possible to translate the index directly in the Index palette, but this will not give you reference information.

Use the Build Index command from the Utilities menu to generate the localized index.

3.1.5   Spell Checking Your Translations

If you want to use the spelling checker on your document, you first need to apply a language to a paragraph or range of paragraphs.

To spell-check your document, follow these steps:

1. Select all text, and select the desired language in the Language pop-up menu of the Formats tab in the Paragraph Attributes dialog box.

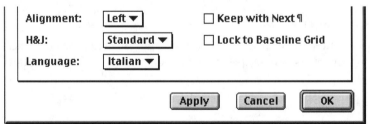

2. Now you can start the Spelling Checker by choosing Check Spelling from the Utilities menu. You need to have the QuarkXPress Dictionary file for the desired language in your QuarkXPress folder.

You can check the spelling of the selected word, story (section) or the entire document.

For more information about QuarkXPress, visit the Quark Web site at www.quark.com.

3.2 Using PageMaker

3.2.1   File Setup

In recent versions of PageMaker, files can contain a book list, which includes all publications that are contained in a book, for example separate chapters. A book list allows you to generate a table of contents or index for multiple publications.

3.2.2   Opening a PageMaker File

If your publication contains graphics that cannot be found, a "Cannot find" window will be displayed. A preview of the image will still be visible, and information about the missing linked image can be displayed by clicking on the image and choosing the Link Info command from the Element menu.

You can jump to the desired page by clicking on the page number icon in the lower left corner of your screen. Clicking on the L or R icon will display the left and right master page, which might also contain translatable text such as headers.

3.2.3   Counting Words

To count words in a PageMaker document (version 6.5 or higher), follow these steps:

1.   From the Utilities menu, select the Plug-ins command.

2.   Select the Word Counter plug-in.

You can count the entire document or just the selected text. Please note that the word count does not include the index markers, so you also need to run the word count on the generated index.

3.2.4   Translating a File

In PageMaker, text can be contained in either text blocks or text frames. All text is part of a PageMaker story; a story can comprise numerous or just one text object. You use the Type tool (T) on the toolbar to type your translations over the original text.

You can translate text in page layout view or in the story editor. You switch between the two views using the Edit Story and Edit Layout commands from the Edit menu. In the story editor you can search and replace text, check spelling and translate index markers. It is recommended to translate PageMaker files in the story editor, mainly because translating in layout mode makes it easy to delete index markers.

When you translate, do not alter the size or position of text boxes. Also, make sure you translate all stories in the publication. Using the Word Counter plug-in you can verify how many stories the publication contains.

3.2.4.1   INDEX MARKERS

You can translate index markers in PageMaker in two ways: in the story editor by opening the index marker, or by using the Show Index command. The best way is to first translate the index markers in the story editor and preview the results using the Show Index command.

To translate index markers in PageMaker, follow these steps:

1. Switch to the story editor.

2. Select the first index marker. Index markers are included in black squares with ◊ symbols.

3. Select the Index Entry command from the Utilities menu.

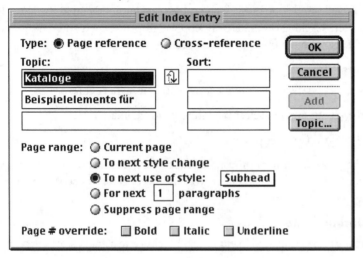

4. Refer to the surrounding text to find the right terminology and type your translations in the Topic fields. There can be up to three index entry levels.

5. Click OK to close the Edit Index Entry dialog box, and continue with the next index marker.

6. When all markers are translated, select the Show Index command from the Utilities menu to view the translated index entries per letter section. To change an entry, click the Edit button.

Indexes can be generated using the Create Index command from the Utilities menu. For more information about indexing in PageMaker, refer to your PageMaker user guide or online help.

3.2.5   Spell Checking Your Translations

To check the spelling of your translations in PageMaker, follow these steps:

1. Switch to the story editor.

2. Set the language of the text by selecting one or more paragraphs and choosing the Paragraph command from the Type menu.

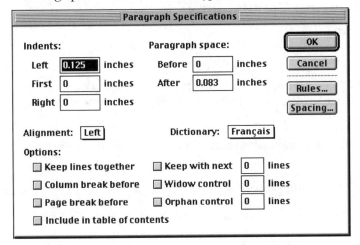

3. In the Paragraph Specifications dialog box, select the desired language. The available languages depend on the selected dictionaries when PageMaker was installed.

4. Choose the Spelling command from the Utilities menu to start the spelling checker.

For more information about Adobe PageMaker, visit the Adobe Web site at www.adobe.com.

4 Proofreading Documentation

It is recommended to proofread documents at the very end of the translation process, after the page layout has been finalized and screen captures have been inserted.

A proofreader should not review documents on-screen. Be sure to proofread on a clean printout of the final file that you are planning to deliver. It is always a good idea to compare the translated printout with the original, English hard copy.

More important is that a proofreader is not supposed to make stylistic changes to the translation; this should have been done in the editing stage. A proofreader should only do a linguistic QA check on the final product.

Typically, a proofreader would be someone who has not been deeply involved in the localization project, such as a freelance language specialist.

The following checklist contains some of the things that a proofreader should check. The list is by no means a complete one, but could act as a starting point for your documentation QA.

4.1 Accuracy and Consistency

Check to ensure that:

- All text is translated.

- All special characters are present, such as ® registered trademark and © copyright symbols. This is especially important for the title page and first few pages of a document.

- Company names, street address, zip code, telephone and fax numbers, including the area code, are correct.

- The legal page displays the proper date, version, and part number of the product.

- References to the running software have been formatted consistently, for example in italics or boldface.

- Punctuation is applied consistently, especially in numbered or bulleted lists.

4.2 Examples and Screen Captures

- The screens and other graphics are displayed correctly.

- The screen captions appear correctly and point to the right place. Ideally, an illustration should appear within one page after its mention. It should not appear before it is mentioned in the text.

- The examples and screen captures match the surrounding text.

- Manually edited graphics contain correct translations.

4.3 General Page Layout

- Page size and layout equals the original text.

- All chapters start on odd (right-hand) pages.

- Page numbering sequences are correct.

- Headers and footers correspond with the chapter titles.

- Font style and size of the footers are correct.

- Odd footers are at the same height on the page as the even footers.

- Spacing between titles, headings, and paragraphs is consistent.

- The alphabetic sorting of both main and sub-entries corresponds to the target language rules in the case of manuals that contain a glossary.

- All listed items (bullets, numbers, etc.) are aligned correctly.

- Final page count is a multiple of four.

- The end of the book is an even page.

4.4 Cross-references

- The entries and page numbers in the table of contents are accurate.

- Cross-references in the body text refer to the correct page numbers.

5 Creating Online Documentation

As mentioned before, software publishers increasingly ship online manuals with their products instead of printed documentation. There are several online file formats, of which Adobe's PDF format has become de-facto industry-standard.

The following sections tell you how to create PDF versions from your translated documentation files.

5.1 Creating Adobe Acrobat PDF Documents

Adobe's Portable Document Format (PDF) is a file format that is used to distribute online documents on all platforms. Adobe Acrobat is a set of programs used to create, enhance, and read PDF documents. PDF documents can be created from any application; hypertext links, forms, movies, sounds, and bookmarks can be added; and they can be viewed on each platform using Acrobat viewers, such as Acrobat Reader, or web browsers.

For more information about Adobe Acrobat, visit Adobe's Web site at www.adobe.com or the Portable Document Format newsgroup at comp.text.pdf.

Many software developers include online versions of their printed manuals in PDF format on the disks that they distribute. Typically, a PDF book is created from a manual after it has been translated. Increasingly, only installation and getting started guides are included in printed form, all other manuals, such as reference or administrator's manuals, are included in PDF format only.

If a manual has been translated in a word processor or document processing application, such as Word or FrameMaker, there are two ways in which the document can be converted to PDF format. It is possible to "print to PDF" directly using the PDF Writer printer driver. Second, the manual can be printed to a PostScript file, which is then "distilled" to PDF using Acrobat Distiller. The first method is mostly used for simple documents without special fonts, formatting or graphics. The second method should be used with complex page layout documents, or documents that contain high quality images.

5.1.1   Using Acrobat PDF Writer

To create a PDF file from a document using PDF Writer, follow these steps:

1. Open the document that you want to convert to a PDF file.

2. Choose the Print command from the File menu.

3. From the Printer Name drop down box, choose PDF Writer (Windows) or open the Chooser and select the PDF Writer printer driver (Macintosh).

4. Enter the Acrobat document information. The information you enter here will be displayed in the Info box for the PDF file.

5. Name the file with a .PDF extension and click OK (Windows) or Save (Macintosh).

PDF Writer allows you to set several options, such as page size and orientation, font embedding and subsetting, and image compression.

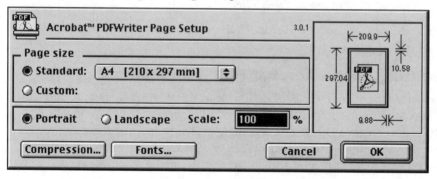

For more information about PDF Writer, refer to the PDF Writer Online Guide that is installed with Adobe Acrobat.

5.1.2   Using Acrobat Distiller

To create a PDF file from a document using Distiller, follow these steps:

1. Open the document that you want to convert to a PDF file.

2. Create a PostScript file by choosing the Print command from the File menu, and selecting Print to File (Windows) or Destination: File (Macintosh). Make sure you are using the correct printer driver and PostScript settings. If you are not sure which settings to use, ask your client.

3. When the PostScript file (.PS) is created, run Acrobat Distiller and open the PostScript file using the Open command from the File menu.

4. Name the file with a .PDF extension and click OK (Windows) or Save (Macintosh).

In some applications, such as Adobe FrameMaker 5.x and higher, you can set Acrobat options when you create a PostScript file. Distiller allows you to set several advanced options, such as page size and orientation, resolution, font embedding and subsetting, and image compression and conversion.

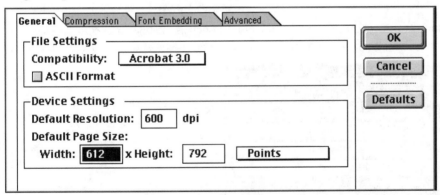

For more information about Distiller, refer to the Distiller Online Guide that is installed with Adobe Acrobat.

5.2 Testing Adobe Acrobat PDF Documents

Because there are several ways in which you can create PDF documents, and many different options you can set, it is recommended to compare translated PDF documents with the original English files to see if any file characteristics have changed.

To test a PDF document created from localized source material, concentrate on:

- File Size – Make sure that the size of the localized file does not differ substantially from the original file. If it does, try to use different compression or font embedding options.

- Graphics – Graphics should display with the same quality as the original files. If the quality differs considerably, try different image compression types.

- Page Size – Localized PDF files should use A4 paper when they are intended as print-on-demand documents.

- View on Open – Make sure the localized file has the same default view on opening as the English original. To check this, select Document Info from the File menu and choose Open.

- Document Info – Check if the document info, such as the title, has been translated by selecting Document Info from the File menu and choosing General.

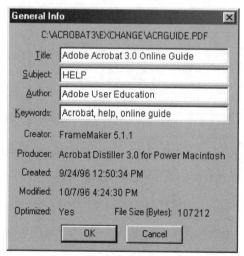

- Font Embedding – Compare the font embedding information by selecting Document Info from the File menu and choosing Fonts.

Also make sure that the PDF file prints without problems or quality loss on different printers, using different resolution settings.

Chapter 5:
Translation Memory
Tools

This chapter contains information about the use of computer-aided translation memory tools in the localization process.

O ver the past ten years, the use of computer-aided-translation tools–CAT tools–has become common practice within the localization industry. Translation memory tools in particular, have been a valuable asset for companies working on large localization projects.

Computer-aided translation tools can be subdivided into three sections:

- Translation Memory tools

- Machine Translation tools

- Terminology Management tools

In this chapter, you will find information about terminology management tools, plus some additional info on machine translation. Terminology Management tools are discussed in Appendix A.

The translation tools discussed in this chapter are computer-aided translation tools that use translation memory and code protection features to simplify the translation process. All tools discussed create a translation memory of the translations entered, which can be used later to quickly update new versions of source files.

Most of the tools discussed have a similar feature set. Every tool has its strengths and weaknesses. This chapter will not tell you which tool is the best, it only introduces the currently available translation memory tools and describes their main features. To learn more about differences between the tools, refer to the LISA Web site or specialized localization and translation magazines.

1   Introduction

Translation memory is a technology that allows you to store translated sentences in a special database for re-use or shared use on a network. Translation memory systems work by matching the terms and sentences in the database with those in the English text. If a match is found, the system proposes the ready-made translation in the target language.

Most translation memory systems support *fuzzy* matching, where translations are also retrieved from memory in cases where the old and the new source sentences are not 100% identical. For example: a translation memory database contains the translation of the sentence "To search for text", and a new sentence like "To search for and replace text" needs to be translated. The translation will be retrieved from the memory with a highlight on "and replace" indicating the difference.

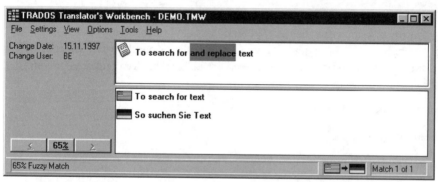

Another feature that most translation memory systems provide is *alignment* of existing translations. When existing translations are aligned, the source and target text are imported and matched to create a translation memory.

1.1.1   Translation Memory vs. Machine Translation

Translation memory (TM) is easily confused with machine translation (MT). The major difference is that in machine translation, a computer translates text whereas in translation memory systems a computer only stores translated sentences. Where a MT system tries to *replace* a translator, a TM system *supports* the translator. Interestingly enough, only low-end MT systems claim to replace the translator. The more powerful the MT tool the more likely that the producer will market it as a translation productivity tool, not as a replacement for the translator.

Although MT systems haven't improved considerably over the past few years, porting to PC, Internet compatibility, and price reductions have renewed the interest in machine translation systems. More and more translation memory systems offer support for MT. For example, Trados Translator's Workbench co-operates closely with the Systran machine translation system.

In a typical setup where TM and MT are both used, the computer first searches the translation memory for a match of the sentence that needs to be translated. If no (fuzzy) match is found, the translator can ask the MT system to translate the sentence, edit the result and store the translation in the translation memory.

Some examples of commonly used machine translation systems:

- Systran – more info at www.systransoft.com

- LANT@MARK – more info at www.lant.com

- Logos Translation System – more info at www.logos-ca.com

- Globalink Power Translator – more info at www.globalink.com

1.1.2 Advantages in Localization

There are many advantages to using translation memory in localization projects. Some examples are listed below:

- Software documentation tends to be repetitive. When a sentence has been translated once, the translation will be automatically inserted when a translator reaches the next instance of that sentence. These sentences, or segments, are called *internal repetitions.*

- Software applications are regularly updated. Existing translations can be re-used in new versions of help files or manuals. These re-used sentences are called *external repetitions.*

- Most translation memory tools are integrated with a terminology management application that automatically displays key terms that occur in the source sentence. This will guarantee consistency in terminology.

- Detailed analysis features reporting word counts and number of internal and external repetitions provide valuable information to project managers scheduling localization projects.

- Several translators can work on one project to speed up translation. Consistency in translation is guaranteed by networked use of translation memories.

- There is no need to train translators in complex word processing application or document creation tools. Most of the translation work is done in standard word processors or integrated text editors. Consequently, coding is protected in tagged file formats such as HTML and SGML.

- On average, productivity levels can be improved by around 30%, sometimes even 50%. Total translation costs can be reduced by 15 to 30%.

Translation memories segment imported text in so-called translation units. Usually, segmentation takes place on a sentence level. Most translation memory tools create the memory automatically during translation.

1.1.3   Translation Memory Exchange

Since the very beginning of the development of CAT tools, different file and database formats have been used to store translated text in translation memory. Because this was causing problems for both software developers and translation service providers, a special interest group was formed in 1997 by LISA, the Localisation Industry Standards Association.

This group of translation providers, tools vendors and customers of translation services, called OSCAR, is developing a file format specification called TMX, short for Translation Memory Exchange. The purpose of TMX is to allow easier exchange of translation memory data between tools and/or translation vendors.

For more information about OSCAR and TMX, visit the LISA Web site at www.lisa.org.

Another standard that is being developed is OpenTag, a single common mark-up format to encode text extracted from documents of varying and arbitrary formats, aimed at translation and natural language processing tools.

For more information about OpenTag, visit the OpenTag Web site at www.opentag.org.

2 Trados Translator's Workbench

Translator's Workbench is a translation memory application developed by Trados. It can be used to translate any kind of document that can be opened by Word or WordPerfect.

Translator's Workbench ships with MultiTerm, a terminology management application that is interactive with Workbench and the word processor that you are using. For more information about MultiTerm, refer to the Trados MultiTerm section on page 285. An additional Trados product is Winalign, a tool that can be used to *align* a translated text with the English text in order to create a translation memory.

The following file formats are supported by Translator's Workbench: Rich Text Format (RTF), Word, WordPerfect ASCII (via RTF), FrameMaker (via S-Tagger), Interleaf (via S-Tagger), Ventura (via RTF with macro), SGML/HTML (via RTF with macro).

Trados Translator's Workbench enables you to create a statistical overview of the number of internal repetitions, and fuzzy or exact matches found in the translation memory. The Translate command in the Tools menu of Translator's Workbench enables you to pre-translate files with translations present in the translation memory.

In 1998 Trados Translator's Workbench 2 was released with major improvements such as a translation memory management tool, Unicode support, and faster matching.

For more information about Translator's Workbench, visit the Trados Web site at www.trados.com. It is also possible to download demo versions of all Trados applications.

2.1 Software

To translate software resource (RC) files using Translator's Workbench, follow these steps:

1. Start Translator's Workbench, create a new project or open an existing translation memory project (TMW file).

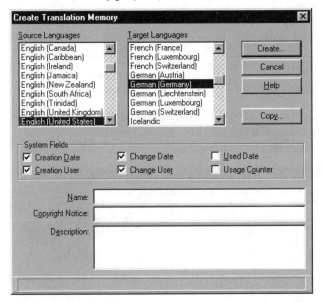

2. Start your word processor and open the RC file that you want to translate.

3. Attach the *Tw4win.dot* template to the document. This template can be found in the folder where you installed Translator's Workbench.

4. Run the *tw4winPrepareRC* macro. This macro will mark all strings in the RC file that are enclosed in double quotes, and that are translatable.

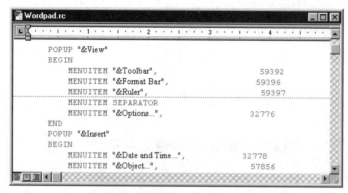

5. Save the file in RTF format and click on the first translatable string.

6. Select Open/Get from the Trados menu in Word, or press Alt-Home. Type your translation in the field directly below the source text. If the source text was already present in the translation memory, the translation will automatically be inserted.

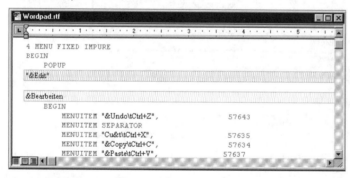

7. In the Translator's Workbench window the string or word will be displayed in the top window, with the fully matching translation or a fuzzy match displaying in the bottom window.

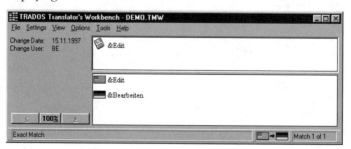

8. Select Set/Close Next Open/Get from the Trados menu, or press Alt-+. This will take you to the next translatable string. The source text of the previously translated term will remain in the file as hidden text.

9. After the file has been translated, save the file in RTF format.

10. Switch to Translator's Workbench and select the Clean Up command from the Tools menu. In the Clean Up window, add the file you have translated.

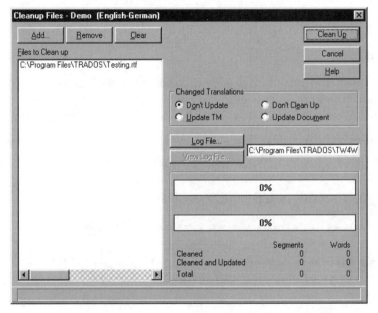

11. Click on the Clean Up button to remove all hidden source text from the file.

After cleaning up, save the file as text only with its original RC file name. If you or somebody else needs to edit the file, leave the hidden source text in the RTF file. When you edit the file without Translator's Workbench running, you can automatically enter the changes in the translation memory by selecting the Update TM option in the Changed Translations field of the Cleanup Files dialog box.

2.2 Help

To use Translator's Workbench to translate Windows Help RTF files, you can follow the same steps as described in the software section above.

The only difference is that you do not need to run a macro to prepare the file for Trados. RTF files can be directly opened, edited and saved in Microsoft Word. Windows Help files do require some additional preparation work before they are translated:

- Check the files for unusual features, and accept all revisions in the document by choosing the Revisions command from the Tools menu and clicking on the Accept All button.

- Mark all bitmap references, such as {bmc image.bmp} as *tw4winInternal* style. Refer to the Turning Graphic References Into Placeables section from the Trados Translator's Workbench for Windows User's Guide for more information.

More information about preparing Windows Help files for translation in Trados can be found in Sharon O'Brien's Workflow manual, which can be downloaded from the Trados Web site.

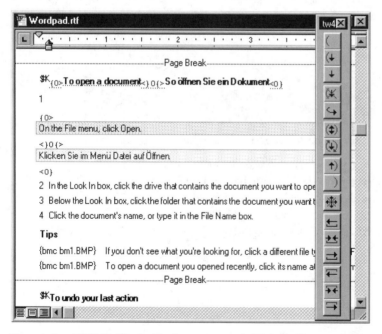

To translate HTML files in Trados, open each HTML file in Word, attach the Trados template and run the *tw4winPrepareSGML* macro to protect all HTML tags.

If a large number of HTML files need to be translated, you can convert all files in batch mode using the HTML tools that have been developed by International Translation & Publishing (ITP). More information about these HTML conversion tools can be found in Sharon O'Brien's Workflow manual. The HTML conversion utilities can be downloaded from the ITP (www.itp.ie) or Trados (www.trados.com) Web site.

2.3 Documentation

To translate documentation files in FrameMaker or Interleaf format using Translator's Workbench, the files need to be converted to a tagged format called STF. STF files can be edited in Word like regular RTF files.

Conversion from FrameMaker MIF or Interleaf files can be done using a tool called S-Tagger. This tool is not part of the standard Translator's Workbench package! Detailed information about preparing documents for conversion by S-Tagger can be found in Sharon O'Brien's Workflow manual and the S-Tagger for Windows User's Guide which can be downloaded from the Trados Web site.

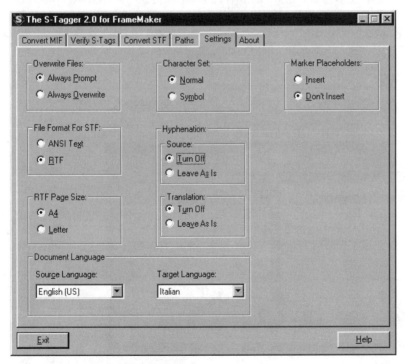

For more information about S-Tagger, refer to the S-Tagger for Windows User's Guide, which can be downloaded from the Trados Web site.

3 IBM TranslationManager

IBM TranslationManager is a computer-aided translation system that combines translation memory features with dictionary lookup and spell checking functionality.

Unlike Trados Translator's Workbench, IBM TranslationManager comes with an integrated word processor and alignment tool.

IBM TranslationManager supports the following file formats (markup codes are included between brackets): Rich Text Format (EQFRTF), Word (EQFWORD*x*), WordPerfect (EQFWP*x*), AmiPro (EQFAMI), ASCII (EQFASCII) Assembler (EQFASM), HTML (EQFHTML2), OS/2 resource files (EQFMRI), and Windows resource files (EQFAMRI). You can separately order the support for the following word processors: FrameBuilder (MIF), PageMaker, Interleaf, QuarkXPress, and Ventura Publisher.

More information about IBM TranslationManager can be found on the IBM TM Web site at www.software.ibm.com/ad/translat. It is also possible to download a demo version of IBM TranslationManager from IBM's FTP server at ftp.software.ibm.com/ps/products/translationmanager.

3.1 Software

To translate software resource (RC) files using IBM TranslationManager, follow these steps:

1. Start IBM TranslationManager and click on the Folder List window.

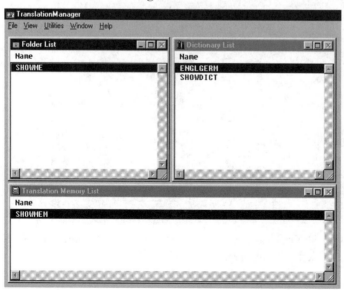

2. Select New from the File menu and enter the project properties in the New Folder dialog box. You need to specify a name for the new project folder, the source and target language, translation memory and database to be used, and the markup method. For software resource files, the markup type is *EQFAMRI*.

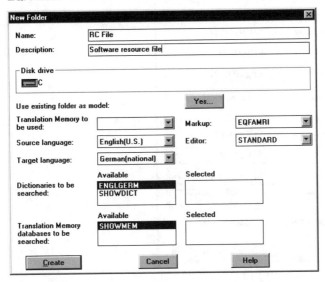

3. Click the Create button to create the new project.

4. Activate the Document List window and choose Import from the File menu. In the Import Documents dialog box, select the file(s) that you want to translate.

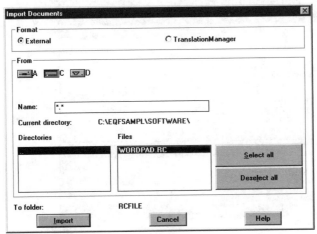

5. Click the Import button. In the Document Properties dialog box, specify the settings you want to use for this file if you want to use settings other than the

ones that you specified for the project. If you want to use the project settings, simply click the Cancel button.

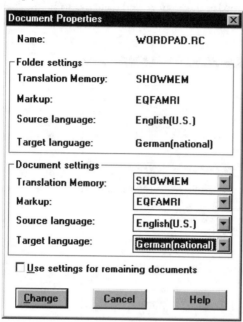

6. In the Document List window, double-click on the file that you want to translate.

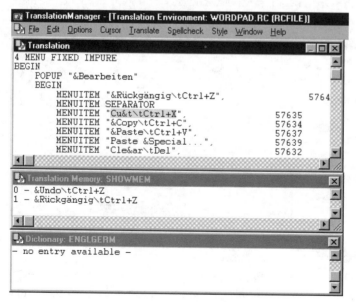

7. In the Translation window, overtype the English text with your translations. To jump to the next untranslated segment, press Ctrl+Enter. If items are found in the translation memory or dictionary, they will be displayed in the Translation Memory or Dictionary window. To automatically insert translations, press Ctrl-*n*, where *n* is the number of the suggested translation or fuzzy match.

8. To save the translated file, select Save from the File menu.

9. To export the translated file from the project folder, select the file in the Document List window and select Export from the File menu. Specify the export options and file locations in the Export Documents dialog box.

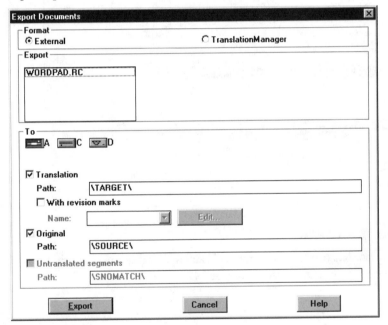

10. Click the Export button. The translated and/or source files will be exported to the folders that you have specified. The default folders are \Source and \Target.

3.2 Help

To use IBM TranslationManager to translate a RTF Windows help source file, you can follow the same steps as described in the software section above. The only difference is that you need to use EQFRTF as markup type in step 2.

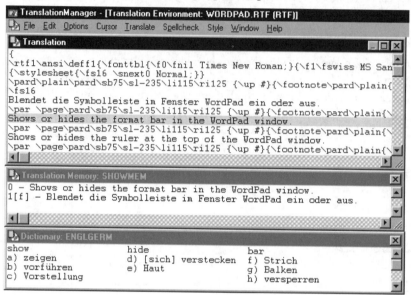

To translate HTML files, use EQFHTML2 as markup method.

3.3 Documentation

IBM TranslationManager does not support FrameMaker files. All supported documentation file formats are listed on page 142.

4 Atril Déjà Vu

Déjà Vu is a translation tool that can be used for documentation, help, and software resource files. It has been developed by Atril, and consists of the following components:

- Déjà Vu Interactive is used to create projects, import files to be translated, and to enter the actual translations.

- Database Maintenance is used to maintain translation memory databases, e.g., importing, exporting, aligning, and editing. Terminology Maintenance is used to maintain terminology databases.

- Database Conversion Wizard is used to convert Déjà Vu memory databases from an older format to the current version format.

- TermWatch is a memory-resident utility that lets you access terminology databases from any other Windows application, using custom key combinations. For more information about TermWatch, refer to the Atril TermWatch section on page 288.

The basic Déjà Vu Interactive application can build and handle projects for the following file formats: Rich Text Format (RTF), Word, and plain text source files. Support for FrameMaker (via MIF), Interleaf, QuarkXPress, HTML, HTML Help, Trados Translator's Workbench, IBM TranslationManager, RC and C/C++ files is available at additional cost.

For more information about Déjà Vu and a demo version, visit the Atril Web site at www.atril.com.

4.1 Software

To translate software resource (RC) files using Déjà Vu, follow these steps:

1. Start Déjà Vu Interactive.

2. To create a new project, select the Create Project command from the File menu. In the Create Project submenu, select RC files or C or C++ files.

3. Specify the name of the work file you wish to create and click OK.

4. Select the Configure Current Project command from the Tools menu.

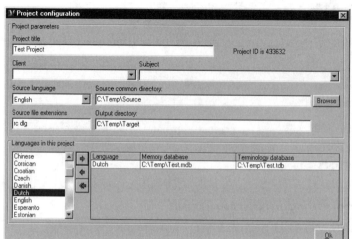

5. In the Project Configuration dialog box, specify the settings for your project.

6. Select the Import RC Files command from the File menu. In the Import Files dialog box, select the RC files that you want to translate, and click on the Go button.

7. In the main translation window, select the string you want to translate, and type your text in the box in the lower right corner. To enter your translation in the active resource file, choose the Propagate in Current File command from the Tools menu. To enter the translation in all resource files of the active project, select the Propagate to All Files command from the Tools menu.

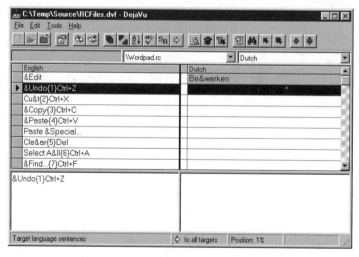

4.2 Help

To use Déjà Vu to translate a RTF Windows help source file, you can follow the same steps as described in the software section above. The only difference is that you need to select RTF from the Create Project submenu in step 2.

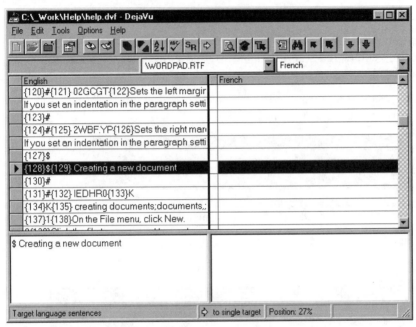

4.3 Documentation

To use Déjà Vu to translate a FrameMaker file, you can follow the same steps as described in the help section above. The only difference is that you need to select FrameMaker from the Create Project submenu in step 2. FrameMaker files first need to be converted to MIF format.

5 Miscellaneous

5.1 Amptran

Amptran Translator's Workbench is a localization tool that is developed by SDL Ltd.

With Amptran, you can translate the following file formats: Rich Text Format (RTF), FrameMaker MIF, Ventura, Interleaf ASCII, HTML, and software resource files (RC, DLG, MNU, and STR).

Amptran only shows the strings that need to be translated, and automatically creates a translation memory of all translated strings.

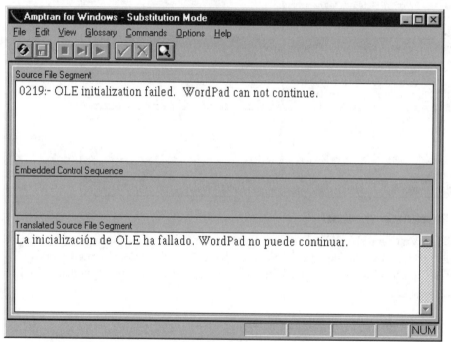

For more information about Amptran and a demo version, visit the SDL Ltd. Web site at www.sdlintl.com.

5.2 STAR Transit

Transit is a translation memory system that is developed by STAR. Transit contains an integrated translation editor that runs in Word or WordPerfect mode, and can open multiple files at the same time. It also contains an integrated terminology management application, called TermStar.

STAR Transit comes with import filters for the following file formats: Rich Text Format (RTF), Word, WordPerfect, AmiPro, FrameMaker, SGML, HTML, Xyvision, Ventura Publisher, QuarkXPress, and software resource files (RC, C or other). Filters are highly customizable and support of custom file formats is possible on special request order. Optional add-ins for the full version are Interleaf and PageMaker filters, spelling checkers in other languages, and an alignment tool.

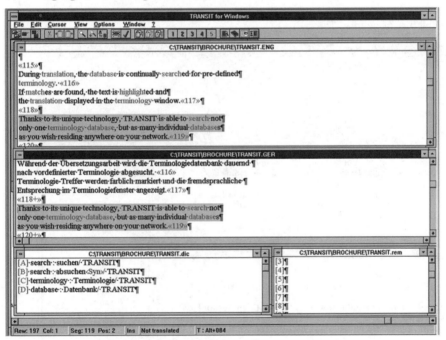

Transit is available in a full version and a light version that does not contain the project management features and TermStar.

For more information about STAR Transit, visit the STAR Web site at www.star-ag.ch.

5.3 TSS/Joust

TSS/Joust is a translation memory system that is developed by Alpnet.

Alpnet's TSS (Translation Support System) is the result of more than 20 years of research and development in the field of MT and CAT tools. TSS is the file management and filtering tool that processes and post-processes files for the translator's component, Joust.

Customized filters provide import and export for the following file formats: Rich Text Format (RTF), Word, WordPerfect, FrameMaker MIF, Interleaf, PageMaker, QuarkXPress, and SGML/HTML, and software resource files (RC).

Joust, the translation editor, is configured in a split-screen mode, which allows translators to view the source and target text and terminology simultaneously. Joust is available in a Pro and a Lite version. Joust Lite is a subset of the complete suite of translation tools and offers the same full functionality as Joust Pro.

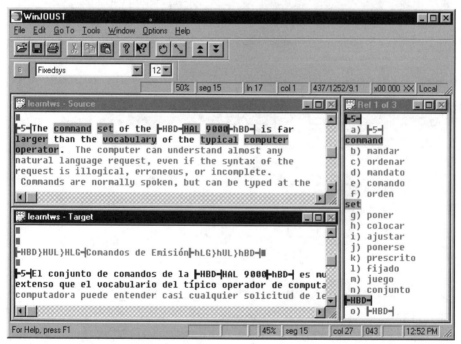

For more information about TSS/Joust, visit the Alpnet Web site at www.alpnet.com.

5.4 XL8 TransPro

XL8 TransPro is a translation tool that is developed by GlobalWare Inc.

With XL8 TransPro, you can translate files in the following formats: Rich Text Format (RTF), Word, FrameMaker, Interleaf, HTML, and software resource files (RC, C/C++, Pascal, and Assembly).

For more information about XL8 TransPro, visit the SAM Engineering Web site at www.sam-engineering.de.

5.5 Eurolang Optimizer

Eurolang Optimizer is a translation memory tool that is marketed, supported and maintained by LANT. Optimizer integrates with word processors.

With Optimizer, you can pre-translate new documents using existing translation memories on a server, then edit the text locally in your word processor and add translations. Next, you can store your newly translated sentences in the translation memory on the server.

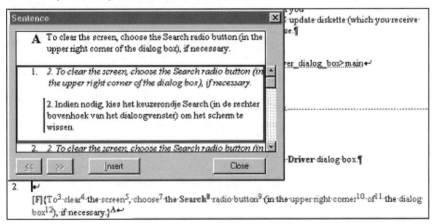

For more information about Eurolang Optimizer, visit the LANT Web site at www.lant.com.

Chapter 6:
Localization Engineering

This chapter contains information about the engineering of localized software and help files for Windows and Macintosh.

U sually, software developers prepare a localization kit that is sent out to the localization vendor. These localization kits are created by the development department of the software manufacturer, and contain all files necessary to translate, compile, and test an application. This file set is called a *build environment*. Mostly, also the build environment for the online help system is included in a localization kit.

This chapter will tell you how to deal with files that are included in localization kits. You will find information about how to prepare files for translators, how to compile software and help files, and how to test localized files.

In this chapter, you will find many references to the Microsoft Developer Network CDs and the Apple Developer Connection CDs:

- Microsoft Developer Network (MSDN) is an online service that you can subscribe to in order to receive a set of CDs containing development kits and tools, translated versions of Microsoft operating systems and applications, glossaries, beta versions of new releases, etc. There are three subscription levels: library, professional, and universal. For more information about MSDN, visit the MSDN Web site at www.microsoft.com/msdn.

- Apple provides a similar subscription to its Apple Developer Connection CD series. This is a series of quarterly CD-ROMs that provide developers with the latest Apple technical information, system software, and development utilities. The Tool Chest CDs, containing localization tools, are part of the CD series. For more information, visit the Apple Developer Connection Web site at www.apple.com/developer or connect.apple.com.

Another valuable source of information for each localization engineer is Nadine Kano's book *Developing International Software for Windows 95 and Windows NT*.

International Language Engineering (ILE) Corporation have developed a set of guidelines and tools for internationalization and localization called Borneo. For more information, visit the ILE Web site at www.ile.com.

1 Windows

Software applications for the Windows environment are usually written in an object-oriented programming environment such as Visual C++ or Visual Basic. A software developer can choose to have the text-only resource files translated, or the compiled executables. In the first case, compilation is necessary. In the other case, the translator will need a tool that supports translation of binary files. Examples of these applications are Microsoft RLToolset, Corel Catalyst, Borland Resource Workshop, or Microsoft Developer Studio.

> ### Important
>
> Always use the resource editor and compiler that your client has been using for the English product. Using different editors or compilers might seriously damage or restructure the files!

Because these tools all have their own features and specifications, we will concentrate on the first case, i.e., engineers compiling text-only resource files that have been translated in a text editor. More information about the tools mentioned above can be found in the Program Files section on page 27 and the Software Localization Tools section on page 37.

1.1 Software

In the following section, we will concentrate on applications written in Visual C++ with standard Windows resource files. For information on localization of applications that are created in other development environments, refer to the Other Environments section on page 247.

1.1.1 Engineering

1.1.1.1 PREPARATION

1.1.1.1.1 Test-Compiling

First, the localization engineer should check if all files are present, and test-compile the original, English files. If there are problems compiling the English product, these problems should be solved before translation starts.

An instruction document that accompanies the localization kit usually describes how the application is compiled. If you are not sure how to proceed, ask your client. Typically, Windows applications are built from a make (MAK) file. This MAK file is opened using Visual C++ (Microsoft Developer Studio) and is linked to numerous resource (RC) files, include (H) files, and other files. Refer to the File Types section on page 162 for a listing of file types that might be included in a build environment.

There are differences between RC files for 16-bit, and RC files for 32-bit applications. Resource script files (RC) are distinguished as being 16-bit or 32-bit on whether they contain 32-bit resource keywords, such as LANGUAGE, EXSTYLE, or DIALOGEX, not by some underlying file structure. If you are not sure which compiler version you should use, ask your client.

When the original application compiles with no errors, check if the file that is being built, such as a DLL or EXE file, has the same size as the file that is installed with the original application. If there is a substantial file size difference, it might be useful to ask your client if the increase in file size will cause a problem.

Also, replace the DLL of the original, installed application with the English DLL that you have test-compiled. Check if the application still runs without problems.

1.1.1.1.2   Check List

If your client does not supply you with detailed instructions, ask the following questions to get a complete overview of the work that needs to be done:

1.1.1.1.2.1   *Compilation*

- How should the application be compiled?
- Which version of which compiler should be used?
- What is the name of the program file that is being compiled?
- Are specific tools required for compiling the software?
- Which path settings are required for compiling?
- Can controls, such as buttons, and dialog boxes be resized?

1.1.1.1.2.2   *Translation*

- Which software resource files need to be translated?
- How should the resource files be translated?
- Which bitmaps or icons need to be translated?
- Are blank or layered versions and font information for the bitmaps available?
- Are there space restrictions that translators should keep in mind?
- Are previously translated versions of the resource files available?

1.1.1.1.2.3   Localization

- Are source files available for each component that contains user interface text?

- Do the files contain country-specific information that needs to be changed, such as default page sizes, currency symbols, etc?

- Should *locale* information be changed in the resource files?

1.1.1.1.2.4   Testing

- Should the localized software also be tested?

- What type of testing should be done, i.e., only linguistic testing, or functionality, compatibility, and regression testing?

- On which platforms should the software be tested?

- Are test scripts available?

A well-constructed localization kit would already answer most of these questions for you.

1.1.1.1.3   Preparing for Translation

After test compiling, you need to identify the files that will be translated, and mark the strings that should or–even more significant–should *not* be translated.

If the localization kit does not contain a list of files that need to be translated, you need to locate them in the build environment. Most of the time, translatable strings are included in RC files, but it might also be possible that programmers have chosen to include text in files with extensions like STR, DLG, or TXT. Refer to the Resource Files section on page 15 for more information. If you are not sure about which files to translate, ask your client.

1.1.1.1.4   Creating Word Counts

You can create word counts using the text-only software resource files, or using the compiled DLL file or executable. If you use the compiled DLL, you need a tool such as Corel Catalyst. If you create word counts from the text-only software resource files, it will take more time to determine translatables, but your count will be more accurate.

There are several things to keep in mind when creating software word counts:

- Do not forget to include components such as the Installer, wizards, or included utilities in your total word count.

- Check if the software application contains graphics with text. You can check this by opening the program file in a resource editor and browsing through the Bitmap resources.

- When UI text is hard-coded in the executable, you cannot create a word count.

1.1.1.1.4.1 *Software Resource Files*

You can create word counts from software resource files in several ways. Tools that support word counting of RC files are Corel Catalyst and Accent Loc@le. Without these tools, the easiest way is just to use your word processor in the way described below.

To quickly create word counts from RC files using Microsoft Word, follow these steps:

1. Open the RC file in Microsoft Word.

2. Select all text and choose the Sort command from the Table menu. Sort all text by paragraphs.

3. You will now have all comment text, define statements, string sections, captions, controls, and menu items in separate text blocks in your document.

4. Browse through the file and delete all lines that do not contain translatable text. Translatable text is enclosed in double quotes.

5. After deleting all non-translatable lines, select all text and convert the text to a table, using the double quote character (") as a delimiter.

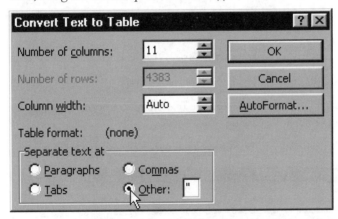

6. The second column of the table will now contain all translatable text. Copy this column to a new document and count the words using the Word Count command. This will give you a rough estimate of the number of translatable words.

Tip

If you want to count multiple RC files you can concatenate the files just for counting purposes by copying them all to one folder and typing the following DOS command: COPY *.RC ALL.TXT. The ALL.TXT file will contain the strings from all RC files.

Another way to create word counts is to import the RC file in one of the computer-aided translation memory tools, such as Trados Translator's Workbench or IBM TranslationManager. After importing the RC files, you can run the diagnosis or statistics command that will tell you the word counts. These tools will also provide you with information about internal or external repetitions. For more information about using these tools for software files, refer to Chapter 5, Translation Memory Tools.

1.1.1.1.4.2   *Binary Program Files*

To create word counts from binary program files, such as DLL or EXE files, you can save the files as text-only RC files using Microsoft Developer Studio and follow the procedures described in the previous section. Alternatively, you can use one of the software localization tools that provide word count features, such as Corel Catalyst.

If you have only received a set of setup disks or a CD-ROM containing the application, the DLL or EXE files containing the user interface text need to be found. To locate the program files that contain interface text, install the application, choose an option from a dialog box, and search the program folder for files containing that option. With the Windows Find function you can search a folder for files containing a certain text string. When you have located the files containing interface text, use a software localization tool to count the words.

To use Corel Catalyst to create a word count from a DLL or EXE file, follow these steps:

1. Start Catalyst and create a new project.

2. Use the Insert Files command from the File menu to import the DLL or EXE file that you want to count.

3. Select the file and click on the Statistics tab to see detailed word counts.

Object	Words	Translatable	Translated
⊟ 🗀 <Project Title>			
⊟-🗀 WORDPAD.EXE			
⊞-🗀 Bitmap	0	0	0
⊞-🗀 Menu	225	225	0
⊞-🗀 Dialog	120	120	0
⊞-🗀 StringTable	959	959	0
⊞-🗀 Accelerator	0	0	0
⊞-🗀 Icon	0	0	0
⊞-🗀 Version	0	0	0

Corel CATALYST - [TTK1]
File View Tools Window Help

📄 All   👥 Filter   📊 Statistics

1.1.1.2 COMPILING

Typically, a make file (MAK) instructs the resource compiler to create a binary resource file (RES) from an ASCII resource file (RC). The RES file is then appended to the executable file (EXE or DLL) of a Windows application. Increasingly, programmers include translatable resources in a separate DLL, called a *satellite DLL* or *resource-only DLL*, which is completely separated from the binary program code.

To compile the translated product, replace all English RC files with localized ones. Now, open the MAK file using Visual C++, and choose the Rebuild All command from the Project menu (1.5x and 2.x) or Build menu (4.x and 5.x).

Tip

You can also change the build environment and create subfolders for the resource files of each language. In this case, you need to create batch files that will set the right paths and instruct the compiler to use localized files.

Don't forget to change the language settings in your compiler before you build the DLL or EXE file. In Microsoft Developer Studio, open the Project Settings window and select the required language in the Resources tab.

Important

Do not edit, save, or compile the RC or MAK file using other versions of Visual C++ than the one it was originally created with because this might change the file structure considerably! Often, the header of the MAK file contains compiler version information.

If you are not sure which version of which compiler you should use, do not edit the RC files directly in the resource editor. Instead, open the compiled file in the resource editor, and enter all changes in the RC files, which can be recompiled to reflect the changes.

If your translated RC files do not compile, you need to find out which string in which file is causing the problem. Try to narrow the problem down as much as possible by gradually replacing the English build with translated files, or even by gradually copying blocks of the translated file into the original English. Even though this can be time-consuming, most errors can be found by "trial-and-error".

Common problems found in translated RC files are deleted quotes, and strings that have become longer than the 254 character limit.

1.1.1.2.1   File Types

The following table lists different file types that are most likely to be included in a localization kit. It also indicates if the file can be localized or translated:

Extension	File Type	Localizable?
.aps	binary version of the resource script file	no
.bat	batch file used for compiling	no
.bmp	bitmap resource file	yes
.clw	class wizard file	no
.cpp	C++ module used for DLL	no
.cur	cursor resource file	yes
.def	module definition file	no
.dlg	dialog resource script file	yes
.dll	dynamic link library	yes
.fnt	font	no
.h	header file	no
.ico	icon resource file	yes
.inf	setup file	yes
.mak or .mdp	file containing project build instructions	no
.mc	messages	yes
.mnu	menu resource file	yes
.rc	resource script file (text-only)	yes
.rc2	resources Microsoft Visual C++ does not edit directly	no
.reg	registry files	yes
.res	resource file (binary)	yes
.vcp	project configuration file	no
.ver	version information header file	no

1.1.1.2.2   Language Settings

Software resource files contain several international settings that you might need to change before you compile translated files.

If you are editing RC files using a text-editor, you can change the header information and the version stamp.

1.1.1.2.2.1   Header

The header of a RC file might contain the following lines:

```
/////////////////////////////////////////////////////////////////////
/////////
// English (U.S.) resources

#if !defined(AFX_RESOURCE_DLL) || defined(AFX_TARG_ENU)
#ifdef _WIN32
LANGUAGE LANG_ENGLISH, SUBLANG_ENGLISH_US
#pragma code_page(1252)
#endif //_WIN32
```

This info block contains four language settings that need to be changed:

- The English (U.S.) resources comment line indicates that the resources following will be English. The end of a language block is defined by #endif // English (U.S.) resources.

- AFX_TARG_ENU indicates the AFX language that will be used. The three letter language codes are only valid in Windows 9x and NT. ENU is the language code for U.S. English. For a complete list of language codes, refer to the Locale Codes and IDs section on page 165.

- The LANGUAGE line defines the locale that will be used in the compilation. LANGUAGE is one of the keywords that were introduced with 32-bit RC files.

- The pragma code page defines the character set that will be used. Code page is a code array that maps the integer code to the character of the character set. The number 1252 stands for the default Latin-1 ANSI code page. Code page 1252 is used for English and most European languages. Other examples of code pages are 1200 (Unicode), 1250 (Eastern European), 1251 (Cyrillic), 1253 (Greek), and 1254 (Turkish).

To set the language of resources when you are using Microsoft Developer Studio, follow these steps:

1. Open the RC file or binary program file (DLL or EXE) that you are editing.

2. Select one or more resources of which you want to set the language.

3. Right-click on the selection and choose the Properties command.

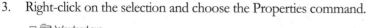
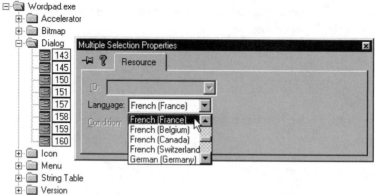

4. In the Properties window, select a language from the Language drop-down menu.

1.1.1.2.2.2   *Version Stamp*

The version stamp in a RC file specifies the company name, application name, copyright, version number, and language edition of a program.

A `Version` section in a RC file contains a language ID in the StringFileInfo and `VarFileInfo` blocks. The `StringFileInfo` block contains the user-defined string information, and the variable file information (`VarFileInfo`) block contains a list of languages supported by this version of the resource file.

```
BEGIN
    BLOCK "StringFileInfo"
    BEGIN
        BLOCK "040904e4"
        BEGIN
            VALUE "CompanyName", "Microsoft Corporation\0"
            VALUE "FileDescription", "WordPad MFC Application\0"
            VALUE "FileVersion", "4.00.950\0"
            VALUE "InternalName", "wordpad\0"
            VALUE "LegalCopyright", "Copyright © Microsoft Corp.\0"
            VALUE "OriginalFilename", "WORDPAD.EXE\0"
            VALUE "ProductName", "Microsoft Windows (TM)\0"
            VALUE "ProductVersion", "4.0\0"
        END
    END
    BLOCK "VarFileInfo"
    BEGIN
        VALUE "Translation", 0x409, 1252
    END
END
```

In the example above, change the language ID "040904e4", "0x409" and 1252 character set specification to reflect the settings for your language. The following section contains a table of language IDs and codes.

To change the version stamp of the resource file when you are using Microsoft Developer Studio, follow these steps:

1. Open the RC file or binary program file (DLL or EXE) that you are editing.

2. Open the Version resource.

3. Double-click on the Block Header line.

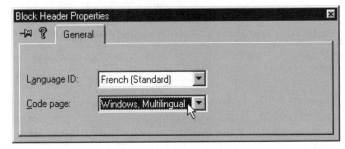

4. In the Block Header Properties window, select a language and code page for the file or project.

If you are working with a large set of RC files, it might be quicker to assign the language to the resources in one of the RC files. Next, copy the language definition heading from one file into the other files using a text editor or word processor.

1.1.1.2.2.3   Locale Codes and IDs

The following table shows the IDs and language codes that are used to identify locales in Windows software resource files. A complete listing can be found on the Unicode Web site at www.unicode.org.

Language	ID	Code	Locale
English	0x409	ENU	LANG_ENGLISH
English (UK)	0x02	ENG	SUBLANG_ENGLISH_UK
English (US)	0x01	ENU	SUBLANG_ENGLISH_US
French	0x40c	FRA	LANG_FRENCH
French	0x01	FRA	SUBLANG_FRENCH
French (Belgian)	0x02	FRB	SUBLANG_FRENCH_BELGIAN
German	0x407	DEU	LANG_GERMAN

Language	ID	Code	Locale
German	0x01	DEU	SUBLANG_GERMAN
German (Austrian)	0x03	DEA	SUBLANG_GERMAN_AUSTRIAN
German (Swiss)	0x02	DES	SUBLANG_GERMAN_SWISS
Italian	0x410	ITA	LANG_ITALIAN
Italian	0x01	ITA	SUBLANG_ITALIAN
Italian (Swiss)	0x02	ITS	SUBLANG_ITALIAN_SWISS
Spanish	0x40a	ESP	LANG_SPANISH
Spanish (Modern Sort)	0x03	ESN	SUBLANG_SPANISH_MODERN
Spanish (Traditional Sort)	0x01	ESP	SUBLANG_SPANISH
System Default	0x02		SUBLANG_SYS_DEFAULT

A locale is a combination of primary (language) and sub language (country) codes. Locale information includes currency symbol, date/time/number formatting information, localized days of the week and months of the year, the standard abbreviation for the name of the country, and character encoding information.

1.1.1.2.3   MFC Components

MFC, short for Microsoft Foundation Class library, is a set of C++ classes that contain standard resources and common dialog boxes for applications running under Windows 9x and NT. Examples of these standard resources are the Open, Print, Print Preview, and Save As dialog boxes, and the OLE Interface. The MFC resource file names are AFXRES.RC, AFXPRINT.RC, AFXOLECL.RC, AFXOLESV.RC, and AFXDB.RC.

Often, the MFC files are referenced in the RC file that you are localizing. For example, your RC file might contain the following code:

```
#include "afxres.rc"  // Standard components
#include "afxprint.rc"  // printing/print preview resources
```

This indicates that the standard resources from the AFXRES.RC and AFXPRINT.RC files are compiled into your DLL or EXE file. If you translate your RC file, but use the English versions of AFXRES.RC and AFXPRINT.RC, the compiled program file will be partly in English.

To get a completely localized DLL file, translate the included MFC file, or use one of the pre-translated files that are included on the Visual C++ disk. By default, the compiler uses the MFC files in the \MFC\INCLUDE folder of your Visual C++ program folder. The

\MFC\INCLUDE\L.* folders contain pre-translated MFC files in some languages, including German, Spanish, French, and Italian.

For example, to use the German MFC files, copy all files from the \MFC\INCLUDE\L.DEU folder to the \MFC\INCLUDE folder. Do not forget to copy the original English files to a folder called \MFC\INCLUDE\L.ENU. If you are building the DLL from the command line, you can also add /IC:\MSDEV\MFC\INCLUDE\L.DEU to your RC command line.

If translation is performed directly in the program files, provide translators with a glossary of the MFC files that are used. The MFC translations can also be found in the Microsoft glossary set that is described on page 283. Using these glossaries will save translators unnecessary work and improve consistency.

Other standard resource files that are included with MFC are PROMPTS.RC and INDICATE.RC. The INDICATE.RC file contains string resources for the status bar key-state indicators, such as CAP or INS. The PROMPTS.RC file contains menu-prompt string resources for each of the pre-defined commands, such as *Create a new document* for the New command. Pre-translated versions of these files can be found in the \MFC\SRC\L.* folders.

1.1.1.3   RESIZING

When software resource files have been translated, the dialog boxes need to be adjusted to make all options fit in the space available.

There are some general user interface rules that should be followed when resizing (controls in) dialog boxes:

- Localized dialog boxes should contain exactly the same number of buttons and options as the English version.

- Default buttons have default sizes, e.g., the Cancel button should be the same size in all dialog boxes.

- If possible, buttons should be the same size within a dialog box.

- Use the same alignment of options as the original version, i.e., left, right, top, or bottom.

- The Tab key order of options in the localized dialog box should be identical to the original version.

- Do not abbreviate text unless there really is no other way to make it fit.

- The dialog box title should fit in the title bar.

- Dialog boxes should fit on a standard VGA screen with 640 x 480 resolution.

Each item in a dialog box has position and size coordinates. In the following example, the position of the Cancel button is 29 units from the left of the dialog box, and 44 units from the top of the dialog box. The button height is 14 units, and the button width is 32 units.

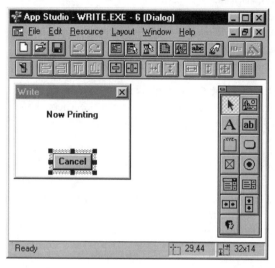

1.1.1.3.1   Visual C++ 1.x

If you are using Visual C++ version 1.x, use App Studio to open the resource or 16-bit program files. RC files can only be opened when all include files are available. For more information about App Studio, refer to the Microsoft App Studio section on page 27.

1.1.1.3.2   Visual C++ 2.x, 4.x and 5.x

Microsoft C++ 2.x and 4.x have an integrated resource editor, so you can simply use the Open command from the File menu to open RC files for resource editing.

Refer to the Microsoft App Studio section on page 27, and following sections for information about opening different resource types.

Open each dialog box and drag the sizing handles of the items that you wish to resize. Be careful not to overlap any hidden items, e.g., controls in which variables such as page numbers will be shown in the running application.

Tip

You can resize a control one dialog unit at a time by holding down the Shift key and using the arrow keys.

If translated text does not fit in an item, you can choose the Size to Content option from the Layout menu.

If there are two or more items, such as buttons, that you want to align, you can use the following commands and shortcuts:

Button	Command	Key Combination
	Make Same Height	Ctrl+\
	Make Same Width	Ctrl+-
	Make Same Size	Ctrl+=
	Align Left	Ctrl+left arrow
	Align Right	Ctrl+right arrow
	Align Top	Ctrl+up arrow
	Align Bottom	Ctrl+down arrow
	Center Vertical	Ctrl+F9
	Center Horizontal	Ctrl+Shift+F9
	Space Across	Alt+right arrow
	Space Down	Alt+up arrow

Some software localization tools, such as Corel Catalyst, contain features that automatically check for clipped text in controls. Refer to the Software Localization Tools section on page 37 for more information.

1.1.1.4 CHECKING HOT KEYS

Each option in a dialog box or menu must have a unique hot key, or mnemonic. In the property window of a dialog box item, you can change the hot key by typing an ampersand (&) in front of the letter that you want as the mnemonic.

In Visual C++ versions older than version 4.x, and in Borland Resource Workshop, you need to check the hot keys manually. Visual C++ 4.x and later contain a Check Mnemonics command that you can use to automatically search for duplicate hot keys in dialog boxes or menus.

To automatically search for duplicate hot keys, follow these steps:

1.   Open the dialog box that you want to check.

2.   Right-click in the dialog box and choose the Check Mnemonics command.

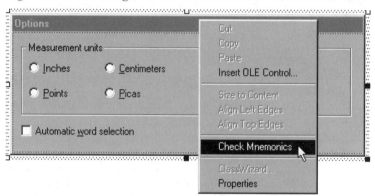

3.   When duplicates are found, a warning dialog box is displayed.

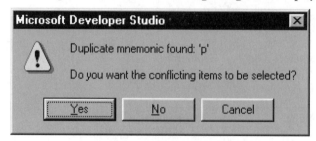

4.   Click Yes to locate the duplicates and change one of the hot keys.

5.   Repeat the command until all mnemonics in the dialog box are unique.

Some software localization tools, such as Corel Catalyst, also contain automatic hot key checking functions. Refer to the Software Localization Tools section on page 37 for more information.

1.1.1.5   BITMAP EDITING

When bitmaps containing text are included in software resource files, these need to be edited using a graphics editor, such as Adobe Photoshop or Paint Shop Pro.

If translation is performed in RC files that are compiled, the `// Bitmap` section in the RC file indicates which bitmaps will be included. If the bitmap section contains a reference like `BITMAP MOVEABLE PURE "bmp403.bmp"`, locate the *bmp403.bmp* file in the build environment and edit it using a graphics editor.

If translation is performed directly in a program file, open the bitmap resource using the integrated bitmap editor of your resource editor. It is also possible to export the bitmap resource and import it again after editing.

Sometimes bitmaps contain images that are very specific for a particular culture, or that may be offensive in other cultures. For example, a mailbox icon displaying a U.S. mailbox might mean nothing to a user in another country. In these cases, consult with your client if the bitmap should be localized or generalized.

If a bitmap contains translatable text that is pasted on a background, ask the software developer to provide you with *blanks* of the bitmap, i.e., bitmaps without the text. Re-creating backgrounds with, for example, gradients or photographic images can be very time-consuming and complex.

1.1.1.6   CREATING INSTALLERS

Although there are many other ways of creating installers for Windows applications, one setup technology will be used by most Windows-based installers that you will see.

Most installers for Windows 9x/NT applications are based on the InstallShield engine. InstallShield is a Setup development system by InstallShield Software Corporation. InstallShield5 International is a special version of InstallShield5 Professional that lets you produce one installation that supports many languages or any combination of localized installations and applications.

A typical InstallShield folder structure looks like this:

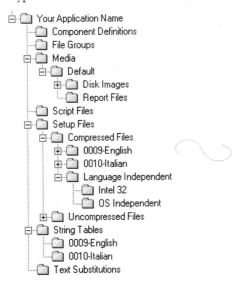

InstallShield International creates separate language folders with localizable files to allow the user to select the language of the installer that needs to be created. These project folders will contain files such as executables, DLLs, sample files, and help files.

Almost the entire Setup interface consists of standard InstallShield windows that are provided in most languages that are supported by Windows.

The following steps are essential for creating a localized version of an installer:

- Translate the string table file with all existing string identifiers. This file is called Value.shl and can be found in the \String Tables\<language> folder. In this file, all text following the equal sign (=) should be translated.

- Include your language-specific resource files. You need to make sure that all <language> equivalents of the 0009-English folder contain localized versions of DLLs or bitmaps. Also, include localized readme and license files.

- Include localized InstallShield files. These files include _setup.dll, _isres.dll, and IsUninst.exe, and including these files in your setup means that all InstallShield and unInstallShield dialog boxes and error messages appear in the desired language. These files will be automatically added when you create an installer using InstallShield5 International. They can also be found in the \Redistributable folder in InstallShield's program folder.

- Set the File Groups to include only localized files.

When you are ready to create your localized installer, click on the Media Build Wizard in the main project window. Click the Next button until the Languages dialog box is displayed.

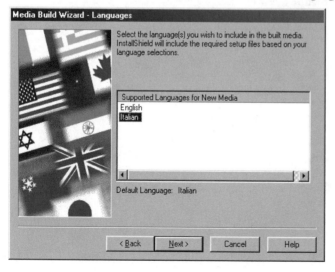

In the Languages dialog box, select the desired language, and click Next and Finish to create the installer. The localized setup will be created in the \Media folder.

For more information about InstallShield5 International, visit the InstallShield Web site at www.installshield.com.

1.1.2   Updating

If software is updated during the localization process, all changes in the English resource files or program files need to be implemented in the already–partly–localized files.

How these updates are processed depends on the way in which the software is translated, i.e., in text-only resource (RC) files, or directly in the program files.

Change management is very important when you handle software updates. You can either create a standard folder structure in which all updated files are clearly traceable, or you can use a version tracking system such as Microsoft's Visual SourceSafe.

1.1.2.1   RESOURCE FILES

The easiest way to process small software updates of RC files is to do a file compare between the old and new source files, and to implement all changes in the already localized resource files.

This method only works when there are only small changes in the update. If the resource files have been completely re-written or re-ordered, translating the new files is recommended.

If you are translating the resource files using a translation memory tool such as Trados Translator's Workbench, or IBM TranslationManager, it is possible to automatically update the new resource files with the previous translations. Most software localization tools also contain leveraging (translation re-use) features.

1.1.2.2   PROGRAM FILES

If you are translating directly in the program files, such as a DLL file, use a localization tool if you want to update updated files with previous translations. Examples of tools that support this functionality are Corel Catalyst, Microsoft RLToolset, and AppLocalize.

1.1.3   Software Testing

Testing localized software often is an essential part of the localization process.

If help and documentation are translated after the software application has been localized, try to involve translators in the testing process as much as possible. They should have access to a bug reporting database or form where they can report errors that they encounter while using the translated software for reference purposes. These error reports usually are an invaluable source of information for testing engineers!

For more information about software testing procedures and tools, visit the Software QA/Test Resource Center Web site at www.charm.net/~dmg/qatest or the Software Quality Engineering Web site at www.sqe.com.

In general, after an application has been localized, there are three testing stages.

- The first step after translation is the *linguistic test*, where the translator validates the translated software in context, with or without the help of an engineer.

- The second test is the *functionality test*, where localization engineers check if the localization of the application did not damage its functionality.

- Usually, at the very end of the software localization process, a *QA, acceptance, or delivery test* is performed. This test implies installing the localized product the way it will be installed by the end user, or checking the final deliverables against the original instructions or localization kit.

The following sections discuss each of these testing types, and any preparation work that should be done before testing of localized files can be done.

1.1.3.1 PREPARATION

The operating environment in which localized applications are tested is very important. First, the application should be tested on an operating system written in the target language of the application. This has several advantages:

- It is most likely that the end user will be using the application with an operating system written in the same language. Bugs caused by operating systems in other languages will be traced this way.

- All default international settings will be there, such as time, date, separator, and currency settings. If the application is using default settings that are not correct for the target language, you will know it is not caused by the operating system.

- It is easier to see if all parts of the application have been translated. English messages or dialog boxes attract less attention when testing is done on an English operating system.

Before starting to test an application, make sure your computer is "clean". This means that all previous, beta or original English versions of the program to be tested either should be removed from the hard drive or be compressed. Removing an application not only means deleting the program files but also all files that are installed by the application to the operating system folders. For example, on Windows computers, the \Windows and \Windows\System folders should not contain INI, DRV or other files from a previous installation of the application. Also, the Registry should not contain any information related to the application.

Tip

When you do *compatibility* testing, do not use a "clean" machine. Instead, use a computer with target language versions of other applications, drivers and hardware installed.

Because localized applications should always be tested on an operating system in the language that the application was translated to, it is recommended to install a new version of a localized operating system on your machine.

It is possible to install multiple language versions of Windows or Windows 9x on one hard drive and then switch between the different versions. To multi-boot different language versions of Windows NT, you will have to create partitions on your hard drive, or use a multi-boot utility that supports Windows NT. Windows NT 5 comes with locale-switching features which allow you to select the interface language that you want to use.

1.1.3.1.1 Setting up multiple language versions of Windows 3.1

For Windows 3.1 applications, the best way to ensure you are testing on a clean Windows version is to install Windows from the installation disks or CD in a folder called WIN*xxx*, where *xxx* is the language code. Refer to Locale Codes and IDs on page 165 for a list of language codes. A German version, for example, would be installed in a folder called WINDEU.

After installing Windows, compress (use PKZIP) all files in the WIN*xxx* and WIN*xxx*\System folder and store them somewhere on your hard disk or on the network. When the testing work is completed, delete the WIN*xxx* folder. When you need the clean Windows version again for testing, just unzip the files. A compressed Windows 3.1 version requires approximately 5MB of disk space.

1.1.3.1.2 Setting up multiple language versions of Windows 9x

You can configure your computer for multi-booting in several ways. If you are only using Windows 9x, you can edit your startup files or use a utility called WinBoot. If you are using other operating systems on the same computer, use a professional multi-boot utility like System Commander by V-Communications, Inc.

The following sections describe how to set up your computer for multi-booting.

1.1.3.1.2.1   Changing Boot Sequence

To install two or more different language versions of Windows 9x on your machine, follow these steps:

1.   Install Windows 9x.

2.   Restart in DOS mode and install another language version of Windows 9x. Make sure you install to a folder with a different name, for example WIN*xxx*, where *xxx* is the language code. Also, add the language code extension to the name of the \Program Files folder because in some languages this folder name equals the English folder name.

3.   After you have installed all required languages of Windows 9x, open Explorer and locate the MSDOS.SYS file in the root of your hard drive.

4.   Open the Properties for this file, and deselect the Read Only option.

5.   Open the file using Notepad, and change the path following the `WinDir=` and `WinBootDir=` options to reflect the folder of the language version that you want to run.

6.   Change the \Program Files folder that belongs to this language version to its original name.

7.   Restart your machine.

Please note that this method only works when you are not concerned about language or code page settings that are loaded from the AUTOEXEC.BAT and CONFIG.SYS startup files. For most European languages this is not important.

1.1.3.1.2.2   Using WinBoot

WinBoot is a multi-boot utility that allows you to install and switch between different language versions of Windows 9x. The tool can be found on the Microsoft Developer Network CD's, and can be downloaded from the Internet at www.microsoft.com/globaldev/gbl-gen/intlboot.htm. Please note that this utility is not a Microsoft product, and will not be supported by Microsoft.

The utility stores all language-specific files (AUTOEXEC.BAT, COMMAND.COM, CONFIG.SYS, IO.SYS, and MSDOS.SYS) with an ISO language code extension in the \Winboot folder. It uses the files of the language that the user selects in the WinBoot screen.

Important

To install Windows 9x from CD, you need to have real-mode CD drivers installed in your CONFIG.SYS and AUTOEXEC.BAT files.

To set up multiple language versions of Windows 9x on your computer using WinBoot, follow these steps:

1. Copy the WinBoot files (WINBOOT.EXE and WINBOOT.HLP) to the root directory C:\ of your system's boot drive.

2. Start WINBOOT.EXE from Explorer, or choose Run from the Start menu and type WINBOOT.EXE in the Run dialog box.

3. In the WinBoot dialog box, select the Click here to install a new language version of Windows 95 option.

4. Press OK in the Setup New Language Version message box.

5. After your computer restarts in MS-DOS mode, install the new language version of Windows 9x. Make sure you install the new Windows version to another folder than the default \Windows folder. For example, install it to a \WIN*xxx* folder, where *xxx* is the language code.

6. A \Winboot folder will be created in the root of your hard drive, containing the settings files for the installed languages.

To switch between different language versions of Windows 9x , follow these steps.

1. Start WINBOOT.EXE from Explorer, or choose Run from the Start menu and type WINBOOT.EXE in the Run dialog box.

2. Choose the language that you want to switch to in the Change Language To drop down box.

The computer will restart and start Windows in the language that you have selected.

1.1.3.1.2.3   *Using System Commander*

System Commander allows you to install and run any combination of PC-compatible operating systems, including Windows 95/98, Windows 3.1, Windows NT, DOS, OS/2, and all of the PC compatible Unix versions.

System Commander makes it possible to have the same operating system in several different languages as well as different operating systems in different languages.

For more information about System Commander, visit the V-Communications Web site at www.v-com.com.

1.1.3.2   TESTING

After a software application has been translated, two things need to be tested: the *language* of the application, and its *functionality*.

1.1.3.2.1   Linguistic Test

The *linguistic test* focusses on the visual aspects of an application, i.e., it is a user interface test. Ideally, linguistic or localization testing is performed by the person who translated the software, with the help of a localization engineer or test scripts.

During this test, the translator should validate each dialog box, menu and as many strings as possible in the running application. Even if the software translator has been using a WYSIWYG localization tool or resource editor to translate the resources, this step is essential, especially to verify strings that are inserted in dialog boxes and menus only at run-time.

For linguistic testing, open the resource files you have translated one by one in a resource editor (binary files) or text editor (text-only resource files). Next, make sure you open every menu, dialog box and alert box that is present in the resources in the running application. Also, browse through the string sections in the resources and try to get error messages or status messages on screen, especially the longer ones and concatenations. For example, type an invalid value in every text box where a value can be entered.

During the linguistic test, focus on the following:

- Is all text translated?

- Do accented characters display OK?

- Are dialog boxes properly resized? Pay special attention to dynamic dialog boxes, where object overlays such as buttons, fields, and drop-down menus are used to change the possible options that a dialog box presents depending on the options selected.

- Do all menu items, status bar messages, and dialog boxes fit on the screen in all resolutions?

- Are all hot keys in dialog boxes and menus unique?

- Do error messages show up OK, without truncations?

- Have any leading or trailing spaces in concatenated strings been deleted by the translator?

- Have any icons, graphics or sounds been used that are not relevant to the target language market?

- Do all concatenated strings display OK? Often, spaces are deleted during translation causing two strings to be merged into one word.

1.1.3.2.2   Functionality Test

The *functionality test* focusses on the tasks that should be performed by the program. If the application has been internationalized well, i.e., if all translatable text has been separated from application code, it is more likely that no bugs have been introduced by translation of the software.

The best way to do a functionality test of a localized application is to set up a team of testing engineers. Testing engineers should also experiment with unusual situations, like write-protected disks, full disks, read-only files, etc. All bugs should be entered in a problem report or database, which is referred to by the engineers that are fixing the bugs.

During functionality testing, the translation should be finalized and stable, and only the technical aspects are considered. Often, software developers provide the localization vendor with test scripts that systematically test the functions of the application, or that guide testers through all screens and menus of the application.

If you have not received any guidelines or scripts for testing, create your own testing environments and testing scripts. In most cases, a test script will be a document explaining how to get to every screen in the application and how to reproduce most possible situations.

During the functionality test, focus on the following:

- Can documents that are saved in the original version be opened in the localized version, and vice versa?

- Is it possible to type accented text, use hot keys, and use control keys with international keyboards and keyboard layouts?

- Do the default settings, such as page size, time, number and currency formats, reflect the language of the localized product? Does the localized application automatically use the regional settings from the Control Panel?

- Can the user copy and paste text with accented characters from the localized application to another application? Does OLE functionality still work?

- Does the application function correctly on a localized operating environment?

- Do language-specific add-ons, such as spelling checkers for a word processor, or character conversion tables for a telecommunication product, work OK?

Often functionality testing includes a *compatibility test*. The purpose of compatibility, or configuration testing is to ensure proper operation of the software under various hardware and software environments. Testing consists of verifying proper functionality and program execution against all applicable processors, (language versions of) operating systems, applications, memory configurations, video adapters, sound boards, and CD drives along with their associated drivers.

Sometimes clients might ask you to do full functional testing and to deliver a *gold master* of the translated software product. A gold master is the final version of the product that has passed all QA and engineering processes, ready for manufacturing and redistribution.

1.1.3.2.3   Delivery Test

The *delivery or QA test* should be performed on a clean system written in the language to be tested, using the final disk images or deliverables.

Especially with large localization projects, it is always a good idea to refer back to the original instructions or localization kit to see if all instructions about file format, folder structure, etc. were followed.

During the delivery test, focus on the following:

- Do the original disks and the localized disks contain the same number of files?

- Open all DLL, EXE or DRV files on the installation disks using a resource editor and browse through all dialogs. Verify that all files are in the right language.

- Install and check all dialogs of the installer.

  1. Try all options with both keyboard shortcuts and mouse buttons.

  2. Try installing on a full disk, in different directories, with different component options, etc.

  3. Quit the installation halfway through and start it again.

- Does the localized version of the application install the same number as files as the original version?

- Are all installed components in the correct language? You can check this by double-clicking on all executables and help files in the program folder.

- Does the application run? A quick functionality test should be sufficient at this stage.

- Does the Uninstaller work OK?

- Have bugs that were reported to your client been fixed during the update cycle? If not, report them again.

- Are no temporary or old versions of files included in the final delivery?

- Are the files delivered in the same folder structure as the original files?

1.1.3.2.4   Writing Bug Reports

Bug reports, or rather *software problem reports*, can play an important role in localization projects and in the communication between localizers and software developers. A bug report is maintained by the localization engineer and contains issues covering the following problem areas:

- Functionality problems in the original application

- Functionality internationalization problems, for example wrong display of accented characters, no support for foreign keyboards, wrong page sizes and other defaults, no support for hardware used in foreign market, etc.

- Localization problems, for example items that cannot be localized properly because they are hard-coded, or problems that were introduced after localization and that cannot be solved by localization engineer

- Questions to the software development department about technical issues

Bugs need to be reproducible. If a problem only occurs once and it cannot be reproduced on the same or other machines, this problem should not be reported.

Problem reports can be created in any format, from basic word-processing documents to advanced bug tracking databases. More important than file format is the content of a problem report. Above all, problem reports should be simple and clear.

A typical localization bug report would contain the following fields:

- Number of the problem

- Product, version, platform, and platform version

- Date that the problem was reported, or software build number.

- File name of the file that contains or causes the problem, or product area

- Location in the file or application where the problem occurs

- Description of the problem, its severity, and the steps needed to reproduce it

- Configuration details about the machine on which the bug was found

- Workaround suggested by localization engineer

- Answer or solution to be entered by client

- Status of the problem, i.e., has it been fixed? The status can be *new*, *open*, *pending*, or *closed*. It can also include options such as *bug in source*, *need more info*, or *no need to fix*.

The following section contains an example of a basic localization problem report:

Problem Report #2

Product: DataView 1.4
Reported by: BE
Date: 23-9-98

Nr.	Date	File	Location	Problem	Status
C001	23-9-98	SETUP.EXE	Opening screen	Product icon is not displayed	Open
C002	23-9-98	LANG.DLL	Dialog box 103	Drop-down list shows up in English	Closed
C003	23-9-98	LANG.DLL			

The easiest way to keep track of bugs is to set up a file that both your engineers and your client can access, such as a Web-based database. If you do not have these facilities, sending a new version of a problem report with every delivery might be a good idea. This also allows you to do regression testing, i.e., tracking if reported bugs have been fixed. If they are, the status field will change to *Closed*.

Try to avoid sending problems, questions, and bugs in separate e-mails or messages because they might get lost during the project. Tracking problems and bugs in one central place will make it much easier for both you and your client to track the status of bugs.

1.1.4   Creating Screen Captures

Screen captures are images containing elements of the user interface of an application or operating system. They are usually embedded in or linked to documentation and help files.

Screen captures can be created by pressing Alt-Print Screen on your keyboard, switching to a graphical application, and choosing the Paste command. This will create a screen capture of the entire screen. On the Internet or other online services, you will find numerous utilities that will allow you to only capture a section of a screen, such as a window or a menu. Refer to the Utilities section on page 185 for more information about some of these utilities.

1.1.4.1   PREPARATION

1.1.4.1.1   Display Configuration

Before you start shooting screen captures, verify the computer configuration and software settings that you need to use to reflect the original images as closely as possible. Settings include factors such as color depth (black & white, grayscale, color, 8-bit, 16-bit, etc.) and screen resolution. If you are not sure which settings to use, ask your client.

In Windows 3.1, the screen resolution can be set by opening Windows Setup from the Main program group and selecting the desired resolution and color depth from the System Settings dialog box.

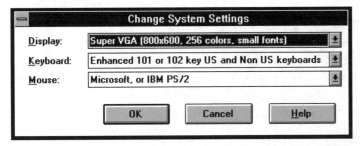

In Windows 9x, you can specify the screen resolution in the Display control panel. The Settings tab contains options for color palette and desktop area.

A typical configuration for Windows 3.1/9x screen captures is 256 colors and a desktop area (resolution) of 800x600 pixels.

1.1.4.1.2   File Format

Always verify with your client which file format is required. If original image files are available, use the format and image settings of the original files.

The following table shows commonly used file formats and the documents in which they are mostly used:

Document	File Format
Printed Document	.BMP (Bitmap) or TIFF (Tagged Image File format)
Help File (.HLP)	.BMP (Bitmap), SHG (Shed Graphic), or WMF (Windows Meta File)
Online Document (.HTML)	.GIF (Graphics Interchange Format) or JPG (Joint Photo. Expert Group)

Also, check the settings or sub-types of the file formats that you are using. For example, GIF files can have different transparency settings or sub-types: version 87a – Interlaced or Non-interlaced, or version 89a Interlaced or Non-interlaced. For JPG files, you can specify the DPI to be saved.

In Paint Shop Pro, select the Image Information command from the View menu to check the format settings of an image.

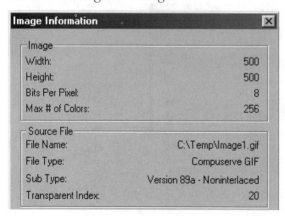

1.1.4.1.3   Cursors

Check if the original screen captures contain cursors. If they do, a cursor should be on the same location in the localized screen capture. Most screen capture utilities have an option to include or exclude the cursor in a screen capture.

1.1.4.1.4   Utilities

Examples of applications and utilities that you can use to create screen captures on a Windows platform are:

- Paint Shop Pro

Paint Shop Pro is a raster format image editing application developed by JASC, Inc. For more information about Paint Shop Pro and a demo version, visit the JASC Web site at www.jasc.com.

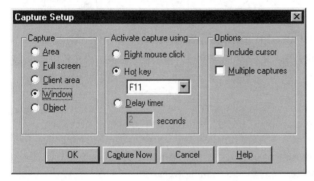

- Collage Complete

Collage Complete is a Windows and DOS screen capture and image handling utility developed by Inner Media, Inc. For more information about Collage Complete and a demo version, visit the Inner Media Web site at www.innermedia.com.

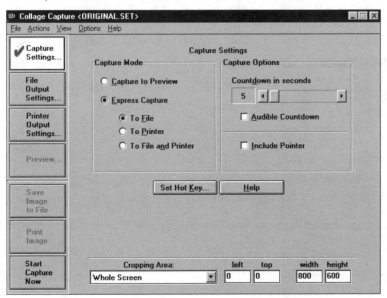

Other examples of screen capture utilities are:

* Hijaak Pro – www.imsisoft.com

* SnagIt – www.techsmith.com

* Capture Professional – www.creativesoftworx.com

1.1.4.1.5   Test

Before creating all screen captures, test some of the localized images in the documentation files where they will be inserted, such as a manual or help file.

For example, when images are linked to a document, replace the original image with your localized screen capture and print the page containing the image. Compare the test page with the original printout to see if the screen capture is scaled and printed correctly.

1.1.4.2   GRAPHICS EDITING

Sometimes it is necessary to *fake* screen captures. For example, this might be necessary when the translation of the application is not yet finished and a screen capture is needed for a marketing brochure. Or, when the original screen capture contains a situation or error that is difficult or impossible to reproduce in the running application.

1.1.4.2.1   Tips

If you need to manually enter text in a user interface screen capture, the font which is used for most Windows applications is Ms Sans Serif size 8. Another commonly used font is Arial.

To check which font of which size is used in error messages or menu items, open the Appearance tab of the Windows Display Properties control panel and click on an item to see its font characteristics.

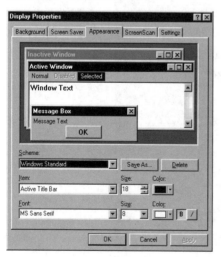

To edit screen captures manually, follow these steps:

1. Start the graphics application, such as Paint Shop Pro.

2. Open the graphic that you want to edit. In this example, we will edit a screen capture from Windows 9x Wordpad.

3. Use the eyedropper to set the background and foreground color to black and gray.

4. Identify the font that you need to use. To do this, use the type tool to insert one of the English menu items and place it on top of the existing command. If it exactly overlaps the item, you have found the correct font. In this case, Ms Sans Serif size 8 is used.

5. Now, use the type tool to insert your translation next to the original item or in a separate file.

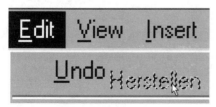

6. Draw a marquee around the translated string using the selection tool, and move the translation on top of the original item.

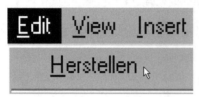

Sometimes you first need to delete the English text in order to paste your translation next to it. In these cases, leave one dot of the original text to make sure you paste the translation in the correct place.

1.2 Windows Help

When the RTF, CNT, and HPJ files of a help project have been translated, all components are compiled into a Windows help file. Refer to the Windows Help Files section on page 72 for more information on translating help project files.

The following sections outline the steps that need to be taken to compile, engineer, and test Windows help files.

1.2.1 Engineering

Apart from just using the HPJ file to compile a set of RTF files into a Windows help file, there are several other things a help engineer needs to do to create a truly localized help file.

1.2.1.1 PREPARING

Before the files of a help project are translated, it is advisable to do some preparation work that might save a lot of problems and manual editing after the files have been translated. It is essential that the source material be correct before it is translated. If an incorrect file is going to be translated into four languages, it is easier to fix a problem in the source file than to fix it later in four translated files.

1.2.1.1.1   Test-Compiling

Test-compiling a help project before it is translated will automatically tell you if all necessary files are included. Missing RTF or image files will be reported by the compiler. Errors will be reported by the compiler in an ERR file. If there are many errors reported by the compiler, ask you client if translation of the online help files should really start.

Before you compile, you need to find out if a help file should be compiled using the HCP (Windows 3.1) or HCW (Windows 9x) help compiler. If a help project contains a CNT file and the HPJ file starts with "This file is maintained by HCW. Do not modify this file directly.", use the HCW.EXE WinHelp 4.x compiler.

1.2.1.1.2   Creating Word Counts

When you have received a localization kit including all help source files, such as RTF, HPJ, and CNT files, you can create word counts of these files using HelpQA or a word processor. For more information about HelpQA, refer to the Using HelpQA section on page 207.

HelpQA will provide you with detailed statistics on the help project, including word count, number of images, number of files, and number of links. You can click on the Reports button to create a text document with all statistics.

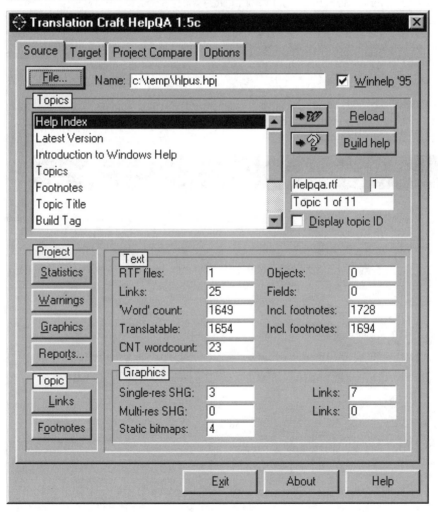

1.2.1.1.2.1   *RTF files*

Rich Text Format files can be opened using most word processors. Please note that different word processors can output different RTF versions that are not necessarily compatible. For example, the RTF file format of Microsoft Word 8 is not compatible with other word processors or older versions of the Microsoft Help Compiler.

Keep the following in mind when doing word counts of RTF files that are used for Windows Help or Macintosh QuickHelp files:

- A true word count of RTF files would not include some of the footnotes, such as the code # and ^{A} footnotes, which are never translated.

- ^{K} keyword footnotes that are separated by semi-colons without spaces are counted as one word. For example, if a ^{K} footnote contains the keywords "file;print", this will be counted as one word.

You can prevent this by clicking in the body text and using the find/replace command to replace all # and ^{A} characters with spaces. Also, click in the footnotes area and replace all semi-colons with semi-colon-space.

> ### Important
>
> RTF files saved in Word for Windows 8 (Microsoft Office 97) contain new tokens that are incompatible with help compilers older than HCRTF 4.02. A freeware utility filters these tokens out. You can download this utility from the Wextech Web site at www.wextech.com. Another solution is the EasyFixRTF utility from Eon Solutions, available from www.eon-solutions.com.

1.2.1.1.2.2   *HPJ Files*

Help Project files usually contain only a very few words to be translated. For more information about this translatable text, refer to the HPJ Files section on page 80.

1.2.1.1.2.3   *CNT Files*

To count the words in a CNT file, follow these steps:

1. Open the CNT file using your word processor.

2.   Select all text and convert the text to a table using the equal symbol (=) as a separator.

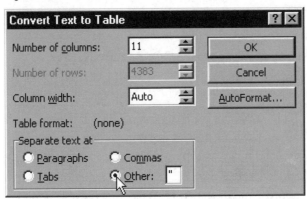

3.   Copy the first column to a new document and count the words.

To count the number of topics or screens in a help file, open the compiled help file (HLP) with the Help Author option in the File menu of Microsoft Help Workshop enabled. This option will display the topic number in the title bar of the help file. Pressing Ctrl+Shift+Home will bring you to the last topic of the help file. The topic number in the title bar tells you the total number of topics.

1.2.1.2   COMPILING

To compile a Windows help file, you need to use the Microsoft Help Compiler. Currently, there are several versions of the Microsoft Help Compiler available: HC.EXE, HC30.EXE, HC31.EXE, HCP.EXE, and HCRTF.EXE.

For Windows 3.0 and 3.1 help files, you respectively use the HC.EXE/HC30.EXE or HC31.EXE compiler. The HCP.EXE is the protected-mode version of the Windows 3.1 help compiler, i.e., it supports extended memory usage.

HCRTF.EXE is the Windows 9x help compiler, for WinHelp 4.x projects. This compiler is activated from within the Microsoft Help Workshop shell, HCW.EXE.

Help compilers are included with most programming languages, and can be downloaded from Microsoft's FTP server at ftp.microsoft.com/softlib/mslfiles. For example, the HCWSETUP.EXE file contains the Microsoft Help Workshop version 4.03, which is compatible with Word 97 RTF files. The HC505.EXE file contains all Windows 3.1 help compilers. They can also be found on the Microsoft Developer Network CDs. The HCW.EXE Windows 9x help compiler needs to be licensed from Microsoft, and is included with most 32-bit SDKs and programming languages.

For downloadable versions of most help compilers and other Windows Help utilities, visit the Help Master Web site at www.helpmaster.com or the Help Universe Web site at www.weisner.com/universe.

1.2.1.2.1   Windows 3.1

To compile a Windows 3.1 help project, go to the DOS prompt and type:

HC31 *help_project_filename*.HPJ

–or–

HCP *help_project_filename*.HPJ

Before compilation, translate all RTF files and appropriate items in the HPJ file, as described in the HPJ Files section on page 80.

If error messages are displayed, refer to the HC31.HLP file for a possible solution. Error messages are recorded in the *help_project_filename*.ERR file. During compilation, a *help_project_filename*.HLP file will be created in the folder where you issued the command.

1.2.1.2.2   Windows 9x

To compile a Windows 9x help project, start Microsoft Help Workshop (HCW.EXE), open the *help_project_filename*.HPJ file and click the Save and Compile button.

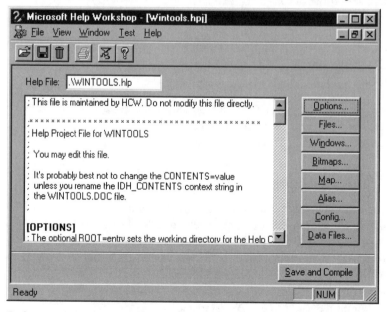

Before compilation, translate all appropriate items in the HPJ file, as described in the HPJ Files section on page 80. Error messages are recorded in the *help_project_filename*.ERR file.

> **Tip**
>
> If compression is enabled in the HPJ file (COMPRESS=TRUE), compilation time will be considerably longer. Therefore, you might want to disable compression until the final release build.

1.2.1.2.3 Using Robohelp

Robohelp is a help-authoring tool that offers a fast and easy way to create help systems. It consists of a series of Microsoft Word templates and macros that guide the help author through the help creation process.

In Robohelp, all processing is based on Word DOC files. Because the Microsoft Help Compiler only supports RTF files, the DOC files are automatically saved as RTF files before compilation. When a help file has been created using Robohelp, it is recommended to translate the DOC files instead of the RTF files.

If a help file is compiled from a set of DOC files, there is always one project file, which is based on the ROBOHELP.DOT template. Additional files use the ROBORTF.DOT template. Typically, the project file has the same name as the compiled help file, i.e., SAMPLE.DOC will be compiled into SAMPLE.HLP.

Translators do not really need the templates to translate the DOC files, but for compilation and page layout, it is necessary to use the Robohelp templates. Opening the project file will display a set of Robohelp tools that are used to configure the help project, to compile and to run the help file.

For more information about Robohelp, visit the Blue Sky Software Web site at www.blue-sky.com.

1.2.1.2.4 Using Doc-To-Help

Doc-To-Help is an application that allows you to create printed documentation and online Help from a single source.

Increasingly, software developers use the "single-source-multiple-output" method for their source documents as well as translated documents. For example, when a printed manual has been translated, the online help for the same application is not translated, but created from the translated manual, or vice versa. Doc-To-Help automatically converts index markers to help keyword entries, titles to help page topic titles, and it automatically generates pop-up definitions, links, and CNT files.

For more information about Doc-To-Help, visit the Wextech Web site at www.wextech.com.

1.2.1.3 RTF FILES

The [FILES] section in the HPJ file defines which RTF files will be included in the help file. Do not change the order of the files listed in this section.

If you have changed the names of the localized RTF files, you need to change the file names in this section accordingly. Typically, file names will not be changed.

1.2.1.4 GRAPHICS

Windows help files can contain graphics of the following types: Windows bitmaps (BMP or DIB), Windows metafiles (WMF), Windows Help multiple-hotspot (SHED) bitmaps (SHG), and Windows Help multi-resolution bitmaps (MRB).

In WinHelp 3.x, only 16-color and, in more recent versions, 256-color bitmaps are supported. WinHelp 4.x supports any number of colors. The color depth is automatically reduced if the user's display driver does not support more colors, which not always gives the best results. A solution is to use multi-resolution bitmaps, which are compiled by the Multi-Resolution Bitmap Compiler (MRBC.EXE), and that compensate for display types differences (CGA, EGA, VGA, or 8514).

Make sure the localized versions of these bitmaps have the same color depth as the original bitmaps. Refer to your help compiler's documentation for more information on graphics in help files.

In the HPJ file, the location of the graphics is set by the BMROOT option in the [OPTIONS] section. When this option is not specified, the compiler will only search in the help project folder for referenced graphics.

1.2.1.4.1 Position

Bitmaps are inserted in help files through bmc, bml, or bmr statements. A bmc statement, such as {bmc bitmap.bmp}, inserts a bitmap in the text as if it were a character. The bml and bmr statements place the bitmap at the left or right margin of the help window, with the text wrapping around the bitmap.

In your localized RTF files, make sure these statements do not change.

1.2.1.4.2 Hotspots

Often, help files contain graphics with hotspots, so-called *hypergraphics*. This means that you can use bitmaps, such as buttons or graphics, as *jumps* to other topics. When a user places the pointer cursor over a hotspot, the cursor changes to a hand with pointing index finger, indicating that the user may click to activate a link.

One bitmap can contain several hotspots. For example, a screen capture of a dialog box can contain a number of hotspots that take you to help information about the window option that you click on in the help file.

These hotspot graphics, with the SHG extension, are created with the Microsoft Hotspot Editor (SHED.EXE). To create a hotspot graphic, open a bitmap (BMP) file in Hotspot Editor, drag a box around the section that you want to define as hotspot, and select Attributes in the Edit menu. In the Attributes window, type a context string (topic ID) of a help file topic, and change additional settings if necessary.

The SHED.EXE utility is available from Microsoft's FTP server at ftp.microsoft.com/softlib/mslfiles. Another SHG editor is included in the HelpScribble shareware application, which is available from www.ping.be/jg.

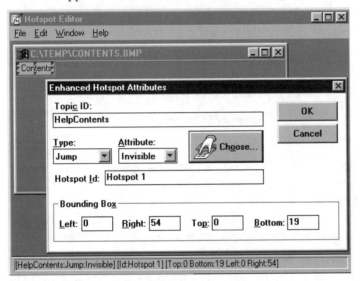

There are several versions of SHED Hotspot Editor available. The following sections describe how to edit SHG files using these versions.

1.2.1.4.2.1   Shed

When you are creating localized hotspot graphics, you can copy the hotspots from the original SHG files to the localized bitmaps. To copy and paste hotspots:

1. Open the original SHG file in Hotspot Editor.

2. Choose the Select command from the Edit menu (Ctrl+Ins).

3. Select the hotspot you want to copy and press the Select button.

4. Open the localized bitmap and choose Paste from the Edit menu (Shift+Ins).

5. Move the bounding box to the right location and resize it if necessary.

6. Save the file with the SHG extension.

1.2.1.4.2.2   Shed 3.50.784

When you are using SHED Hotspot Editor version 3.50.784 or higher, there is a faster way of creating localized SHG files. This version of SHED contains a new Replace feature in the Edit menu.

Suppose you have an English SHG file with 5 hotspots, and a localized bitmap file that you want to convert into a SHG file. To use the Replace feature, follow these steps:

1. Start SHED Hotspot Editor and open the English SHG file.

2. Open the localized bitmap file using any graphics application that can read BMP files, such as Windows 3.1 Paintbrush or Windows 9x Paint.

3. Copy the bitmap to the clipboard by choosing Select All and Copy from the Edit menu.

4. Go back to SHED Hotspot Editor and select Replace from the Edit menu.

5. Adjust the size or position of the bounding boxes and save the SHG file.

1.2.1.4.2.3   Shed 1.4 or 2

A disadvantage of using the Replace function is that the SHG file size might increase. To avoid this, use version 1.4 or 2 of SHED Hotspot Editor. You can download these versions from the Help Master Web site at www.helpmaster.com. Version 2 can also be downloaded from Microsoft's FTP server as part of the MMVIEWER.EXE file that can be found at ftp.microsoft.com/developr/MSDN/UnSup-ed.

These versions contain an Import command. Instead of using the clipboard, open the English SHG file, import the localized bitmap using the Import command from the File menu, and adjust the hotspot boxes.

1.2.1.5   BROWSE SEQUENCE

A browse sequence is the order in which help topics will be displayed when the user clicks on the browse buttons (>> and<<) in the compiled help file. A help file can have one browse sequence, which means the user can browse from the first page to the last page of the help file, or several smaller browse sequences.

Browse sequences are mostly used in WinHelp 3.x help projects.

Often, help files contain glossaries, which are alphabetically sorted. When the glossary text is translated, the sorting order changes. Instead of manually sorting all glossary entry pages in the RTF file, you can also change the browse sequence of every topic.

The footnote mark for browse sequences is the plus sign (+). The footnote itself consists of a code string and a number, with the number indicating in which order the topic in question will be called.

To change the browse sequence of a subset of topics, follow these steps:

1. Open the RTF file containing the topics in your word processor.

2. Open the footnote section and go to the first topic of the sequence.

3. Go to the lowest number for that sequence, which is not necessarily number 1.

4. Change the sequence numbers following the + footnote symbol to the correct alphabetical order.

The translated word that should be on top of the list will have the lowest number.

1.2.1.6   FORMATTING

As a rule, help file formatting should stay the same as in the original files. Sometimes, it might be necessary to change the column width of tables or to change tab settings, but in general all text wrapping and page layout will be adjusted automatically in the compiled help file. This means that you should never insert manual line or page breaks in RTF file text.

As far as character formatting is concerned, if you are compiling a help file using the Windows 3.1 help compiler, you might experience problems with curly quotes, emdash, endash, and bullet symbols. You can manually search and replace these symbols in your word processor, but there is also a tool available that will do this work for you.

This tool is called Rich Text Format Modifier and is available from Microsoft's FTP server at ftp.microsoft.com/developr/drg/Multimedia/RTFMod.

In the WinHelp 4.x help compiler, these problems are solved. In this version of the help compiler, you can even automatically localize quotation marks. For example, if the RTF files contain the string "example", and you compile the help file using the French language setting, this string will be displayed in the compiled help file as «example», or in German as „example".

1.2.1.7   CHARACTER SET

You specify the character set used in a localized help file using the CHARSET option in the [OPTIONS] section of the HPJ file.

If you have edited the RTF files using Microsoft Word 6.0 or higher, you don't need to include this statement, because Word specifies the character set. If you have used an earlier version of Word or a RTF editor that does not specify the character set, specify it in the HPJ file.

This option only works for WinHelp 3.x projects. Microsoft Help Workshop 4.x supports all RTF characters sets, i.e., ANSI, Windows, Macintosh, OEM code page 437, International English code page 850.

To change the default character set, open the HPJ file using Microsoft Help Workshop, click the Options button, select the Fonts tab and select an option from the Character Set list.

1.2.1.8   SORT ORDER

Specifying the language of the help file in the HPJ file will adjust the sort order of the keywords in the search index. For example, in Scandinavian languages, words starting with ä, å, or ö are sorted at the end of the alphabet, and not under the **A** section.

1.2.1.8.1   Windows 3.1

In WinHelp 3.x, only English and Scandinavian sorting is supported. If the help file is translated into a Scandinavian language, add the following option to the [OPTIONS] section of the HPJ file:

```
LANGUAGE=scandinavian
```

1.2.1.8.2   Windows 9x

In WinHelp 4.x, the LCID= option defines the language of the help file. The LCID= option is followed by a language code, such as **0x409** for American English. This option will also automatically determine whether topic files use a double-byte character set (DBCS). If the LCID= option is followed by an Asian language code, the DBCS= option is forced to YES.

To change the language identifier using Microsoft Help Workshop, click the Options button, select the Sorting tab, and choose a language from the Language of Help file drop-down list.

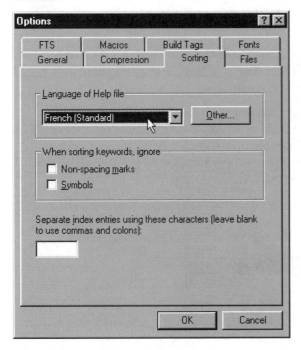

1.2.2   Testing

After a help file has been translated, reviewed, proofread, formatted and compiled without errors, it needs to be tested.

Several elements need to be tested or checked:

- Project statistics

- General page layout

- Window titles

- Jumps

- Search keyword list

- Context help from within application

- Contents (CNT) file (WinHelp 4.x help only)

- Custom buttons or menus

1.2.2.1   PREPARATION

Always test localized help files on an operating system of the same language. Because many items in a Windows screen originate from the standard WinHelp viewer that is included with every translated Windows version, it will not be possible to do a reliable help file test using a WinHelp viewer in another language.

If you do not want to install a localized version of the operating system just for testing a help file in that language, copy the Winhelp.exe (16-bit help) or Winhlp32.exe (32-bit help) from the Windows setup disks of the desired language.

For example, if you need the help viewer files in French, open the folder containing the setup disks for the French version of Windows 9x. All localized versions of Windows 9x can be found on the Microsoft Developer Network CDs. The Setup disks are compressed CAB files. To open these files, you need to install the Microsoft Power Toys cab viewer, which can be downloaded from Microsoft's Web site at www.microsoft.com.

With the cab viewer, locate the help viewer files in the CAB files on the setup disks, right-click on the file names, and choose Extract to copy the files to a folder on your hard drive. Now, open the localized help file with the help viewer of the same language.

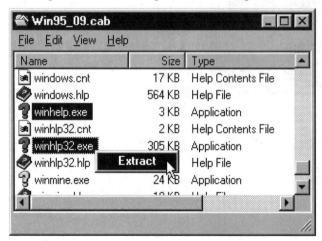

1.2.2.2   PROJECT STATISTICS

When a help file is compiled using Microsoft Help Workshop, the error file that is generated will contain project statistics, such as the number of topics, jumps, keywords, and bitmaps. In addition, the file size of the compiled help file is given.

After you have compiled the localized help file, check if the number of topics, jumps, keywords, and bitmaps is still the same. It is possible that the number of keywords has changed, if the translator has decided that not all entries were necessary for the search index, or when two English synonyms only have one translation.

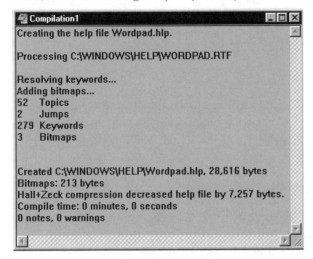

The file size is also important, especially in cases where the help file will be distributed on diskette.

1.2.2.3   GENERAL PAGE LAYOUT

In this step, check the following:

• Is the paragraph formatting correct? This includes font sizes, alignment, and line spacing.

• Do all accented characters display correctly?

• Are all graphic elements, such as icons, bitmaps and screen captures placed and displayed correctly?

• Do the tables wrap, scroll, and resize correctly?

• Do numbered and bulleted lists display correctly?

The best way to test the general page layout is to browse through every page of the compiled help file. Using the browse buttons (<< and >>) is not the best way to do this because a browse sequence often contains only part of the help file. Refer to the Browse Sequence section on page 196 for more information.

Both WinHelp 3.x and 4.x allow you to browse through a compiled help file page-by-page. The following sections describe which settings should be changed to enable this feature.

1.2.2.3.1   Windows 3.1

To configure your system for WinHelp 3.x help file testing, follow these steps:

1. Open the WIN.INI file with a text editor.

2. In the WIN.INI file, go to the `[Windows Help]` section, or create this section if it is not there.

3. Enter the following line: `seqtopickeys=1`.

4. Save your changes, and restart Windows.

Now, open the help file that you want to browse. Press Ctrl+Shift+Home to jump to the first page of the help file. Next, press Ctrl+Shift+right-arrow to browse through the help file page-by-page.

1.2.2.3.2   Windows 9x

To configure your system for WinHelp 4.x help file testing, follow these steps:

1. Install Microsoft Help Workshop (HCW.EXE).

2. Start Microsoft Help Workshop, and make sure the Help Author option in the File menu is enabled.

3. Exit Microsoft Help Workshop.

Now, open the help file that you want to browse. Press Ctrl+Shift+Home to jump to the first page of the help file. Next, press Ctrl+Shift+right-arrow to browse through the help file page-by-page.

You will see the topic number in the title bar, plus an indication that the Help Author is active. If you disable the Help Author function, the help window titles will be displayed.

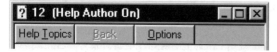

You can also browse backward using the Ctrl+Shift+left-arrow key combination. Pressing Ctrl+Shift+End will bring you to the last page of the help file. Pressing Ctrl+Shift+J will prompt you to enter the number of the topic that you want to jump to.

To view topic information, right-click in a help window, and select Topic Information. In the Topic Information window, the Help File field will show you the name of the HLP file and its version, i.e., 3.1 or 4.x.

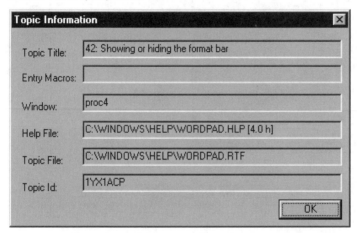

If you need to make a correction in this specific topic, open the RTF file that is indicated and search for the string that is displayed in the Topic Id field.

By default, the Topic File name and Topic Id fields will be unavailable. To make sure this information is included in the HLP file, follow these steps:

1. Start Microsoft Help Workshop and open the HPJ file of the help project that you want to compile.

2. Click the Compile button on the toolbar or choose the Compile command from the File menu.

3. In the Compile a Help File dialog box, activate the Include RTF filename and topic ID in Help file option in the Temporary settings field.

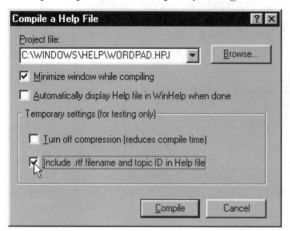

4. Click the Compile button.

In your compiled help file the RTF file name and topic ID of the selected topic will be displayed in the Topic Information window.

1.2.2.4 WINDOW TITLES

In this step, check the following:

*   Do the titles fit in the window title bars?

*   Are accented characters displayed correctly?

To view Window titles in WinHelp 4.x help, you first need to disable the Help Author option in the File menu of Microsoft Help Workshop.

Try to check all titles, including the secondary window titles. In the HPJ file, you will find the main help window title in the TITLE= option. Secondary window titles can be found in the [WINDOWS] section.

If accented characters do not show up correctly, save the HPJ file as DOS text only instead of Windows text only.

1.2.2.5 JUMPS

Depending on the size of the help file, it might not be feasible to check all jumps in the file. If there are too many, do a spot check of the jumps. Just click on a jump and choose the Back button.

Do not forget to test the hotspots in graphics. For more information on hotspots, refer to the Hotspots section on page 194.

1.2.2.6 SEARCH KEYWORD LIST

You check the search keyword list by clicking on the Search button (WinHelp 3.x help) or the Index tab (WinHelp 4.x help). This alphabetized index is generated from the K keywords in the RTF files that are compiled into the HLP file.

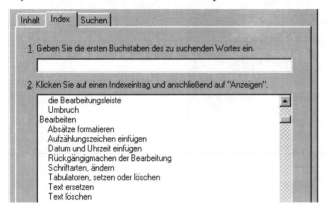

In the search list, check the following:

* Are all entries translated?

* Do all entries fit in the box?

* Does the list contain any unnecessary entries?

* Is the list sorted correctly according to the standards of the target language?

* Are the main and sub entries organized correctly?

In general, the search index should look like an index in a printed manual. For more information and general guidelines, refer to the Translating Indexes section on page 120.

1.2.2.7 CONTEXT HELP

Context-sensitive help means that online help can be accessed from within the application.

To test if localized context-sensitive help still works, copy the localized help file to the folder with the localized application. Run the application, and choose the commands in the Help menu.

Also, press the F1 key or Help button in some dialog boxes. Many Windows 9x applications also offer "What's This?" help. To check this help text, click on the question mark button in the upper right corner of a dialog box, and click on a field or option. Alternatively, right-click an option or field and choose the What's This? command.

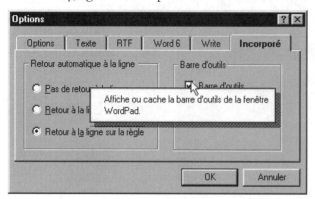

1.2.2.8   CONTENTS FILE (WINHELP 4.X ONLY)

The CNT contents file contains the text that is displayed when you click on the Contents tab of a WinHelp 4.x help file.

To check if all items in a localized contents file are still linked to topics in the help file(s), follow these steps:

1. Start Microsoft Help Workshop.

2. From the Test menu, choose Contents File.

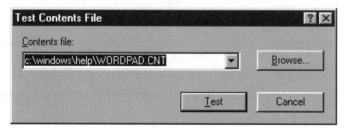

3. Select the CNT file that you want to test. This file should be in the same folder as the corresponding HLP file(s).

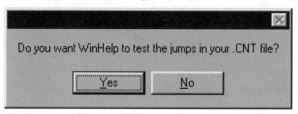

Microsoft Help Workshop will test if all the jumps in the contents file work. If errors are reported, open the CNT file and correct the link to make it match the actual topic ID in the RTF file that is referred to.

1.2.2.9 CUSTOM BUTTONS OR MENUS

If custom buttons or menus have been added in the translated HPJ file, check to make certain the hot keys used in these buttons or menu items do not conflict with the hot keys of the default WinHelp buttons and menus.

For example, when a Glossary button has been added to the WinHelp button bar of the help file, make sure that the hot key that is used for the translation of Glossary does not conflict with any of the hot keys used in the default menu and button bar of the WinHelp viewer window of the target language.

In the following example, there is a hot key conflict between *Sommario, Opzioni* and *Glossario*. The first two are errors in the default WinHelp viewer localization, the second one is an error in the localized HPJ file of the help project that you are testing.

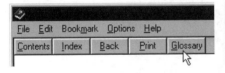 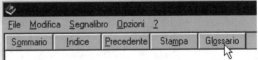

1.2.2.10 USING HELPQA

HelpQA is a utility designed specifically for the localization industry, technical translators and localization engineers in particular, which manages all aspects of the quality assurance of multiple language Windows help files.

HelpQA analyzes localized help projects or help source files against the original ones. It not only provides you with a full report of the help file, i.e., word counts, graphic references, and CNT file analysis, it also checks whether the localized file functions in exactly the same way as the original help file. This means that there is no longer any need to click manually on every link in a help file to verify that the link has been preserved.

HelpQA provides the following features:

- Full support for all help project source formats, including help project files (HPJ), rich text format (RTF), Windows 9x contents files (CNT) and the BMP, WMF, SHG and MRB graphic file formats

- Consistency verification of all standard footnotes

- Full verification of links in the RTF source and in hypergraphic files

- Reporting features that include project, file and topic word counts, graphic lists, macro lists, button lists, external reference and unresolved internal reference lists.

- The WinHelp navigator which controls two instances of the help viewer, allowing you to view the localized help file alongside the source help file

- Reporting features that will tell you if jumps to topic titles have been translated consistently

To test a help project using HelpQA, follow these steps:

1. Open the source and target help project files (HPJ) using the Source and Target tabs.

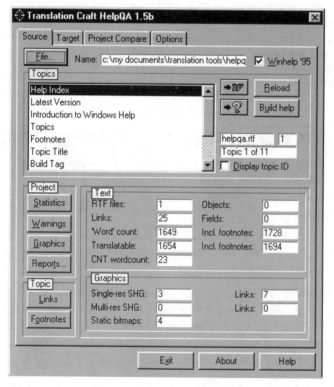

2. Click on the Project Compare tab to test the number of topics, links, footnotes, commands, formatting, graphics and CNT file.

3. Click on the Visual button in the Project Compare tab window to view the source and target help files side-by-side.

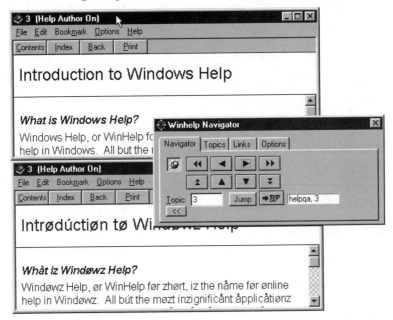

For more information about HelpQA and a demo version, visit the Translation Craft Web site at www.tcraft.com.

1.2.2.11 HELP TESTING CHECK LIST

The following checklist can be used to see if you have covered all items while testing a localized help project. Check the following items:

Compilation

-   No errors are reported when compiling the help file.

-   The number of topics, jumps, and bitmaps equals the English project statistics. The number of keywords may differ slightly.

-   The file size does not differ substantially from the English file.

-   The same compression algorithm is used as in the English project.

HPJ File

- The sorting language is set correctly.

- The help file title has been translated.

- All window titles have been translated.

- All custom button or menu items have been translated. They will not cause hot key conflicts in localized help viewer.

Help File

- All window titles fit in the window title bars.

- Accented characters are displayed correctly in the window title bars.

- All topic and page titles are translated.

- All graphics are translated.

- All jumps, hotspots, and pop-ups work.

- The paragraph formatting, including font sizes, alignment, line spacing, is correct.

- All accented characters are displayed correctly.

- All graphic elements, such as icons, bitmaps and screen captures, are placed and displayed correctly.

- Tables display translated text, wrap, scroll, and resize correctly.

- If a glossary is included with the help file, the entries are sorted according to target language standards.

- The keyword index list is alphabetized according to the target language conventions.

- In the keyword index list, all entries are translated.

- In the keyword index list, all entries fit in the box of the localized help viewer.

- In the keyword index list, there are no unnecessary entries.

- In the keyword index list, the main and sub entries are organized correctly.

- The help file can be accessed from within the localized application, for example by using the Help menu items, or pressing F1.

- The What's This? help can be accessed from within the localized application.

CNT File

- The title is translated.

- All items are translated.

- Topic title references are translated consistently.

- All jumps in the contents files work.

2 HTML Files

Due to the enormous growth of the Internet in the past few years, the HTML format has become popular amongst designers and developers of Web sites and online help systems. HTML files can be read on all platforms, editing HTML is quite easy, and files sizes are small.

One of the disadvantages of HTML was the display of accented characters of non-Western languages. However, this problem will be solved with the introduction of HTML 4.0, which is based on Unicode. For more information about HTML development, visit the HTML Help Web site at www.htmlhelp.com.

2.1 Localizing Web Sites

More and more Web sites on the Internet will be multilingual in order to reach a large international audience. Currently, most multilingual Web sites have an English front page containing icons and jumps to pages in another language.

If your client does not provide you with a set of files to translate, in most cases it is possible to download a copy of the entire site to your hard disk, preserving its folder structure. An example of an application that you can use to download Web sites is Teleport Pro by Tennyson Maxwell. For more information, visit the Tennyson Maxwell Web site at www.tenmax.com. Please note that downloading Web sites to your local hard drive will probably not capture CGI scripts, programs running on the Web server, or embedded files.

For more information about multilingual Web site development, visit the Internationalization and Localization web page from the World Wide Web Consortium at www.w3.org/International. Another good reference point for Web site internationalization is the Worldpoint Web site at www.worldpoint.com. A good book about web site internationalization is *How To Build A Successful International Web Site* by Mark Bishop.

2.1.1 Folder Structure

If the Web site has been *internationalized*, a multilingual folder structure will allow for localization. An internationalized Web site will have a folder structure that makes efficient use of disk space and image files.

For example, the folder structure of a multilingual Web site may look as follows:

```
index.html
\us
\us\images
\fr
\fr\images
\de
\de\images
\shared images
```

The *index.html* page will contain links to all language folders. The \us, \fr, and \de folders will contain the English, French, and German files. Each language folder has its \images folder to store localized images, and there will be a \shared images folder containing non-localized art, such as logos or symbols.

If the Web site that needs to be translated has been designed like this, localization is quite easy. It is merely a matter of copying the entire contents of the \us folder to one of the language folders and translating the HTML and image files. Do not forget to change the path statements and internal links in the localized HTML files to reflect the new language path. For example, if an English HTML file contains a link to an image, such as `<img src=..\us\images\topic.gif>`, the French version of this HTML file needs to be changed to `<img src=..\fr\images\topic.gif>`.

If the Web site has not been internationalized and only contains one folder structure with English files, discuss the following issues with your client:

- What will be the folder structure of the multilingual Web site?

- Who will be responsible for creating this folder structure?

- Who will be responsible for changing the paths in the localized HTML files?

Usually the easiest solution will be for the localization engineer to suggest a folder structure, and completely reconstruct this for all languages in which the site is being translated.

2.1.2   Localization

Web sites often require more real *localization* work than software documentation. Examples of web content that often needs to be localized are product prices, contact information such as e-mail addresses and telephone numbers, and new links to sites in the target language.

Before translation starts, make sure you know which information needs to be adapted, and ask your client all necessary questions. Clients need to decide whether they want to simply translate the content, change information that is different for the local market, or completely recreate the content for the target countries.

2.1.3   Images

If a Web site contains many images containing text, it might be worth asking your client for original, layered art files. Often the graphic artists who created the art files will have used layered files, with a separate text layer. Translating the text on a text layer is much easier and less time-consuming than completely re-creating the background and the text of an image.

One important aspect of GIF images that are used in HTML pages is their subtype. GIF images can have several transparency settings and subtypes, such as 89a Non-interlaced. Make sure your image editor supports all subtypes and transparency settings. For more information about image file format, refer to the File Format section on page 184.

2.1.3.1   TRANSPARENCY

If an image is transparent, this means that one of the colors in the color palette of the image is selected as the transparent color. For example, if a GIF image has a white background with red text, selecting the white color index number from the color palette as the transparent color will only display the red text on the HTML page. The white background will be replaced by the color defined in the HTML page.

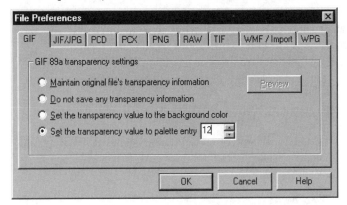

Make sure your image editor supports transparency in GIF files. Always check if the translated GIF files display correctly on the HTML page.

2.1.3.2   ANIMATED GIF

Animated GIF files consist of a sequence of separate images, which need to be edited. First, use an animated GIF utility that separates the images, edit the images and paste them back in the sequence.

Because images take longer to load into the browser than text, Web site developers have started using Java applets to overlay text on images. For more information about translating Java applets, refer to the Java Applets section on page 92.

2.1.4   Language Tags

HTML was designed around the ISO 8859-1 character set (also known as ISO Latin-1), which only supports representation of Western European languages.

For languages that are not supported by this character set, such as Cyrillic languages, it is useful to add the following line to your localized HTML documents just below the <HEAD> tag, where ISO-8859-1 is replaced with the MIME name of your chosen character set:

```
<META HTTP-EQUIV=
"Content-Type"
CONTENT="text/html;
charset=ISO-8859-1">
```

Since version 4 of the HTML standard is based on Unicode (ISO 10646), specification of separate character set codes will not be necessary anymore. Most recent browsers support the Unicode standard, so character sets coming in from all over the world are transmitted without corruption.

A new feature in HTML 4.x is *language identification*. Many aspects of document presentation depend not only on the character set, but also on the language of the text. For this reason, HTML 4.x introduces the new LANG attribute, which can be used with most HTML elements to describe the language of the element contents.

A language definition statement looks like this:

```
<P LANG="fr">Ce paragraphe est en Français</P>
```

The LANG attribute takes as a value a two-letter abbreviated language tag. A list of these codes is defined by the ISO 639 standard, which can be found at the ILE home page at www.ile.com.

2.1.5   Testing Localized Web Sites

There are two types of tools available for testing localized Web sites:

* General Web site testing tools

* Localized Web site testing tools

The first type of testing tools will analyze one set of (localized) HTML files and will verify if all internal and external links are valid, if all images are present, if there are no corrupt HTML tags, etc. Most HTML editors offer verification features for Web sites or collections of HTML files. Examples of HTML testing applications are SiteBoss (www.siteboss.com) and LinkBot (www.linkbot.com).

For more information about Web site testing procedures and tools, visit the Software QA/Test Resource Center Web site at www.charm.net/~dmg/qatest or the Software Quality Engineering Web site at www.sqe.com.

The second type of tools will compare a localized set of HTML files with the original files. This type of testing is useful to see if anything was corrupted or lost during translation. It is recommended to run both tests on your localized Web sites.

There are currently two tools available to compare a localized set of HTML files with the original source files. These tools are HtmlQA by Translation Craft and Trans Web Express by Berlitz.

2.1.5.1 USING HTMLQA

HtmlQA is an analysis and quality assurance tool that is used to verify the functional identity of two HTML-based files or groups of files, typically an untranslated source project and a translated target project.

HtmlQA is not only useful for engineers, who can test localized Web sites, but also for project managers who can create detailed reports of sets of HTML files, listing word counts, number of files and images, problems in source material, etc.

To test a localized Web site using HtmlQA, follow these steps:

1. Load the source and target HTML files using the Source and Target tabs.

2. Save the file list in a project file by clicking on the Save Project button.

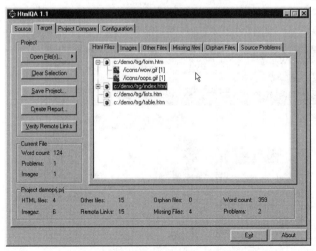

3. Check the project statistics in the bottom of the screen. Switching between the Source and Target tab will show you the source and target statistics.

4. Check the source and target project specifications listed in the six tab windows from the Source and Target windows. These tabs will indicate the differences between the source and target sets of HTML files. The results of the six tabs can be saved using the Create Report button.

5. Click on the Project Compare tab in the main window to run a detailed comparison between the source and target files. You can execute a specific comparison by clicking on the appropriate button on the left of the page, or execute all the checks by clicking the Run all Checks button.

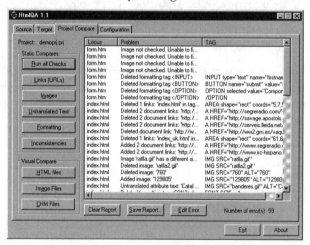

6. Click one of the buttons in the Visual Compare field to perform a visual comparison of the source and target HTML, image or CHM files side-by-side.

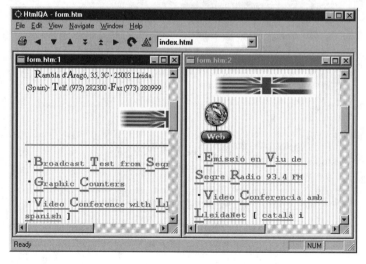

HtmlQA uses Internet Explorer or Netscape Navigator for the visual comparison. You can select your preferred browser in the Configuration tab. Please note that both browsers contain a language selection setting for viewing multilingual web content.

For more information about HtmlQA and a demo version, visit the Translation Craft Web site at www.tcraft.com.

2.1.5.2 USING TRANS WEB EXPRESS

Trans Web Express has been designed specifically for the localization of Internet pages and HTML help. It includes a comprehensive set of utilities which cover areas including translation, engineering and testing of the files as well as a feature allowing for resource planning through its Project Management utility.

With Trans Web Express, you can navigate through an entire HTML project viewing files as HTML code or as web pages. The navigator can view one window or two windows side-by-side. Trans Web Express can be used on any HTML project and is particularly suited to Web projects and HTML help.

To test a localized Web site using Trans Web Express, follow these steps:

1. Open the source and target files using the Open command from the File menu or the Source and Target buttons. The HTML file that is selected first is displayed in the Source and Target tab window.

2. Choose the Project Analysis tab and click on Compare in order to perform a functional comparison of the source and target tags.

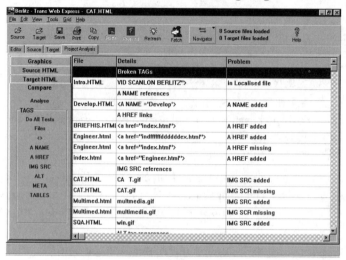

3. You can fix errors by double-clicking on an error in the Compare window and editing the HTML code in the internal editor.

4. Click on the Navigator button to perform a visual comparison of the files.

Trans Web Express has a Project Analysis function which can provide a detailed analysis of HTML files for project management and scheduling purposes. It not only counts the words and images, but also calculates a complexity factor, indicating how complex the files are for translation.

For more information about Trans Web Express and to download a fully functional version, visit the Berlitz Trans Web Express Web site at www.berlitz.no/twe.

2.1.5.3 HTML TESTING CHECK LIST

The following checklist can be used to see if you have covered all items while testing a localized HTML project or Web site. Check the following items:

2.1.5.3.1   Links

- The number of translated files must exactly match the number of original files.

- The number of hyperlinks must be the same as the original file.

- There are no broken links (internal and external, to bookmarks and to other files).

2.1.5.3.2   Visual

- Correct fonts, colors and styles are used in headings and text.

- Tables display translated text and appear as in the original files.

- HTML page titles in the browser's title bar have been translated.

- All meta-info, such as keywords, in the header of the HTML file has been translated.

- Text displayed in the status bar and pop-up text has been translated.

- All indices and glossaries are sorted according to target language standards; extended characters are sorted according to language defaults.

2.1.5.3.3   Syntax

- The HTML syntax must exactly match the original files. No tags have been added or deleted, unless they were added intentionally such as <B> and </B> formatting text surrounding software references in some languages.

- There are no broken tags in the HTML code.

- No carriage returns have been deleted from the HTML code.

2.1.5.3.4   Images

- Images (GIF of JPG files) must be fully translated and legible.

- Image placeholders have been translated. Image placeholders will show up when images are not available or being loaded into the browser.

- Images match the original files with regard to transparency or animation.

2.2 HTML Help

Microsoft HTML Help is the next-generation online authoring system from Microsoft
Corporation and is based on Microsoft WinHelp 4.x.

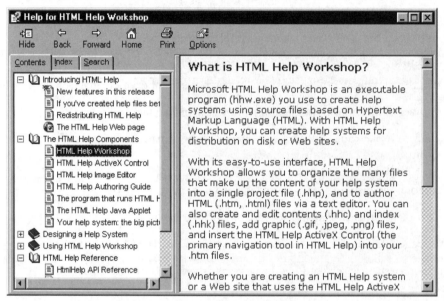

HTML Help is a help system that allows you to create help files or Web pages in HTML
format. Like WinHelp, HTML Help uses a project file to combine help topic, contents,
index, image, and other source files into a compressed help file. Part of the HTML Help
authoring system is the HTML Help Workshop, an authoring tool that allows you to view,
manage, and edit your files in a graphical user interface.

In HTML Help Workshop, a project file is used to manage all the files in your help system.
This project file is comparable to the Windows help HPJ file. HTML Help Workshop takes
all the information about the help project stored in the help project file and all the related
files that make up the content of your help topics, and compiles this into a single help file
with the CHM extension.

The HTML Help window is the browser in which the content of the help project is
displayed. This executable, a host for the layout engine, can be evoked directly through the
HTML Help API or indirectly through the HTML Help executable, HH.EXE, which is
located in your \Windows folder.

The following files are used by HTML Help Workshop:

- Topic files, in HTML format

- Graphics and multimedia files, which are linked to HTML topic files

- Help project files–the files that are compiled. These files have the HHP extension.

- Contents files, which contain the information that appears in the Table of Contents for your help system or Web site. These files have the HHC extension.

- Index files, which contain the information that appears in the index for your help system or Web site. These files have the HHK extension.

The topic, contents and index files need to be translated. These files are regular HTML files, so they can be translated using an HTML editor or translation tool. For more information about the translation of HTML files, refer to the HTML Files section on page 86. Please note that in the contents and index files, only the text following the "value=" attribute should be translated.

2.2.1 Compiling HTML Help projects

A typical HTML Help project consists of a help project (HHP), a contents file (HHC), and an index (HHK) file, and two folders containing the topic files (\HTML) and graphics (\Images).

To compile an HTML Help project, follow these steps:

1. Make sure all translated HTML files and graphics have been copied over the original English files.

2. Start HTML Help Workshop and open the project file (HHP) using the Open command from the File menu.

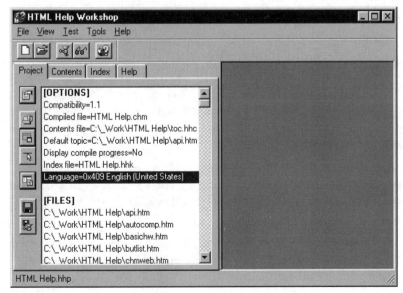

3. Click the Change Project Options button on the Contents tab.

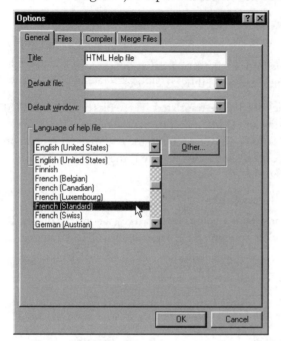

4. In the Options dialog box, ensure that the Title is translated, and set the language of the help file.

5. Choose the Compile command from the File menu to compile the help project.

2.2.2   Testing HTML Help Projects

After compilation, the translated help file needs to be tested.

HTML Help Workshop contains a Test menu that allows you to test pop-up attributes, keywords and the HTML Help API. Refer to the HTML Help Workshop online help for more information about testing HTML Help projects.

To test localized versions of HTML Help projects against English versions, you can use HtmlQA or Trans Web Express. For more information about these utilities, refer to the Using HtmlQA section on page 215 and the Using Trans Web Express section on page 217.

For more information about HTML Help, visit Microsoft's HTML Help home page at www.microsoft.com/workshop/author/htmlhelp or the HTML Help Web site at www.htmlhelp.com.

3 Macintosh

Translating Macintosh software using a resource editor such as ResEdit or Resorcerer does not require much programming or engineering knowledge. In addition, no compilation or post-processing is necessary. For this reason, most resizing and relevant engineering information is included in the Macintosh section of Chapter 2, Translating Software.

The following sections contain typical engineering tasks that need to be done when Macintosh software is localized, such as the use of software leveraging (translation re-using) tools, testing software, creating screen captures, and compiling Macintosh help files.

3.1 Software

3.1.1 Resizing

To resize items in dialog boxes using ResEdit or Resorcerer, do not drag the boxes with the mouse. Instead, change the coordinates in the properties window of each control. This will ensure a consistent look, and avoid sizing mistakes.

For more information about resizing controls using ResEdit and Resorcerer, refer to the Dialog Boxes sections in the Translating Software chapter on page 54 and 60.

3.1.2 Engineering

3.1.2.1 BITMAP EDITING

If you are editing bitmaps from Macintosh resources in an image editor like Adobe Photoshop, you first need to find out which font was used. On a Macintosh, the fonts used mostly are Geneva, Helvetica or Charcoal. To see which font was used, try putting an English text block on top of the original bitmap text. For more information, refer to the Graphics Editing section on page 186 and the Editing section on page 241.

When you copy a colored bitmap resource via the Clipboard to Photoshop, it will be opened in RGB mode by default. Make sure you convert the image to indexed color before you paste it back into the resource because RGB image resources would increase the size of the application and not display correctly on some monitors.

Instead of copying and pasting, it is also possible to import a bitmap resource into Photoshop. To import a bitmap resource, follow these steps:

1.   Start Photoshop.

2.   From the File menu, select Import - Pict resource.

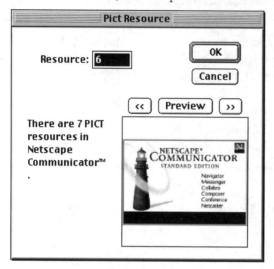

3.   In the Pict Resource window, use the browse buttons to locate the bitmap that you want to edit. Click OK to open the resource in Photoshop.

4.   Use the Type tool to add translated text. You can add your translations directly or copy and paste text from a text editor or word processor.

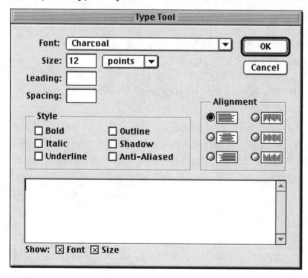

5. Choose Mode – Indexed Color from the Image menu to convert your image from RGB mode to indexed color.

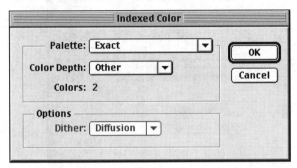

6. In the Indexed Color window, select Exact palette and Other color depth, saving only the colors that are actually used in the image.

7. Press Command-A to select the entire image, and press Command-C to copy the image.

8. Switch to your resource editor, like ResEdit or Resorcerer. Next, open the resource you have edited and press Command-V to paste the localized image into the resource.

3.1.2.2   CREATING INSTALLERS

Most Installers for Macintosh applications are created using Installer VISE, which is a graphical interface tool for building master installation sets for disks, CD-ROM, or network distribution.

3.1.2.2.1   Using Installer VISE

The basic components of an installer that is created using Installer VISE are *archives* and *packages*. The archive contains all the files that may need to be installed. Packages are different combinations of files that the customer can choose during a custom install. The following sample archive is called My App.cvt and contains all files in the Sample Archive Materials folder.

In this archive, file packages are defined. The Installer VISE localization features allow you to create installers for different languages without the need to completely recreate the archive in the new language. The file names, package names, descriptions, and messages are translated, while package definitions, disk information, etc. remain the same as the original archive. Installer VISE ships with installer files in many languages.

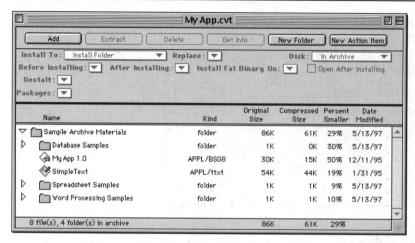

Installers can be single-language or multi-language, which means that the installer checks the languages of the operating system and then runs in that language.

To create a single-language installer from an archive, you first need to create and import a translator application for all the items, such as files and folders, in the archive. The translator application can be edited by the translator to change the names of the files, packages, install text, and disks.

To create a translator application, follow these steps:

1. Start Installer VISE and open the archive that you want localized.

2. From the Extras menu, select the Create Translator command.

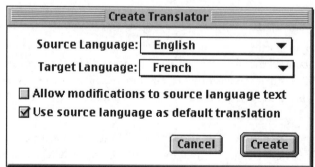

3. Select the source and target languages, and save the translator file using the default name, i.e., English to *language*.

For more information about translating Installer VISE translator applications, refer to the Translating Installers section on page 69.

When the translator application has been translated, you need to create a localized installer.

To create a localized installer, follow these steps:

1. Run Installer VISE and select the Archive Settings command from the Archive menu.

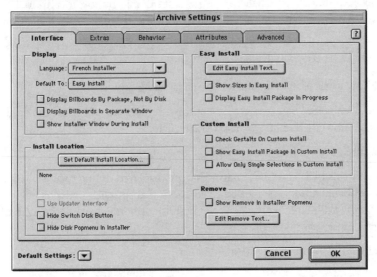

2. In the Archive Settings window, select the Advanced tab, and click the Set Language button.

3. In the Language File Setup window, click the Language File button and import the desired language file from the Installer VISE Extensions folder.

4. Next, click on the Import File button in the Language File Setup dialog box. Select your translator file, English to *language*, and click on OK. Do not forget to select the desired language at the bottom of the import dialog box.

Tip

To build a multilingual installer, use the Import File button to import the language files and translator applications from the languages that you want supported.

5. Click OK to close the Language File Setup dialog box.

6. In the Archive Settings window, select the Interface tab and select the desired language from the Language drop-down menu.

7. Click OK to close the Archive Settings dialog box.

If an Installer contains billboards, i.e., images that are displayed during the installation process, these probably need to be localized. To check if an Installer contains billboards, check if the Display Billboards by Package, not by Disk option in the Interface tab of the Archive Settings window is selected.

To localize billboards, follow these steps:

1. Translate the image files that need to be used as billboards.

2. Open the image file using an image editor and copy the entire file to the clipboard.

3. Select the Edit Packages command from the Archive menu.

4. In the Packages window, select a package name and click on the Edit Package button.

5. In the Edit Package window, click on the Setup Billboard button.

6. In the Setup Billboard dialog box, select Black and White for 1-bit images, and Color for 8-bit images.

7. Press Command-V to paste your localized billboard in the Setup Billboards window.

Before you do a final build of your localized installer, assign the localized readme file and license agreement. To do this, follow these steps:

1. Choose Archive Settings from the Archive menu.

2.   In the Archive Settings window, click on the Extras tab.

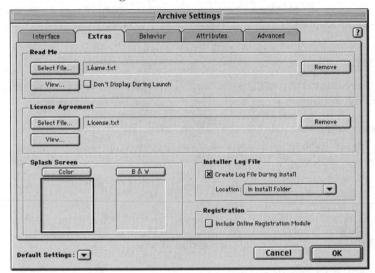

3.   Click the Select File button in the Read Me and License Agreement fields to select the localized files.

4.   If the splash screen has been translated, paste the localized image file in the Splash Screen dialog box.

5.   Press OK to close the Archive Settings dialog box.

To build your localized installer, select the Build Installer command from the File menu.

3.1.3   Processing and Updating Software

3.1.3.1   USING MPW

Macintosh Programmer's Workshop (MPW) is a powerful development system developed by Apple. For the purposes of localization, MPW allows you to extract the translatable resources from a Macintosh program, edit the text strings in the dialogs, menus and messages, and then build the localized version of the software.

Because translating Macintosh software with ResEdit, Resorcerer or PowerGlot is much more intuitive, MPW is usually only used for automatically updating new versions of applications or to verify that no resources have been corrupted during localization.

The localization scripts that Apple provided to automatically update localized versions of Macintosh applications are no longer publicly available. If you are using these scripts, Daniel Carter's book *Writing Localizable Software for the Macintosh* will provide good reference material.

For more information about MPW, refer to the Apple Developer Connection Web site at www.apple.com/developer.

3.1.3.2   USING APPLEGLOT

AppleGlot is a Macintosh software localization tool. It is designed to speed up the process
of localizing Macintosh applications and resource files. It accomplishes this by doing two
things:

- AppleGlot extracts text from resources within files and later merges your
  translations back into the localized resources. These extracted text files can be used
  to translate all user interface text, such as menus, dialog boxes and strings.

- AppleGlot does incremental updates from previously localized versions of the
  software. This minimizes the amount of effort needed to update a new release of a
  file by preserving previously localized resources, or portions of resources, thus
  avoiding the need to repeat earlier work. You only need to work on those items
  that have changed, or are new.

AppleGlot can be downloaded from Apple's FTP server at
ftp.apple.com/devworld/Tool_Chest/Localization_Tools.

3.1.3.2.1   Extracting Resource Text

If your translators are not familiar with translating Macintosh applications using ResEdit or
Resorcerer, you might consider extracting text from the application's resources and have
these translated in text-only files.

To extract text from a Macintosh application, follow these steps:

1.   Create a new environment by selecting the New Environment command
     from the File menu. An environment is a set of specifically named folders that
     AppleGlot uses to process a project.

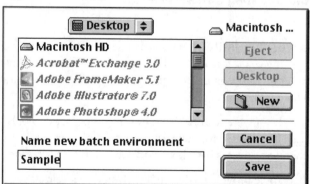

2.   Use the Finder to copy the files to the proper folders. If you are localizing a
     new piece of software, you only need to move a copy of that piece of software
     into the _NewUS folder within your Environment folder. If you are updating

a previously localized version of the application, refer to the Updating Software section on page 233.

3. If you have language glossaries of previously translated applications, copy them to the _LG folder. All translations found in these language glossaries will be used in the work glossaries as guesses. Apple is providing language glossaries with standard Apple interface terminology at the Apple FTP server at ftp.apple.com/devworld/Tool_Chest/Localization_Tools/ Apple_Int'l_Glossaries.

4. Return to AppleGlot and open the environment using the Open command from the File menu. Locate your environment folder, select it–do not open it– and click the Select Folder button.

5. In the AppleGlot environment window, mark the files that you want to translate, and click the Translate Only button.

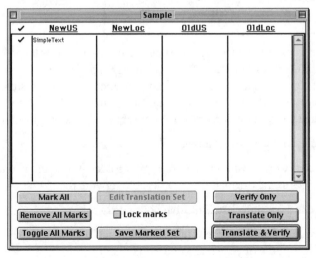

6. Save the batch file in the environment folder. The batch file contains all the information that AppleGlot produced automatically or which you provided manually using the Environment window.

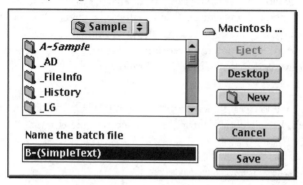

7. AppleGlot now starts extracting the text from the resources, and creating work glossaries.

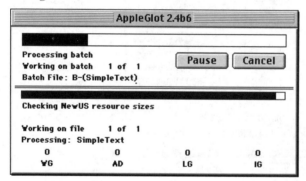

When text extraction is completed, the work glossary file(s) in the _WG folder can be translated using a text editor or word processor. Before giving work glossary files to translators, you may add comments to the file containing specific localization instructions. Comments in work glossary files should be enclosed in { and } braces. Refer to the Using AppleGlot section on page 65 for more information about translating work glossaries.

To update the program file with your translations, follow these steps:

1. Copy the translated work glossary files to the _WG folder. Make sure you use the same file names as the original files in order to overwrite the old files.

2. Start AppleGlot and open the batch file that you saved in step 6.

3. Select the Translate & Verify button. This command will also compare and verify the resources in the original and localized files.

Your localized application version will be placed in the _NewLoc folder.

3.1.3.2.2   Updating Software

To update localized software to a new version, do the following:

1. Create a new AppleGlot environment, as described in the first 3 steps of the previous section.

2. Now copy the old English files to the _OldUS folder, copy the new English files to the _NewUS folder and copy the old localized files to the _OldLoc folder.

3. Open the environment by choosing Open from the File menu, selecting the environment folder and clicking the Select Folder button.

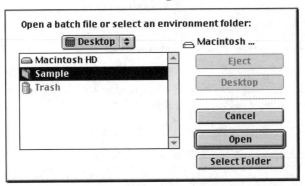

4. Choose Mark All in the Environment window and then click Translate and Verify.

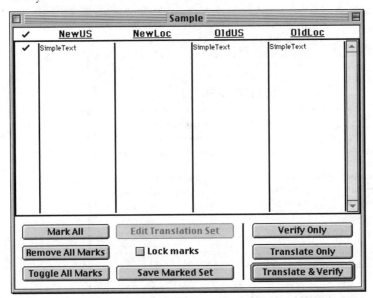

5. The updated localized files will be placed in the _NewLoc folder and the _WG folder will contain a work glossary file that needs to be translated/updated.

The work glossary file(s) in the _WG folder can be translated/updated using a text editor or word processor. The tags in the work glossary will tell the translators which strings were taken from the previous translation and which ones are new. Refer to the Using AppleGlot section on page 65 for more information about translating work glossaries.

To update the program file with the new and updated translations, follow these steps:

1. Copy the translated work glossary files to the _WG folder. Make sure you use the same file names as the original files in order to overwrite the old files. Also, ensure that the work glossary is in text-only format.

2. Start AppleGlot and open the batch file that you saved when you created the project.

3. Select the Translate & Verify button. This command will also compare and verify the resources in the original and localized files.

Your localized application version will be placed in the _NewLoc folder.

When you update Macintosh applications, please note that all exact matches will be included in the application database in the _AD folder, and all guesses and new text in the work glossary. Exact matches are text items in the new application that have exactly the same resource type, ID, name and position as in the previously translated version.

If you want to include all text, exact matches, new text and guesses in the work glossary, you need to enable the All Text -> WG option in AppleGlot's Preferences window.

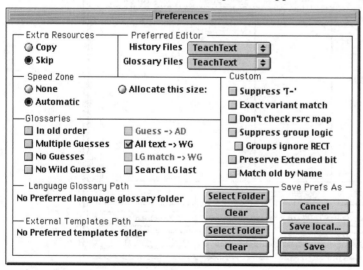

More information about the AppleGlot features can be found in the user manual, which is included with the AppleGlot application.

3.1.3.3   USING POWERGLOT

PowerGlot uses databases and glossaries to store translated strings. A database consists of a single file with references to the included work files, the extracted text, translations, and comments that were added by the translator or localization engineer.

For more information about translating software using PowerGlot, refer to the Using PowerGlot section on page 67.

A glossary is a file that contains a list of terms and their translations. Glossaries can be used to pre-translate a project database. For example, you can use a glossary that was created from the project database of a previously translated program file to automatically pre-translate a new version of the application.

To update software files using PowerGlot, follow these steps:

1. Open the project database of the previously translated application.

2. From the Database menu, choose the Build Glossary command.

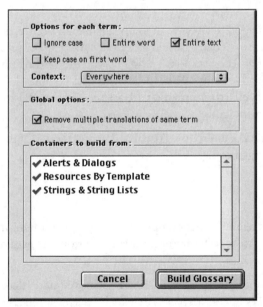

3. Select the desired options for the glossary and click the Build Glossary button.

4. Choose the Save command from the File menu to save the glossary.

5. Create a new project database and import the program file(s) that you want to translate using the Add Work Files command from the Database menu.

6. Select the Translate Using Glossary command from the database menu, and open the glossary you created in step 4 and 5.

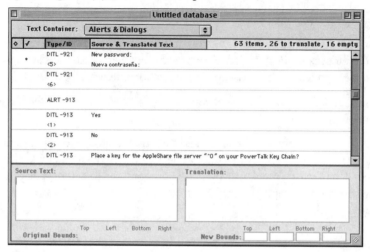

7. All translations that are found in the glossary are inserted in the project database.

If the previous version of the application that you want to update has not been translated using PowerGlot, you can create a project database and glossary by merging the previous English version with the previous translated version. To do this, add the old English version to a new project database, and select the Merge Localized Files command from the Database menu to merge the old translated version. PowerGlot will automatically insert the translations underneath the English strings.

For more information about PowerGlot and a downloadable demo version, visit the PowerGlot Web site at www.powerglot.com.

3.1.4   Testing

3.1.4.1   PREPARATION

Before starting to test a program, make sure your computer is "clean". This means that all previous versions of the application to be tested should be removed from the hard drive or compressed.

On a Macintosh, all related files in the System Folder should be removed or deleted. Examples are extensions, preferences or control panels that are installed with the program.

For more information about software testing procedures and tools, visit the Software QA/Test Resource Center Web site at www.charm.net/~dmg/qatest or the Software Quality Engineering Web site at www.sqe.com.

It is possible to multi-boot different language versions of the Macintosh operating system on one machine. Therefore, it is advisable to install a new version of the operating system in the target language of the localized application before you start testing.

3.1.4.1.1 Setting up multiple language version of the Macintosh Operating System

To set up multiple language versions of the Macintosh Operating System you need the System Picker utility, which can be found on the Apple Developer Connection CDs. It can also be downloaded from Apple's FTP server at dev.apple.com/devworld/utilities/System_Picker_1.1a3.sit.hqx.

To set up your computer for switching between different language versions of the Mac OS, follow these steps:

1. Locate the currently blessed (active) System Folder on the hard disk where you wish to install the new Mac OS. A blessed System Folder has a Mac OS symbol on the folder icon.

2. Change the name of the active System Folder. For example, add the system version number or language extension to the folder name, e.g., *System Folder 7.6*.

3. Open this folder and drag the Finder file out of the folder window to any location.

4. Close the folder window. The folder icon no longer has the Mac OS symbol.

5. Insert the installation disk from the new operating system and double-click the Installer icon. Click OK in the first window that appears.

6. In the Installer's Easy Install window, select the hard disk that previously contained the blessed System Folder. Make sure the window says *Click Install to place*. If it says *Click Install to update* then you know you have not successfully de-blessed the System Folder and you need to quit and go back to step 2.

7. After the installation has successfully completed and you've restarted your Macintosh, drag the "Finder" back into the folder you moved it from in step 3. If you don't do this, the original System Folder will not show in System Picker's list.

8. Repeat these steps for other system languages you might want to install.

To switch between multiple installed language versions of the Macintosh operating system, follow these steps:

1. Double-click on the System Picker icon to run the program.

2. In the System Picker window, select the name of the System Folder of the desired language and click Restart.

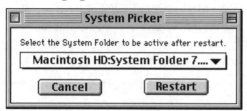

If you choose Options > Search Depth in the System Picker, you can determine how many folders System Picker will search on the mounted disks to find system folders.

3.1.4.2 TESTING

For general interface and functionality testing guidelines, refer to the Testing section on page 178. In addition to all the issues listed in that section, some Mac-specific features require special attention:

- Try balloon-help on the program icon to see if product-specific information shows up. This info balloon is usually translated in the Estr resource.

- Get Info on the program icon to see if the information fits.

- Compare the memory allocation of the original English file to the memory settings of the localized file.

- Is a Preferences file created? Sometimes, when the name of the preferences file in the strings is longer than 31 characters, no file is created.

Apple distributes some tools that you can use to test localized applications. These tools, Verifier and SDB, can be found on the Apple Developer Connection Tool Chest CDs and on the Internet.

Verifier is an MPW-based localization tool that detects improper resource localization by comparing all resources and data forks of a localized application with the original application. Verifier can be downloaded from Apple's FTP server at ftp.apple.com/devworld/Tool_Chest/Localization_Tools.

SDB, short for Show Dialog Boxes, is a tool that shows the dialogs and alerts of a localized application as they are displayed at run-time. The tool can be downloaded from Apple's FTP server at ftp.apple.com/devworld/Tool_Chest/Localization_Tools.

3.1.5   Creating Screen Captures

By default, the Macintosh operating system enables you to create screen captures of the entire screen. When you press Command-Shift-3, a screen capture of the entire screen is created and stored in a file called Picture 1 in the root of your hard drive. Additional screen captures are called Picture 2, Picture 3, etc.

MacOS System 7.6 and later contain more advanced screen capture features:

- Press Command-Shift-3 to save a capture of the entire screen in a file.

- Press Command-Shift-Control-3 to copy a capture of the entire screen to the clipboard.

- Press Command-Shift-4 and drag to save a part of the screen in a file. To constrain the section to a square, hold the Shift key as you drag.

- Press Command-Shift-Control-3 and drag to copy a part of the screen.

- Press Command-Shift-4 with Caps Lock on, and click on a window to save a capture of the window in a file.

- Press Command-Shift-Control-4 with Caps Lock on, and click on a window to copy a capture of the window to the clipboard.

The MacOS screen capture features are only useful for basic screen captures of windows or folders. When you need to include cursors or menu screen captures, it is better to use a screen capture utility. For more information, refer to the Utilities section on page 240.

3.1.5.1   PREPARATION

3.1.5.1.1   Display Configuration

Before you start shooting screen captures, verify the software settings that you need to use to reflect the original images as closely as possible. Settings include factors such as color depth (black & white, grayscale, color, 8-bit, 16-bit, etc.) and screen resolution.

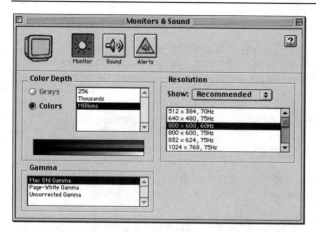

A typical configuration for Macintosh screen captures is 24-bit color (Millions of colors), and a 800x600 resolution.

3.1.5.1.2   File Format

Always verify with your client which file format is required. If original image files are available, use the format and image settings of the original files.

For more information about document types and image file formats, refer to the File Format section on page 184.

3.1.5.1.3   Utilities

Examples of applications you can use to create screen captures on a Macintosh platform are:

• Flash-it

Flash-it is a freeware utility that can be downloaded from www.shareware.com.

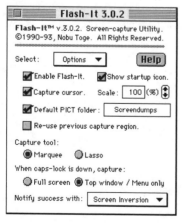

- Captivate

Captivate is a screen capture utility that has been developed by Mainstay. For more information about Captivate and a demo version, visit the Mainstay Web site at www.mstay.com.

Captivate Select can be used to capture any portion of the screen. A pull-down menu, pop-up list, or dialog box can be captured with or without the pointer, scaled, and converted to black and white, as desired. A captured image can be placed on the Clipboard or the Scrapbook, or saved in a desired folder using one of five file formats: GIF, TIFF 5.0, TIFF 4.0, PICT, and MacPaint.

Other screen capture applications you could use are:

- Snapz – more info at www.ambrosiasw.com

- Exposure Pro or ScreenShot – more info at www.beale.com

3.1.5.1.4 Test

Before creating screen captures, test some images in the location where you will insert them, such as a manual or help file.

For example, when images are linked to a document, replace the original image with your localized screen capture and print the page with the image. Compare the test page with the original printout to see if the capture is printed and scaled correctly.

3.1.5.2 EDITING

Sometimes it is necessary to *fake* screen captures. For example, this might be necessary when the translation of the application is not yet finished and a screen capture is needed for a marketing brochure. Or, when the original screen capture contains a situation or error that is difficult to reproduce.

3.1.5.2.1   Tips

If you need to manually enter text in a screen capture, the font that is used for most Macintosh applications is Helvetica size 10. Other commonly used fonts are Geneva, Chicago, and Charcoal. Often a spacing of 0.5 is applied to text in dialog boxes or folders.

To check which font is used in the Mac OS interface, open the Appearance control panel.

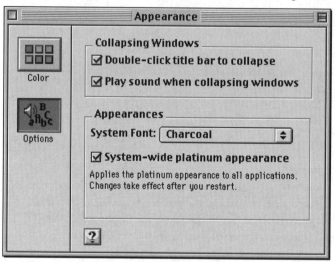

For more information about editing screen captures, refer to the Graphics Editing section on page 186 and the Bitmap Editing section on page 223.

3.2 Help

3.2.1 Apple Guide

The Apple Guide help system was introduced with System 7.5 in 1994. An Apple Guide help system consists of one or more guide file databases, which are created using a word processor or text editor in combination with a help authoring tool, such as Apple's Guide Maker.

Apple Guide files can contain text, sound, graphics and movies. A typical Apple Guide help file contains an access window with Topics overview, an index, and search screen.

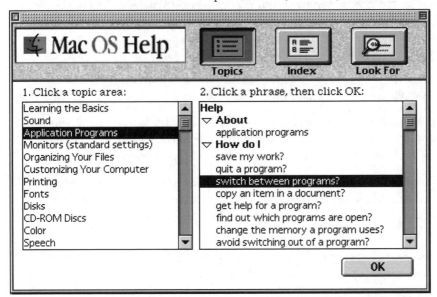

Apple Guide files are based on Guide Script, a mark-up language that identifies Apple Guide elements, and controls content layout and sequence panels. Apple Guide files are compiled versions of text files containing Guide Script tags and instructions written by the developer. These text files can be edited using a word processor or text editor. A Guide database is a compiled set of instructions or information that works with the Apple Guide extension. The tool that is used to compile Apple Guide files is called Guide Maker.

Guide Maker only compiles word processor documents containing Apple Script and instructions. However, there are several Apple Guide authoring tools available that provide a what-you-see-is-what-you-get content entry. Examples of these tools are Apple Guide Starter Kit and Guide Composer. If you are not sure which tool to use, ask your client.

Guide Maker offers authoring tools that allow you to build guide files, test files, and import/export text for localization. This means that Apple Guide files can be translated in two ways: either directly in the Guide Script text files, or by exporting and importing localizable text from a Guide database using Guide Maker. For more information about translating Apple Guide files, refer to the Macintosh Apple Guide Files section on page 93.

For more information about Apple Guide, visit Apple's Web site at www.apple.com/macos/apple-guide.

3.2.1.1   COMPILING APPLE GUIDE FILES

Apple Guide files can only be compiled with Guide Maker or Guide Maker Lite. Guide Maker Lite is a leaner, faster version of Guide Maker that only compiles files. It does not contain the Localize, Import/Export, Diagnose, and Conversion features from Guide Maker. Both compilers can be downloaded from the Apple Guide developer area at www.apple.com/macos/apple-guide/dev/dev.html.

Before you compile your Apple Guide files, make sure that:

- The Apple Guide fonts are installed on your Macintosh. These fonts, Espy Sans and Espy Serif, are included with most Apple Guide authoring kits, such as the Apple Guide Starter Kit, which is available from the Apple Guide Web site.

- All Apple Script source files are in a format that Guide Maker can read. The best format to use is MacWrite II. To convert files to MacWrite II format from your word processor, make sure the XTND Power Enabler is in your Extensions folder.

If you are compiling a large Apple Guide file, it is recommended to use Guide Maker Lite because compiling with Guide Maker could take hours.

3.2.1.1.1   Using Guide Maker

An Apple Guide project includes a build file, which contains only `<Include>` and `<Resource>` commands. This file specifies which source files will be compiled.

When you build an Apple Guide file, all source files that are referenced in the build file must be placed in the same folder as the build file.

To compile an Apple Guide file using Guide Maker, follow these steps:

1. Start Guide Maker and select the Build command from the Utilities menu.

2. Click in the Source file area of the Build window and select the build file from your Apple Guide project.

3. Click in the Guide file area of the Build window to specify the Apple Guide file that you want to build. You will be asked to open an existing file or to create a new file. If you create a new guide file, you need to specify its name.

4. Click the Compile button to start building the Apple Guide file.

3.2.1.1.2   Using Guide Maker Lite

To compile an Apple Guide file using Guide Maker Lite, follow these steps:

1. Start Guide Maker Lite, and select the Compile command from the File menu.

2. Locate your build file and click Open.

3. Specify a name for the guide file in the Save Guide File As window and click Save.

3.2.1.2   TESTING APPLE GUIDE FILES

There are several items that need to be tested in Apple Guide files, such as:

*   interface

*   coachmarks

*   context checks

3.2.1.2.1   Interface Test

The interface test shows you whether the order of the panels is correct, the art looks OK, all text fits in the space available, etc.

To test the guide file interface, follow these steps:

1. Choose the Diagnose command from the Utilities menu.

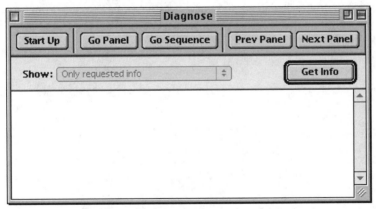

2. Use the Start Up button to display your guide file's startup window. If apple guide file does not display, open the guide file from within the application it belongs to, and open the same guide file using Guide Maker's Open command.

3.   Use the Go Panel and Go Sequence buttons to jump to a specific panel or sequence in your guide file.

4.   Use the Prev Panel and Next Panel buttons to browse through the panels of the guide file.

5.   Use the Get Info button to see information about the current panel, such as the sequence it belongs to, the ID number, and the panel name.

Please pay special attention to the Topics list. The text needs to fit in the available space. If the topic titles are longer, they will not be wrapped, but truncated.

3.2.1.2.2   Coachmarks Test

There are five coachmark types: menu, item, object, window and AppleScript. Coachmarks highlight items in the application's user interface using red circles or underlining. The coachmark items in the source files need to be translated exactly as the translated items in the application that they are referring to. Otherwise, they won't work. Coachmarks need to be tested by opening each panel with the application running in the background.

An example of a coachmark command in a Guide Script source file is:

```
<Coach Mark>   "Menu: File|Save As"
```

In this line, the translations of File and Save As should exactly match the translations of the menu items used in the application.

3.2.1.2.3   Context Check Test

A context check determines certain conditions in the user's environment. For example, some panels will only be displayed when the Date & Time control panel is opened. These context checks need to be tested in a localized environment.

4 Other Environments

4.1 Visual Basic

Microsoft's Visual Basic is a programming language that is quite similar to Visual C++.
A project file is a collection of the forms, modules, and custom controls that make up an
application. A form (FRM) is a window or dialog box containing controls, such as text
fields or buttons.

Each form, control and custom control has a set of properties that are displayed in the
Properties window.

Properties - Form1	☒
Form1 Form	▾
Appearance	1 - 3D
AutoRedraw	False
BackColor	&H8000000F&
BorderStyle	2 - Sizable
Caption	Form1
ClipControls	True
ControlBox	True
DrawMode	13 - Copy Pen
DrawStyle	0 - Solid
DrawWidth	1

The Caption property contains the text that will be displayed on the control. This is the
only property that needs to be translated. A form can also contain menus, which are edited
in the integrated menu editor. Each menu item, like a control, has a property window with a
Caption field where the text is translated and the hot key is defined by an ampersand (&).

In Visual Basic 4.0 and later, it is possible to add a resource (RES) file to a project that
centrally stores all translatable text and bitmaps for an application. This RES file can be
created from a RC file that is compiled using a resource compiler, for example the one that
is shipping with Microsoft Visual C++.

For Visual Basic projects that are not designed using a resource file, translation needs to be
performed directly in the forms. Since this can be time-consuming and error-prone, a
company called WhippleWare has developed an application that extracts text from Visual
Basic forms.

WhippleWare's Visual Basic Language Manager instructs Visual Basic to save all binary files
in the project in ASCII format, then it extracts all strings for translation. Translation can be

performed in Visual Basic Language Manager's integrated Language Table Editor, or in an LMX export text-only file.

After translation, a translated version of the project can be built. Visual Basic Language Manager also contains updating and string size checking features.

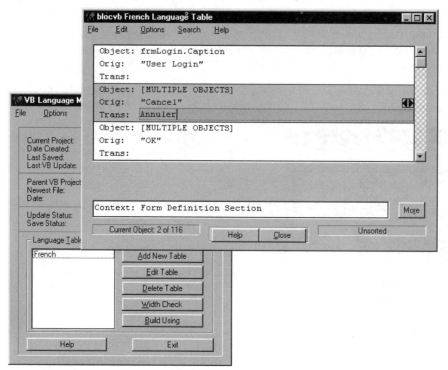

For more information about VBLM and a demo version, visit the WhippleWare Web site at www.whippleware.com.

Another localization tool that supports Visual Basic is the Innoview Multilizer Suite. For more information, visit www.multilizer.com.

4.2 Delphi

Delphi is Inprise's set of visual client and server development tools for creating distributed enterprise and Web-enabled applications. All Delphi applications build 32-bit stand-alone executables. No interpreter or run-time library is required. Delphi applications are typically built using forms (DFM files) and code (PAS files). The forms contain all user interface components, translatable items in .PAS files are considered "hard-coded" and need to be exported.

Inprise's Delphi Translation Suite contains an internationalization/localization environment for Delphi applications. It automates the process of translating Delphi applications, and it includes translated versions of Delphi files for several Western European languages. The Delphi Language Pack is a subset version of the Translation Suite, which contains pre-translated commonly used forms, messages, and project templates.

The tools in the Delphi Translation Suite extract the language-dependent text prompts, captions, and other strings in your project. This text can then be packaged with translation tools into a Translation Kit, ready for a translator to provide local-language versions of the strings. The Translation Kits that you create include a Form and Menu Editor that are specifically designed for translating. These editors present a WYSIWYG view of the forms and menus being translated, so translators know immediately what impact their translations will have on the user interface layout. There is no need for re-compiling, and the development environment and the translation environment are entirely separate.

For more information about the Delphi Translation Suite and Language Pack, visit the Inprise (formerly Borland) Web site at www.inprise.com.

Most localization tools available for Delphi contain both internationalization and localization features. Examples of such tools are:

- Lingscape MultLang – more info at www.lingscape.com

- Innoview Multilizer Suite – more info at www.innoview.fi or www.innoview-data.com or www.multilizer.com.

- Helicon Translator – more info at www.helicon.co.at

Some manufacturers of software localization tools are integrating support for Delphi forms. For more information about these tools, refer to the Software Localization Tools section on page 37.

4.3 Java

Java, developed by Sun Microsystems in the mid-1990s, is a programming language with language features similar to C++. Java also is a software-only platform that runs on top of other, hardware-based platforms.

Java *applets* are small applications that travel with HTML code and execute on the user's computer in a Java-enabled web browser. Java *applications* are complete stand-alone programs that do not require a Web browser or HTML to execute.

Sun's Java Development Kit contains everything you need to create Java applets and applications. Release 1.1 of the Java Development Kit introduced internationalization and localization features that will be enhanced in new releases.

JDK 1.1 allows programmers to develop *global* programs by isolating the language-dependent parts from the actual Java code. Apart from support for locales, Unicode and locale-sensitive settings, programmers can isolate all strings and other language-dependent objects in so-called *resource bundles*.

In resource bundle property files, items have the format <key><separator><value>. An example of the contents of a property file:

```
accesspath.writepath.text=Write:
appletviewer.menuitem.restart=Restart
confirm.overwrite.file.prompt=The file already exists.\nDo you want
to replace it?
```

In the above example, the text that follows the equal sign separator needs to be translated. The key can provide some reference information to translators, but a linguistic check of the translated strings in the running application is essential. Keys are referenced in the actual Java code, and the string is loaded into the application or applet at run-time. Comment text is marked with # or !. Standards for the file format and structure of property files are still under development, therefore it is not yet possible to exactly define the translatable sections in these property files.

Typically, there will be one set of Java code or HTML files, with resource bundles in several languages. These resource bundles will have a locale extension added to the file name, so the desired language is loaded at run-time in the language of the active locale. The locale extensions are based on the ISO 639 standard for *language* and ISO 3166 for *country*, which can be found at the ILE home page at www.ile.com. An example of a file name is *file_fr_CA* for Canadian French.

For more information about localizing Java applets, refer to the Java Applets section on page 88.

Java software applications are difficult to localize, especially when they were not designed with localization in mind. There is no current standard for GUI types for localization purposes so localizers will typically be translating out of context, which requires additional linguistic testing. It might be that a layout manager was used to create the forms and panels in the English product. If you are not sure, contact your client's developer.

In Java software projects, each file type needs to be analyzed carefully to see if it contains translatable text and to identify exactly what needs to be localized.

For more information about Java, visit the Sun Microsystems Web site at www.sun.com or www.javasoft.com or java.sun.com.

Chapter 7:
Project Management

This chapter contains information for project managers of localization projects.

Most large localization service providers employ dedicated project managers for localization projects. Depending on the number and size of the projects, project managers can be dedicated to a client, or to one or more projects.

Often, project managers have a language or translation background. Experience in localization is undoubtedly very useful in identifying problem areas and in finding the right resources and procedures. Project managers should know and understand the business and product because they will be dealing with multiple team members, multiple languages, last-minute updates, etc.

A localization project manager typically is responsible for the following tasks:

- Overall project coordination

- Scheduling and status tracking

- Client contact

- Budget control

- Resource management

- Monitoring the actual project scope

With regard to the last task: It is very common that the scope of a localization project is not clear when translation starts, not even to the client. One of the most important tasks of a project manager is to monitor the scope of the project and compare it to the specifications and schedules that were estimated in the quotation. This monitoring task also includes signaling and invoicing extra activities or updates to the original files.

Many smaller localization agencies do not have dedicated project managers. Instead, senior translators often double as project manager or localization engineer.

1 Creating Quotations

Most localization projects start with a Request for Quotation (RFQ) or Request for Proposal (RFP) from a software developer to a localization service provider. When you create a quotation for a potential localization project, you need to make sure that all translatable components of the software application have been identified.

For quotation purposes, word counts of all components, and time estimates or indications for engineering, testing and desktop publishing need to be provided.

If you have not received any specific project-related or detailed information from the software developer, it is recommended that you ask some general questions about the project first in order to make your quotation as detailed as possible, such as:

- Into which languages will the product be translated? When the product is translated in several languages, much of the preparation work only needs to be done and invoiced once.

- What exactly will need to be translated, i.e., software, help and/or documentation, sample files, etc.?

- Which other tasks need to be performed, for example page layout, printing, software functionality testing, and help testing?

- Will there be updates during translation? If yes, how many rounds of updates, and how extensive will the updates be? Often, updates are estimated in percentages, for example "10% new, 20% changed, 70% unchanged".

- Should a translation memory tool be used? If yes, which tool, and is translation memory available?

- Are glossaries available containing existing terminology equivalents?

- What will be the final deliverables/output? And how should the files be delivered?

- Is any special, or expensive, software or hardware required for localization of the product? Examples are a client/server setup or a specific version of an operating system.

- Does the product require any specialized knowledge or experience with regard to subject matter?

When all components and tasks have been identified, each unit or task needs to be linked to a price. Most localization vendors maintain standard pricing for certain tasks, for example a fixed word price for software translation into German, a word price for help translation into Italian, and help testing rates that are based on the number of topics.

Although standard prices are used, they might not necessarily apply to the project you are quoting on. For example, the complexity level of the translation work is higher than average, dialog boxes are more difficult to resize, and the graphics are extremely difficult to edit. In these cases, you might consider adjusting the standard unit prices.

Please keep the following in mind when creating a quotation:

- Instead of time estimates, software developers increasingly demand unit prices to enable them to budget all work for the different languages.

- Try to use as many fixed unit prices as possible. Quoting too many tasks with a general hour price may make the client suspicious. Only in those cases where "units" such as graphics or dialog boxes are very different, quoting on an hourly basis could be more realistic.

- Clearly indicate which activities are included in a unit price. For example, does the word price for translation work also include editing, and proofreading? In most cases, these tasks will be included in the word price, plus one client validation pass.

- When you have established a good working relationship with your client, you might consider issuing quotations that are based on post-calculation. This implies that all hours spent on certain tasks are calculated after the project and invoiced to the client.

After all components have been analyzed, specifications need to be linked to company prices and included in a quotation, or proposal for localization.

This proposal will not only contain a cost estimate for all services, but also a general time schedule and suggestions for the most efficient way to localize the product.

The following sections contain detailed information about all components and activities that could be included in a quotation for a particular localization project.

1.1 Components

A quotation should be as specific as possible and you should try to clearly separate all tasks and activities. On the other hand, the quotation should leave room for modifications and changes in the course of the project. Of course, all quotations are subject to revision if there are additional files or updates that should be paid for.

In general, a quotation contains the following activities and components, which can be linked to the following unit prices:

Activity	Component	Charged By
Translation	Glossary	hour/term[1]
	Software	word[2]
	Help/Documentation	word
	Sample Documents	hour/word
Engineering	Software	dialog box/hour[3]
Testing	Software (Linguistic)	hour
	Software (Functional)	hour
	Help	topic/hour[4]
Desktop Publishing	Documentation	page
	Collateral Material	page/hour
Graphics	Software	screen/hour[5]
	Help/Documentation	screen/hour
Printing/conversion	Documentation	page
Project Management		% of total cost/hour[6]

Some of these entries require further explanation:

1. Depending on the complexity of the glossary and the amount of terminology research that needs to be done, translation of product-specific terms should be charged per hour or term.

2. The word price for translation of software is usually approximately 20-30% higher than the word price for help and documentation. Some localization agencies even charge double, but this unit price will often include resizing and linguistic testing of the software. For more information about software translation, refer to Chapter 2, Translating Software.

3. Engineering typically encompasses resizing dialog boxes, checking hot keys and compiling the software. Whether you need to quote per hour or per dialog box depends on the complexity of the dialog boxes and the way in which they need to be resized. Resizing that can be done directly in the resource editor is done much quicker than manually changing coordinates of

boxes in text-only resource files. For more information about resizing dialog boxes, refer to the Resizing section on page 167.

4. Whether you need to quote per hour or per topic depends on the size of the help topics, or *help screens*. A help topic can be ten A4 sized pages long or it can be three lines. If the average size of a help topic is an A4 sized page, it is safe to quote on a topic basis. If topics are much longer or shorter, it is better to quote on an hourly basis. For more information about help testing, refer to the Testing section on page 199.

5. Quoting a fixed price per screen may be risky when the images are very complex and require much manual editing. Graphics can be screen captures that are captured in seconds, or complex graphics with bitmapped backgrounds that require hours of editing. In the latter case, getting layered source images (with the translatable text on a separate layer) can be a huge time and cost saver. For more information about graphics editing, refer to the Graphics Editing section on page 186.

6. A common charge for project management is 10 to 15% of the total project costs. Sometimes, an additional 2 to 5% is charged for communication costs.

Analysis of the received localization kit should provide you with the following information:

*   Word counts for software, help and documentation

*   Number of dialog boxes in software application

*   Number of topics or screens in online help; number of pages in documentation

*   Number of graphics in software, help and documentation

Please note that in some countries it is common to charge translations per line–approximately 55 characters–or per number of translated words, i.e., target text. However, in localization it is common to count the words of the source text.

1.1.1   Software

1.1.1.1   WORD COUNTS

If you have received a full localization kit to base your quotation on, you need to identify which files will need to be translated. In most cases, your client will provide you with a list of files that need to be translated. For more information about creating word counts from software resource files, refer to the Creating Word Counts section on page 158.

In some cases, it is impossible to do detailed word counts, for example when the text has been hard-coded in the program files; in those cases, you will have to ask your client for an estimate.

1.1.1.2 DIALOG BOXES

If resizing is performed in a resource editor or translation tool, you can choose to charge per dialog box. To count the number of dialog boxes, open the resource file or application file in a resource editor or localization tool and count the resources in the Dialog section. For more information about resource types, refer to the File Contents section on page 15.

Some software localization tools, such as Corel Catalyst, will automatically calculate the number of items of each resource type. For more information about localization tools, refer to the Software Localization Tools section on page 37

1.1.1.3 TESTING

Estimating the hours needed to compile, engineer and test software and help is the most difficult task in a quotation. Only after you have done some localization projects, is it possible to estimate the duration of these activities.

Each localization vendor will have different standards for estimating time required for technical work. Make sure you know what type of testing is required: linguistic testing, functional testing, or both. For more information, refer to the Testing section on page 178.

One way to achieve correct estimates is to compare hours spent on projects that were done in the past. Unless the analysis of the received files tells you it will be more complicated or time-consuming than similar projects, it is safe to use statistics from similar projects.

Always make sure you track the hours spent by engineers on certain tasks carefully. This will help you adjust estimates you make for future projects.

1.1.2 Help

1.1.2.1 WORD COUNTS

With Windows-based help projects, the following files must be counted: RTF files, CNT files, HPJ files, and images. Refer to the Creating Word Counts section on page 189 for more information about creating word counts from help files.

To create word counts from HTML projects, use one of the tools mentioned in the Testing Localized Web Sites section on page 214. Most translation memory tools will also give you detailed word counts and internal or external repetition counts. For more information, refer to Chapter 5, Translation Memory Tools.

1.1.2.2 TOPICS

If engineering and testing will be based on the number of topics in the help file, you need to specify the number of topics in the help file. Refer to the Creating Word Counts section on page 189 for more information about counting topics in help files.

The automated help testing tool HelpQA will also tell you the number of topics in the help file. For more information about HelpQA, refer to the Using HelpQA section on page 207.

1.1.2.3 GRAPHICS

The statistics displayed after compilation of a Windows Help file will tell you how many bitmaps are included in the help file. HelpQA will also display the number of graphics.

Please note that not all graphics included in a help file are necessarily localizable bitmaps. Bullet or icon symbols are also included in embedded bitmaps. Check the graphics visually before including the total graphic count in your quotation.

1.1.3 Documentation

1.1.3.1 WORD COUNTS

Most word processors or document editors will have a word counting function. If no such feature is present, export the text to a word processor and run a word count. In Chapter 4, Translating Documentation, you will find information about creating word counts using different word processors and desktop publishing applications.

To create word counts from a PDF document, open the file in Acrobat Exchange and select the Copy File to Clipboard command from the Edit menu. Next, switch to a word processor, paste the text, and count the words. For more information about Adobe Acrobat, refer to the Creating Adobe Acrobat PDF Documents section on page 129.

1.1.3.2 PAGES

Most word counting features will also tell you how many pages the document contains. If not, count the pages by going to the last page of the document, and adding any preface, table of contents or title pages if applicable.

1.1.3.3 GRAPHICS

Typically, graphics will be linked to the document files from a separate graphics folder. To determine how many graphics are included in the document, just count the files in this graphics folder. If you are not certain if all graphics are actually linked, or when graphics are embedded or pasted in the documents, count the graphics manually. Check the graphics visually before including the total graphic count in your quotation.

Make sure you look at the types of graphics used. If the graphics are regular screen captures or if they all require similar editing effort, you can use a price per graphic. However, if some of the graphics require a great deal of and others very little manual editing and retouching it is better to quote on an hourly basis.

1.2 Profile Information

Because the quotation will often give the software vendor the first impression of your capabilities, it is important to include information about the strengths of your organizations, the technical infrastructure, the resources available, etc.

When selecting localization vendors, software developers are not only interested in costs. They will also be looking at issues like:

- Company profile, services offered

- Available resources

- Current customers

- Engineering skills, project management skills

- Translation tools used

- Marketing materials expertise

- Linguistic quality

Make sure you include these items with the detailed information about your company.

2 The Localization Process

No localization project is the same. Each project will have its surprises, in a positive or negative sense. Sometimes, projects that were announced as huge, technically complex operations are over before you know it. On the other hand, it is also very well possible that small projects can turn into never-ending nightmares.

If no statement of work listing tasks and responsibilities is provided by your client, start the project by finding out what exactly is expected from you by the software vendor. You need to create a list of tasks that will function as a template for your project schedule.

To avoid surprises, there are several questions worth asking before the start of a localization project. These questions include:

- All questions listed under Creating Quotations in the beginning of this chapter.

- Who will be the contact person? Will there be different contact persons for issues regarding engineering or desktop publishing?

- What is the preferred communication method?

- Will there be a language, software or desktop publishing validation by the client? It is recommended to request a preliminary client validation of translated material very early in the project.

- What is the desired frequency of status reports?

- What are the deadlines? Often deadlines are closely related to the shipping of the English product, or trade shows where localized versions need to be presented.

- Will invoicing be done in installments or upon completion of the project? How will updates during the project be invoiced?

- Will there be different language *tiers*? Large software developers release different language versions of their applications in tiers. For example, French and German can be tier one languages that ship in February, and Italian and Spanish tier two languages that ship in April.

Each step in the localization process, including linguistic, technical and management steps, needs to be defined to oversee the scope of the project. The workflow of a typical localization project can be summarized in the following steps:

1. **Analysis of Received Material**

2. **Scheduling and Budgeting**

3. **Glossary Translation or Terminology Setup**

4. **Preparation of Localization Kit**

5. **Translation of Software**

6. **Translation of Help and Documentation**

7. **Processing Updates**

8. **Testing of Software**

9. **Testing of Help and DTP of Documentation**

10. **Product QA and Delivery**

11. **Post-mortem with Client**

The following sections will provide you with a more detailed overview of these steps and other issues that need to be taken into consideration.

Important

Please note that the order of these steps can differ substantially depending on the project. Besides, two or more tasks can run simultaneously.

2.1 Analysis of Received Material

When files for a localization project are received from a client, they first need to be analyzed by localization engineers. Mostly, files are sent directly from your client's development department and would include the following:

- A running version of the English product

- Build environments for the software

- Build environments for the online help

- A document folder containing all book files, chapter files and graphics

- If appropriate, previously translated versions of the product

Often localization kits coming from software developers include some instructions, but these instructions will typically not be sufficient for translators to understand the material received and tasks required.

The file analysis performed by the localization engineers focusses on the following questions:

- Are all necessary files included?

- Are all files to be translated? Often, old versions of files or unused files are included by software developers. These need to be filtered out.

- Are all word counts provided by your client correct?

- How much re-use of existing text will there be in the source material? Refer to Chapter 5, Translation Memory Tools, for more information about re-using translations.

- Does a pseudo-translation work? A pseudo-translation means replacing all English text with–accented–characters of a certain length in order to test whether translations will corrupt files. This is also called internationalization testing.

- If applicable, is the client's proprietary software localization tool stable and useful?

- What will be the most efficient way to localize the product?

First, it is always a good idea to ask engineers to do a test-compilation of the source material. Compiling the English software and help will tell you whether all necessary files are included, and whether the source material is working. If the source material is not correct, chances are that you will end up correcting the same mistakes in all localized versions!

For more information about analyzing software build environments for localization, refer to the Preparation section on page 156.

The documentation files should also be analyzed. First, check if the index markers that generate the index correspond to the actual generated index file. Secondly, verify if importing and exporting the documentation files from the translation memory system works fine.

For more information about analyzing documentation files for localization, refer to the Preparation section on page 104.

Information that localization engineers should provide to project managers for scheduling purposes includes the scope of the project, the volumes, the approach that will be taken, and additional costs that are likely to be made.

Many software developers organize kick-off meetings for translators, localization engineers and project managers to provide an overview of the project, to explain the localization procedures and methods, and–last but not least–to meet. Project managers should evaluate training needs, especially when translators are entirely new to the product or technology.

2.2 Scheduling and Budgeting

Scheduling is a critical task in localization. Many issues endanger the time schedule set at the beginning of a project, the most likely one being late delivery of the source material by the client. Since many software developers are aiming for simultaneous release–also called *simship*–of all language versions of their product, most localization agencies will experience heavy workloads towards the end of a project.

As in software development, time to market is critical in software localization. To ensure simultaneous or timely shipping of a localized software product, translation work often starts before the English product is finished or complete. Consequently, change management and scheduling dependencies caused by updates are among the most important responsibilities for a project manager.

The first thing you do to create a schedule is to define tasks and activities. Each task will cover a certain period and each activity will be assigned to a certain resource.

Detailed scheduling can only be done once the material has been received and analyzed. Especially analyzing new material using an existing translation memory from a previous version of the product can greatly influence the time necessary to translate help or documentation files. Once you have all the information you need, you can set milestones for the project. A milestone is a task with no duration, a point in time, such as a delivery from or to the client.

As part of project scheduling, you need to schedule and allocate resources, such as translators, engineers and desktop publishers. Try to limit the number of translators working on a project as much as possible to maintain consistency.

When finding people who can do the translation and engineering work, please remember the following:

- Translation should always be performed by native speakers.

- If multiple translators will be working on the same project, assign one of them as project lead who will be responsible for terminology consistency, contacting the client about linguistic issues, and ensuring stylistic consistency.

- Try to find translators who have worked on similar projects or previous versions of the same product.

- Limit the number of freelance staff working on a localization project because it is likely that they will not feel responsible for terminology management, bug tracking, and problem solving.

- Find technical staff who will ensure bug-free software. A localization engineering team should ideally be a mix of people with language and technical backgrounds.

- Make sure all people involved in the project track their hours carefully in connection with a task specification. This will help you explain the final costs to your client.

For projects that are translated into multiple languages, determine where you want certain activities, such as engineering or desktop publishing, to take place. Centralizing these activities might cause a bottleneck towards the end of the project because all languages need to be finalized within the same period.

Each scheduled activity needs to be budgeted. The cost estimates from the quotation need to be compared with the costs of the resources that you have scheduled to use.

In general, the following pricing policy is followed by localization vendors: The profit margins are the amounts that have been invoiced to the client minus all direct and indirect costs. Direct and indirect costs are interpreted differently by each vendor. Some vendors include communication and project management costs as indirect costs, others will charge these costs as direct costs for the project.

Tip

If a software application contains a license agreement or copyright text, consult with your client whether they want it simply "localized" or re-written in the target language by a lawyer familiar with the copyright laws of the target country. In the latter case, budget separately for this item. Never simply translate these texts without any consultation or localization.

2.2.1   Schedule

A project manager creates a time schedule in the very beginning of the project, outlining the start and end dates of all activities in the localization project. These activities would include:

- Translation of glossary or terminology setup

- Translation or updating and review of software, online help and documentation

- Testing of software and help

- DTP of documentation

- QA

A project schedule can be created using an application like Microsoft Project, or a spreadsheet application. A project schedule can be created in many different ways, for example using flow charts or Gantt charts. A Gantt chart is a bar chart used as an aid in planning and scheduling, in which project activities or tasks are shown graphically as bars drawn on a horizontal time scale.

Task Name	Duration	Start	End	1997			
				29/06	06/07	13/07	20/07
Software translation	83.00 d	30/06/97	22/10/97				
Prepare/check glossary	5.00 d	30/06/97	04/07/97				
Prepare software files	2.00 d	07/07/97	08/07/97				
Datalink core resources	71.00 d	09/07/97	15/10/97				
Translate	5.00 d	09/07/97	15/07/97				
Internal linguistic review	3.00 d	16/07/97	18/07/97				
Preliminary build & review	3.00 d	21/07/97	23/07/97				
Client review	5.00 d	28/07/97	01/08/97				
Update to 4.01	8.00 d	06/10/97	15/10/97				
Remaining software (excl samples)	70.00 d	14/07/97	17/10/97				
Translate	5.00 d	14/07/97	18/07/97				
Internal linguistic review	3.00 d	21/07/97	23/07/97				
Preliminary build & review	2.00 d	24/07/97	25/07/97				

Most of the software engineering and testing activities will be scheduled based on input from the localization engineers, who can only estimate the required time for compiling and testing software and help once they have seen the material.

A localization project can be scheduled in two ways: backward and forward. In backward scheduling, the client sets a milestone for an activity or deadline for the project. In this case, the project manager will schedule resources and tasks based on these milestones. In forward scheduling, the project manager will schedule all tasks and resources and propose milestones for the project to the client. Usually, localization projects will combine these two methods.

When a preliminary schedule has been created, it is sent to the client for review or approval. If the schedule is approved, translation can start. It is recommended to schedule some time for the translators to familiarize themselves with the product and for setting up the hardware and software required for the project.

2.2.2   Tracking Sheet

Once the project has started, dates will most likely change. These changes should be monitored by the project manager in a tracking sheet or in the project management software. A tracking sheet shows the differences between the estimated start and end dates from the project schedule and the actual work in progress. It will show you if the project is on schedule, ahead of schedule, or behind schedule.

Another way to track the status of a project is the use of Gantt charts, which will automatically display and process project interruptions, changes in resources, and other changes that will affect the workflow of the project. Usually, a task will have one predecessor and one successor. Changing the duration of one of these tasks will automatically adjust the Critical Path of the project, which is the sequence of tasks that determines the end date of the project.

Tracking sheets may be sent to the client on a regular basis, along with or included in a general status report, which lists any outstanding project-related issues. If any cost changes arise during the project, these should also be included in the status report with reasons and estimated amount.

2.2.3   Status Report

A status report from a localization vendor to a client would include the following items:

- Scheduled start and end dates versus actual start and end dates (tracking sheet)

- Scheduled costs versus actual costs

- Outstanding issues and problems

- Expected progress for the following week

Often, delivery of a status report is followed by a meeting or conference call to discuss the issues raised in the report.

2.3   Glossary Translation or Terminology Setup

Often localization projects start with the translation of a product-specific glossary, which needs to be approved by the client before any localization work can be done.

This glossary, also called project glossary, would typically contain product-specific terms. A project glossary would also clearly indicate which essential terms, such as product names, should *not* be localized, and new and strategic terminology should be marked. For more information about this type of glossary, refer to the Project Glossaries section on page 278.

To obtain accurate translations from the very beginning of the project, provide terminology researchers or translators with sufficient reference material, such as the running application or help file. Translating key terms without any contextual information about the product may result in major terminology changes later in the project.

Typically, the project glossary is sent to the client for validation. After validation of the glossary, translation can start.

2.4 Preparation of Localization Kit

When the localization engineers have analyzed the source files, spotted potential problems and test-compiled all source material, a localization kit is created for the translators.

Preparing a localization kit includes investigating leveraging possibilities for the software, i.e., checking if existing translations can be automatically re-used. If previous translations exist of the software resource files, the localization engineer should try to re-use these translations as much as possible to avoid unnecessary work being done by the translators. This not only improves consistency, it also decreases the number of words to translate, i.e., speeds up the software translation process. For more information about this leveraging of software files, refer to the Updating section on page 173.

The same applies to the online help files and documentation. If translation memories exist, they need to be included with the localization kit, along with files that have been pre-processed for use in the translation memory tool. For more information, refer to Chapter 5.

During the preparation of the localization kit, a folder structure and file naming conventions should be defined. This will make files easier to find and allow for accurate and easy file control. For more information about setting up a folder structure, refer to the File Management section on page 12.

A localization kit contains everything that a translator needs to localize the product, such as:

- A schedule detailing the deadlines for all components, and all tasks required

- The files that need to be translated, i.e., software, help and/or documentation

- A running version of the application that is translated, including online help file(s)

- Instructions explaining to the translator what is included in the localization kit, what needs to be translated, which tools should be used, and which procedures should be followed

- Reference material, such as an overview of the product, a project glossary, glossaries from previous versions of the product, other applications from the same client, previously translated versions of the product, client style guides, or operating system glossaries

- Translation standards, i.e., style guides

- Procedures, i.e., the order in which components should be translated

The technical and linguistic information should be combined into one coherent instruction file that is given to the translator along with all source material.

2.5 Translation of Software

Traditionally, software is translated first in localization projects. Translators edit resources in text-only files, in a resource editor or in a software localization tool. For more information about software translation, refer to Chapter 2, Translating Software.

Depending on the complexity of the application and the procedures and tools being used, software translators will translate approximately 1500 words per day.

The best order in which to translate software resources is: dialog boxes, menus and strings. Usually, the string section contains most of the translatable text: error messages, status messages, and help text.

When dialog box resources and menus are translated, it is already possible to create a preliminary glossary–or even preliminary software build–of these translations, which can be used as a reference for translators of help and documentation. Most of the software references in help and documentation will be references to dialog box items and menu names, so starting translation of help and documentation after these items have been localized will give you a head-start. For more information about creating software glossaries, refer to the Creating Software Glossaries section on page 279.

After software resource files have been translated, the software needs to be compiled and resized. Then, a linguistic test needs to be performed to validate the translations in context in the running applications. Next, if the client requires this from you, functional testing is performed. For more information about testing software, refer to the Testing section on page 178.

When a linguistic test of the localized software has been completed, the terminology of the application should be final. This means that a localized software version can be sent to the client's validator for an acceptance test. In addition, you can start creating screen captures for the online help and documentation.

Tip

It is recommended to start translating sample files along with the software files. Sample files typically contain sample data that can be translated by a different translator from the one translating the software. Because screen captures in help and documentation often contain graphics from sample files, screen capturing can commence early in the project.

After the linguistic test of the software and acceptance by your client, do not accept terminology changes in the software unless they are needed to correct serious errors. Last-minute terminology changes will require too much change management in all other files that are being translated.

2.6 Translation of Help and Documentation

As soon as a software glossary or a preliminary build of the localized software is available, translation of help and documentation can start.

For more information about translating help and documentation, refer to Chapter 3, Translating Online Help, and Chapter 4, Translating Documentation.

Typically, the software glossary will be merged with the project glossary and loaded in the terminology management software that runs in conjunction with the translation memory system in which the help and documentation files are translated. For example, when the help files are translated using Trados Translator's Workbench, the software glossary would be loaded in MultiTerm. For more information, refer to the Trados Translator's Workbench section on page 136.

If software translations are not yet available or finalized and translation of help and documentation needs to start for scheduling reasons, instruct translators to leave all software references in English to be filled in later. In the case of updates, you might choose to translate all references that can be found in the previously translated version or glossaries of the previous versions. These translations will need to be checked against the actual running software later!

> **Tip**
>
> Sometimes it is necessary to start translating help and documentation *before* the software will be translated. In this case, instruct the translators to translate all software references and to create a glossary of all these translated references. This glossary can be used to–automatically–translate the software resource files.

For reference purposes, provide translators of help and documentation with a running version of the (localized) software application. You cannot always completely rely on software glossaries because certain terms may have different translations depending on context, location, or grammatical form. The only way to make sure the correct translations of software references are used is to have the translator verify all referenced options and commands in the running application on a localized operating system.

Tip

If translators constantly refer to the running software, not only do you get accurate software reference translations in your help and documentation, but you can also ask translators to track any linguistic or functional problems that they encounter. This will help the localization engineers doing their testing!

A typical help and documentation translation workflow would involve translation, revision/editing, and proofreading.

2.6.1   Translation

For consistency purposes, try to keep the number of translators working on a project as limited as possible, especially when no translation memory tools are used. If translation memory tools are used, make sure the memory database is shared over the network by translators working on the same project. For more information, refer to Chapter 5, Translation Memory Tools.

Translators can translate approximately 2000 words of running text per day. Of course, this number can change depending on the use of translation memory and machine translation. A well-designed combination of well-structured source material, translation memory and machine translation can increase productivity up to 50%. For more information, refer to the Translation Memory vs. Machine Translation section on page 134.

2.6.2   Revision/Editing

First, translators should review their own work and run a spell-check on their documents. This review is a linguistic one, which can be done on-screen in the translation memory tool.

All–or sections of–translated materials should be revised and edited by a senior translator or localizer who is assigned as project lead. Make sure that translations by new or inexperienced translators are reviewed in a very early stage!

There are some issues to keep in mind when translated documents are being reviewed and edited:

- Check whether there has been any unnecessary editing. Rephrasing perfectly clear sentences just for stylistic reasons is a waste of time and often bad for consistency. Online help and documentation files do not require perfect style; accuracy and consistency are factors that are much more important.

- Make sure that edits are implemented by–or at least shown to–the original translator of the document. This is the only way to prevent the same mistakes from being made again.

- Special attention needs to be paid to the index in a printed manual, and the Search Keyword index in an online help file. A preliminary index generation or help file compilation might be needed. For more information about indexes, refer to the Translating Indexes section on page 120.

Often, terminology changes are introduced in the translated software because of limitations or bugs found in the localized software or linguistic reasons. In this case, or if help translation started before the software localization was finalized, it is recommended to verify all software references in the text with the actual running software. Many localization agencies include this software vs. documentation check, or software consistency check, in their standard procedures.

2.6.3   Client Validation

Most software developers will require samples of the translated material for their internal evaluation during a localization project. This validation will concentrate on the following aspects:

1. Accuracy of translations: Has everything been translated? Do translated software references match the translated software?

2. Terminology: Have provided glossaries been used? Is terminology used consistently?

3. Language Quality: Is the general style and grammar correct? Does the translated text contain any typing errors?

4. Localization: Has the text been adapted to reflect cultural differences?

The result of this evaluation often is expressed in a *pass* or a *no-pass*. If a no-pass is returned by the client, implement the client's suggestions and corrections and send the revised translations for a new quality check. Direct contact between translators and the client's validators often helps to prevent or resolve language or terminology problems.

Try not to base your deliveries of translated material on the timely arrival of your client's validation comments. Often, this review is performed by marketing personnel who do not have much time for this type of work. Discuss with your client whether the validation is important enough to delay the project. This is an internal problem that the client's project manager needs to resolve with the language validator.

2.7 Processing Updates

Translation often starts when the English product is not yet finished. This means that first one or more beta versions or releases of the product are translated before the final version is released for translation.

If you are not using a translation memory system for your translations, you need to process updates using file compares, copying and pasting, etc. Translation memory systems will allow you to process the new files and automatically re-use the translations that were already completed. Refer to Chapter 5, Translation Memory Tools, for more information about the use of translation memory.

When desktop publishing for printed documentation and testing of online help has already started, it is more difficult to process updates. Most of the time, files are converted back to their original formats after translation and are no longer editable in the translation memory tool. In case of these last-minute updates, you can either process the updates using the translation memory tool and lose your desktop publishing or testing work, or insert the changes in the files that are being worked on. In the latter case, your translation memory will not be up-to-date anymore.

Most of the time, there will be too much time pressure to re-do desktop publishing and testing work, and the latter procedure will be chosen.

> **Tip**
>
> When many textual corrections or updates have been entered in the files during testing or DTP, you might consider aligning the translated files with the original files to create a new, up-to-date translation memory. For more information about alignment, refer to the Introduction section on page 134.

To prevent unnecessary software engineering, testing, or desktop publishing work, always consult with your client if–and when–updates can be expected.

2.8 Testing of Software

As explained in the Testing section on page 178, different types of testing are possible in a localization project. The first type, linguistic testing or user interface testing, is often seen as part of the translation process and needs to be done by a translator, if possible with the help of an engineer or test scripts.

If listed in the localization statement of work, functionality testing is performed by localization engineers or dedicated testing engineers. Often the client will provide test scripts, which will guide engineers through the testing process. If no guidelines or scripts are provided, ask your client how much time should be scheduled for functionality or compatibility testing of the localized versions of the software.

Apart from testing the localized product on different (language) versions of the target operating system, also installers need to be tested. Finally, a regression test should be scheduled to check if and how previously reported bugs or problems were fixed.

For large functionality testing jobs, assign a testing lead who designs test scripts and procedures for all people involved in testing. Make sure you schedule sufficient time for this preparation.

2.9   Testing of Help and DTP of Documentation

Screen captures are an essential component of each localization project. Without screen captures of the localized software, no help file or manual can be finalized. Therefore, it is recommended to start creating screen captures as soon as the linguistic testing of the software is completed.

As soon as all graphics are translated and reviewed, desktop publishing of documentation and testing of help can start. It is possible to do DTP and help testing with the original, English graphics but this will require an additional check after the graphics have been translated. Image sizes might change in localized versions, for example, because of resizing of dialog boxes. Consequently, page flows might change so DTP work needs to be re-done.

2.10   Product QA and Delivery

Before delivery, a Quality Assurance check should be performed on all translated material. At this stage, your client might also request a final validation.

This QA would include:

- Proofreading all translations. For more information about proofreading documentation, refer to the Proofreading Documentation section on page 127.

- Delivery test of the software. For more information about this type of testing, refer to the Delivery Test section on page 180.

- Finalizing bug or problem reports. For more information about bug reports, refer to the Writing Bug Reports section on page 181.

- Reviewing the instructions given in the initial hand-off or statement of work from the client to see if all steps were covered.

Proofread help and documentation on a printout after all desktop publishing and graphics embedding has been finalized. For more information about proofreading help and documentation files, refer to the Proofreading Documentation section on page 127.

When the QA checks have been completed, the translated material can be delivered to the client. It is important to deliver translated files in an organized, structured manner. Preferably, an exact duplicate of the source material should be delivered, without any old versions of translated files or internally used instruction files.

If files are delivered electronically in a compressed file, it is advisable to number the delivery. For example, the translated help files for DataLink should not be called *dlink_hlp.zip* but *dlink_hlp1.zip*. If files are updated after delivery or corrections need to be implemented, you can number your deliveries sequentially: *dlink_hlp2.zip*, *dlink_hlp3.zip*, etc. For multilingual projects, also include a language code in the delivery file.

The way in which files are to be delivered, should be discussed in the beginning of the project. For example, should files be delivered by e-mail, FTP, disk, CD, tape, etc.? Also ask your client if a printout of the translated documentation needs to be delivered along with the electronic files.

After all translated files have been delivered and approved by the client, archive all materials. Make sure that not only the translated files are archived, but also the files that you received for translation and the files that you delivered.

2.11   Post-mortem with Client

Many clients organize a post-mortem—or project audit or wrap-up meeting—with the localization vendor after a project has been completed. Issues discussed in these meetings include:

- Evaluation of the completed project

- Evaluation of technical and linguistic quality of deliverables

- Identification of areas for improvement

- Suggestions for process modifications for future projects

Please note that these meetings should work both ways; both parties need to provide input on each other's performance.

During the post-mortem meeting one of the attendees should take notes and distribute a summary to both parties of all topics discussed. This document could function as a starting point for new projects.

3 Communication

Communication is the essential factor in managing localization projects. Project managers will be communicating with clients, translators, technical resources, linguists, validators, and all other people involved in the project.

It is good to keep every person involved in the project informed about the status of the project. However, try to avoid "over-informing" people with information they do not need to know.

3.1 Translators

Mostly, translators will be native speakers of the target language(s) of the localization project. They will be familiar with computer and software terminology, but not necessarily with project process-related terms. Try to communicate project-related information using English that is understandable for non-native speakers.

In dealing with freelance translators, contractors, in-house staff, partner vendors, and client validators, always try to avoid conflicts about terminological or stylistic issues. Discussions about details or regional preferences should be prevented; it should be clear who has the last say in such issues. Although this may prove to be difficult at times, try to convince all people involved that the only way to deliver a high-quality localized version of the product is to work together and accept input from others.

One issue that is very important in multilingual projects is the management of questions by translators and corresponding modifications across different languages. Setting up online forms or databases containing questions and answers that are accessible for all translators is a way to make sure that each language version will contain identical modifications or interpretations.

3.2 Clients

Dealing with clients is a tricky part of project management in localization. It is not easy to communicate missed deadlines or major problems to clients during the project. Try to always keep the client informed of problems that you encounter. Informing your client of delays as soon as they occur will allow you to figure out a solution with your client.

Common issues that make dealing with clients in localization difficult are:

- Unrealistic deadlines caused by lack of understanding of localization

- Unclear or incomplete information about the scope of the project and responsibilities

- Unannounced product updates

Discussing these issues before the project starts will help preventing misunderstandings or conflicts.

Inside your organization, try to make perfectly clear who will be communicating with whom, and about what. For big localization projects, a solution is to maintain direct contact between your lead localization engineer and the client's lead software developer concerning all technical issues. For linguistic issues, a senior translator or project lead could contact the client's validator.

Also, try to agree on the distribution of communicated material, for example who will be copied on all e-mails to and from the client.

Make sure that revised milestones are communicated clearly in a status report. One of the worst things you can do to clients is to inform them of delays on the day of the deadline!

4 Structured Project Management

There are numerous publications and training courses for project managers. However, not many of them focus on localization project management. ETP is a company based in Ireland that specializes in project management workshops aimed at the localization industry. ETP's approach is called *Structured Project Management* which is based on a number of standard, consistent steps.

4.1 Successful Project Management

According to ETP, the ten steps to a successful (localization) project are:

PLANNING

1. Visualize the goal: set your eyes on the prize.
2. Make a list of jobs that need to be done.
3. There must be one leader (*trail boss*)
4. Assign people to jobs.
5. Manage expectations, allow a margin for error, have a fallback position.

VISUALIZATION

6. Use an appropriate leadership style.
7. Know what's going on.
8. Tell other people what's going on.
9. Repeat steps 1 to 8 until step 10 is reached.
10. The prize.

LISA, the Localisation Industry Standards Association has selected Structured Project Management as the preferred and most dynamic project management method for use by the localization industry.

4.2 Why Projects Fail

ETP's top ten reasons why projects fail were listed in Deborah Fry's article on localization project management in Language International, Vol 10.3 (1998):

1. The goal of the project isn't defined clearly.

2. The goal is defined properly, but changes to it aren't controlled.

3. The project isn't planned properly.

4. The project isn't led properly.

5. The project is planned properly but then isn't resourced as planned.

6. The project is planned such that it has no contingency.

7. The expectations of project participants aren't managed.

8. Progress against the plan isn't monitored and controlled properly.

9. Project reporting is inadequate or non-existent.

10. When projects run into trouble, people believe that the problem can be solved simply, e.g., by working harder, extending the deadline, or adding more resources.

For more information about ETP and Structured Project Management, visit the ETP Web site at www.etpint.com.

Appendix A: Terminology

This chapter contains information about terminology, terminology management, tools, and the use of glossaries.

Glossaries are essential in each localization project, for consistent use of terminology is very important. First of all, the terminology used in the online help and documentation should correspond to the terms used in the software. Secondly, the terminology of the translated program should be consistent with the environment in which the product is used. Windows terminology, for example, can differ substantially from the terminology used in the Macintosh environment.

Translators also need to make sure that they use consistent terminology between different products from the same client or older versions of the same product.

In this chapter you will find detailed information about which glossary types are typically used in localization projects, how glossaries are created, which tools can be used, and where specific terminology can be found.

1 Glossary Types

Glossaries are essential in each software localization project. Different glossary types include operating environment glossaries, project glossaries, and software glossaries.

1.1 Operating Environment Glossary

When translating a product for a certain operating system, such as Windows or Macintosh, it is important to use the terminology that is used in the localized version of the operating system.

Some software developers, such as Microsoft, maintain their own style guides and glossaries. All basic Windows terms, for example, can be found in the Microsoft Press publication *Microsoft GUI Guide*. In the GUI Guide you will also find translations for standard software elements like dialog boxes, drop down lists, and check boxes. Complete Microsoft operating system and application glossaries can be downloaded from Microsoft's FTP server.

Standard Macintosh terminology can be found in Daniel Carter's *Writing Localizable Software for the Macintosh* and in the localization guides published by Apple Computers. Complete operating system glossaries can be downloaded from Apple's FTP server.

For more information about Microsoft's and Apple's glossaries, refer to the Multilingual Glossaries section on page 283.

1.2 Client Glossaries

Most clients will provide localization agencies with their internal glossaries. These glossaries would typically include:

- Terms from previously translated versions of the product

- Terms from other translated products from the same client

- Terms from the marketing or documentation group

- Feature and concept names

Along with the operating environment glossaries, these glossaries should be provided to translators that will localize updates to previously translated software applications.

1.3 Project Glossaries

If there is no previous version of the translated product, the software translator creates a preliminary glossary with key words and phrases before translation of the software starts. This glossary should be reviewed by a senior translator or by your client.

A project glossary would typically contain the following terms:

- Industry-specific terminology

- Translations for keywords, both verbs and nouns, appropriate for the product

- Product-related names that should not be translated

- Phrases that are repeated throughout the project, such as "Note", and "Select"

- Feature and concept names

- Names of help files or manuals

Because this glossary will function as a base terminology source for the project, it is very important that term equivalents are correctly established from the very beginning.

If the source material of the product, such as the help file, contains an explanatory glossary, this glossary can be used to function as a basis for your translated project glossary. Another way to create a project glossary is to run a terminology extraction tool on the source documentation or help files. Some translation memory tools contain terminology extraction features.

1.4 Software Glossaries

After all software files have been translated and reviewed, a glossary of the software should be generated for reference purposes during the translation of the documentation, help files, etc. This type of glossary is also called a user interface glossary.

Apart from source term and target term, software glossaries might also include:

- Hot keys

- Product name and version

- Category, i.e., button, menu, dialog box title, etc.

Several software localization tools can create text-only glossaries from software resource files or binaries. For more information about some of these tools, refer to the next section.

2 Creating Software Glossaries

Ideally, software glossaries need to be created from the translated software files before online help and documentation is translated. This will ensure consistency of the software references in the documentation and help as compared to the actual running software.

In most cases, translation of help and documentation will already start before the software translation is finalized. To provide the translators of help and documentation with sufficient terminology reference, it is recommended to create a software glossary of just the menus and dialog box items, which will cover most of the software references found in the help files and documentation. It is not a good idea to include all software strings in a software glossary anyway, because including all error messages, status messages, and other long strings could make the glossary too large.

For translators it can also be very useful to provide context information with each glossary item. For example, it might be useful to know if a term is a menu item, a dialog box option, or a dialog box title. Some glossary tools will add this information, in other cases it might be a good idea to add this information in cases where the contextual reference is unclear.

2.1 Windows

Windows-based applications can be translated in two ways, in text-only resource files that are compiled into binary files, or directly in the binary program files. Subsequently, glossaries can be created in two ways. Most software localization tools contain glossary features. For more information about these tools, refer to the Software Localization Tools section on page 37.

The following sections describe two ways to create software glossaries from Windows applications: from text-only resource files using SDL Amptran, and from resource files or program files using Corel Catalyst.

2.1.1   Using Amptran

With Amptran, you can create glossaries from text-only software resource files, such as RC, DLG, MNU, and STR files.

To create a software glossary using Amptran, follow these steps:

1. Choose the Align Translated Segments option from the Mode menu.

2. Choose the Create Alignment List from Existing Files command from the File menu.

3. Select Program Localisation in the File Selection Filter dialog box.

4. Select the source file(s) and translated file(s).

5. Choose the Export Segment List from the File menu to export the alignment list as a tab-delimited glossary file with source, target, and comment fields.

For more information about Amptran, visit the SDL Ltd. Web site at www.sdlintl.com.

2.1.2   Using Catalyst

With Catalyst, you can create software glossaries from one or more program files, such as EXE, DLL, and OCX files, or software resource files such as RC and DLG files.

To create a software glossary using Catalyst, follow these steps:

1. Create a new Catalyst project, and insert the English file using the Insert Files command from the File menu.

2. In the resources window, click on the file name of the imported file.

3. Choose the Import Translations command from the Object menu, and select the translated program or resource file.

4. Choose the Extract Glossary command from the Tools menu.

5. In the Extract Glossary dialog box, type a name and specify a path for the glossary file.

6. The glossary is saved in tab-delimited text format.

For more information about Corel Catalyst, visit the Catalyst Web site at catalyst.corel.ie.

2.2 Macintosh

Macintosh applications are localized directly in the program files. It is possible to create software glossaries from these files. The tool that is mostly used to create software glossaries, is AppleGlot.

2.2.1 Using AppleGlot

To create a software glossary using AppleGlot, follow these steps:

1. Start AppleGlot.

2. Create a new environment by selecting the New Environment command from the File menu. An environment is a set of specifically named folders that AppleGlot uses to process a project.

3. Use the Finder to copy the files to the proper folders. Move copies of the previous English version into the _OldUS folder, the _NewUS folder, and a copy of the accompanying localized version into the _OldLoc folder.

4. In the AppleGlot environment window, mark the files that you want to translate, and click the Translate Only button.

5. Save the batch file in the environment folder. The batch file contains all the information that AppleGlot produced automatically or which you provided using the manual Environment window.

6. When text extraction is completed, the _AD folder will contain an application dictionary that contains all localized strings.

To convert an AppleGlot language glossary to tab-delimited format, follow these steps:

1. Open the AppleGlot glossary in Microsoft Excel or another spreadsheet application.

2. Delete the first column.

3. Copy the remaining column to a word processor document.

4. Search and replace the > character followed by a paragraph mark with a tab character (search >^p and replace with ^t).

5. Search and replace all < and > characters.

6. Save the document as text-only.

There is one disadvantage to this method: If there are strings that include carriage returns, the section after the carriage return is deleted when you delete the first column. However, for common resource items, such as menu and dialog box items, the method should work.

For more information about AppleGlot, refer to the Using AppleGlot section on page 230.

3 Finding Terminology

The Internet contains a huge number of terminology resources, such as online dictionaries, glossaries, and encyclopaedias. Below you will find some sites that contain interesting terminology resources for localizers, both English and multilingual.

The Translator's Home Companion Web site at www.lai.com/lai/companion.html contains many links to online glossaries and dictionaries on the Internet.

3.1 English Computer Terminology

3.1.1 General

3.1.1.1 SUN

Sun's glossary that covers those terms that are specific or unique to Sun's business can be found at www.sun.com/glossary.

A glossary of Java-related terms can be found at java.sun.com/docs/glossary.html.

3.1.1.2 MICROSOFT

Microsoft's Glossary of International Technology can be found at Microsoft's Web site at www.microsoft.com/globaldev/gbl-res/glossary.htm.

3.1.1.3 APPLE

Apple's Publication Glossary can be downloaded from Apple's FTP server at ftp.apple.com/devworld/Technical_Documentation/Publication_Guides.

3.1.1.4 IBM

IBM's Software Glossary can be downloaded from IBM's Web site at www.networking.ibm.com/nsg/nsgmain.htm.

3.1.1.5 NOVELL

Novell's Glossary of Networking Terms can be found at Novell's Web site at www.novell.com/catalog/glossary.html.

3.1.1.6 O'REILLY

One of the best technical dictionaries on the Internet is the "Dictionary of PC Hardware and Data Communications Terms". The online version is updated regularly with new terms. The dictionary can be found at www.ora.com/reference/dictionary.

3.2 Multilingual Glossaries

3.2.1   Microsoft Glossaries

The operating system and application glossaries from Microsoft can be found on the Microsoft Developer Network CD-ROMs and on Microsoft's FTP server at ftp.microsoft.com/developr/MSDN/NewUp/Glossary.

These glossaries are comma-delimited CSV format files, and can be opened using a spreadsheet application or word processor. The glossaries not only include the operating systems, but also several Microsoft applications, such as the Office programs.

To search these Microsoft glossary files, you can either use the Find function from your word processor or spreadsheet, or use a utility called MSG Browser. This tool enables you to quickly find translations of any English term included in any of the glossary files.

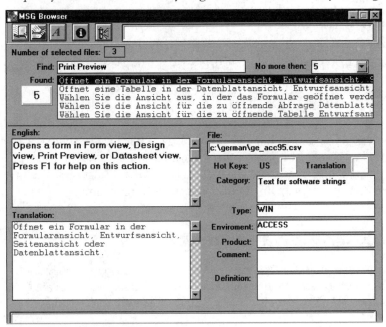

For more information about MSG Browser and a free working demo version, visit the MSG Browser Web site at www.icactive.com/msgb.

Some terminology management applications, such as Lingo and Translation Assistant, contain import features for Microsoft's CSV glossaries. Refer to the Terminology Management section on page 284 for more information.

3.2.2   Apple Glossaries

Apple Computer is providing operating system glossaries in all languages of the MacOS.

The Apple international glossaries can be found on the Apple Developer Connection CDs and at Apple's FTP server at ftp.apple.com/devworld/Tool_Chest/Localization_Tools/Apple_Intl_Glossaries.

The glossaries are available in three different formats: ClarisWorks spreadsheet (SS) tables, tab-delimited text (TXT), and AppleGlot language glossaries (LG). The AppleGlot glossaries can be used to pre-translate products. For more information about translating with AppleGlot, refer to the Using AppleGlot section on page 65.

3.2.3 Novell Glossaries

Novell product glossaries in several languages can be found on the Internet at Novell's FTP server at ftp.novell.com/pub/updates/tresorce/gloss. The glossaries are in tab-delimited text format. At ftp.novell.com/pub/updates/tresorce/stygui you will find translation style guides for several languages.

3.2.4 Lotus Glossaries

Lotus product glossaries in several languages can be found on the Internet at Lotus' FTP server at ftp.lotus.com/pub/lotusweb/product/ngd/glossaries. The glossaries are in Lotus Notes database format. They are part of the Lotus Notes Global Designer translation environment, which is used to translate Notes database files.

3.2.5 NetGlos

NetGlos is The Multilingual Glossary of Internet Terminology. It is maintained and updated on a voluntary basis by translators and other language professionals. It contains an English list of Internet terms with translations and explanations in many languages. The NetGlos glossary can be found at wwli.com/translation/netglos/netglos.html.

4 Terminology Management

Especially in large localization projects, it is not easy to keep track of the terminology used by the translators. To ensure consistent terminology use, most localization agencies use terminology management tools. These tools typically have the following features and functionality:

- Storing terms, translations and definitions

- Lookup features, to find translations

- Automatic insertion, so translators do not need to copy and paste or re-type

To prevent glossaries or terminology databases from getting too large or cluttered, many localization agencies separate their terminology databases in the four types that are described in the beginning of this section: operating environment glossaries, client glossaries, project glossaries and software glossaries.

4.1 Glossary Tools

Because most terminology lookup features are required within a translation memory system, many TM systems come with integrated terminology managers. Below you will find some examples of terminology management applications used, some of which are integrated in TM systems.

4.1.1 Lingo Translator's Assistant

Lingo offers a way to speed up the time-consuming task of creating, consulting and managing bilingual translation glossaries. Glossaries once created can be consulted using a dedicated search function. Glossaries can be imported and exported, and are compatible with any Windows word processor.

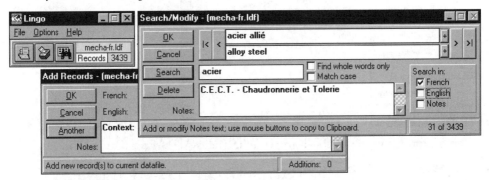

There is also a special Microsoft Glossary Converter available that automatically imports Microsoft's CSV glossaries.

For more information about Lingo and the Microsoft Glossary Converter, visit the Julia Emily Software Web site at ourworld.compuserve.com/homepages/SAbbo.

4.1.2 Trados MultiTerm

MultiTerm is a database program that lets you create, manage and present terminology. For each English term, or concept, you can add equivalents in up to 20 languages. The database can be searched in any language direction. Searches support wildcards and fuzzy matching.

Apart from equivalents, you can also enter a variety of user-defined text and attribute fields or graphics in the records. Records can be cross-referenced, imported and exported, and shared over a network.

MultiTerm can be used in combination with Trados Translator's Workbench. It will automatically display translations of words found in a sentence that is fed into translation memory. For more information about Translator's Workbench, refer to the Trados Translator's Workbench section on page 136.

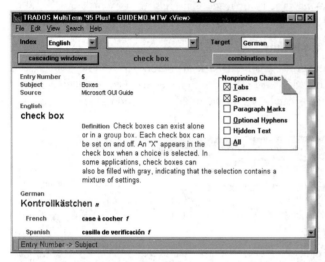

For more information about MultiTerm, visit the Trados Web site at www.trados.com.

4.1.3   Wordwork Glossary Maker

Wordwork Glossary Maker is a freeware tool with which you can create glossaries by inserting text, or by importing glossaries that have been created in other applications. You can search and replace text in any glossary field.

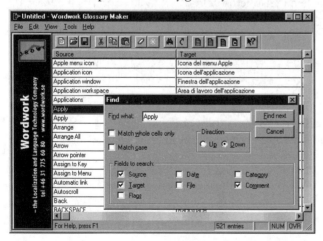

For more information about Wordwork Glossary Maker, visit the Wordwork Web site at www.wordwork.se.

4.1.4   Avalon Glossary Assistant

Glossary Assistant is an eight-language glossary containing terms used in the Localization Industry. Avalon supplies the base glossaries, which can be customized and expanded by the users. Avalon updates the glossaries regularly and makes these glossaries available to their customers.

The Glossary Assistant's interface is very basic and easy to use. The glossary tab shows you the searchable list of terms, the Options tab enables you to add terms to the list.

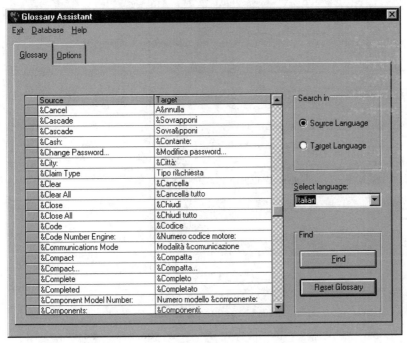

A Glossary Assistant database can be shared over a network, so different users can work with the same glossary, both searching and adding.

For more information about the Glossary Assistant, visit the Avalon Technologies Ltd. Web site at www.freeyellow.com/members/lingualizer.

4.1.5   Atril TermWatch

TermWatch is an application that lets you access terminology databases from any Windows application. You can define key combinations that, when pressed, will look up the selected word in the terminology database and paste the target term into the calling application, or copy the target term to the clipboard, or present all matches in a table in the Déjà Vu translation memory system.

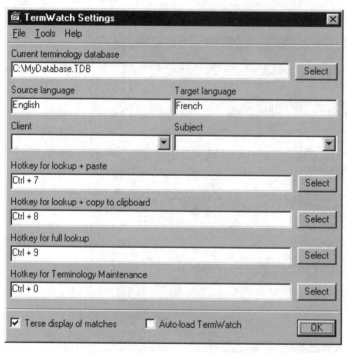

To import, export, create and maintain terminology databases, you need the Terminology Maintenance utility, which is installed with the Déjà Vu translation memory system.

For more information about Déjà Vu and Terminology Maintenance, refer to the Atril Déjà Vu section on page 147 or visit the Atril Web site at www.atril.com.

4.1.6   STAR TermStar

TermStar is a multilingual Terminology Management System that runs under Microsoft Windows.

TermStar is part of the Transit translation memory system. For more information about Transit, refer to the STAR Transit section on page 151.

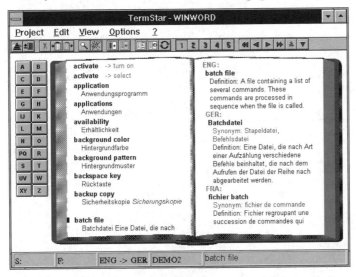

For more information about TermStar, visit the STAR Web site at www.star-ag.ch.

4.1.7   The Translation Assistant

The Translation Assistant is a tool by Language Partners International that offers a full range of dictionary management and lookup features that work with any single-byte language.

There are two look-up functions, allowing you to either type in a word you are looking up in the search box or to paste it in directly from your work environment. TTA has powerful lookup and import/export features.

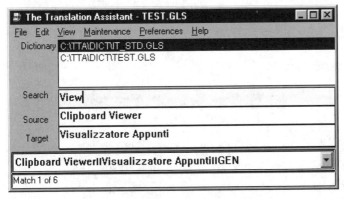

For more information about the Translation Assistant, visit the Language Partners Web site at www.languagepartners.com/translation.assistant.htm.

5 Standard Terminology

5.1 Keyboard Key Names

English	French	Italian	German	Spanish
Alt	Alt	Alt	Alt	Alt
Backspace	Retour arrière	Backspace	Rücktaste	Retroceso
Caps Lock	Verr maj	Bloc Maiusc	Feststelltaste	Bloq mayús
Ctrl (Control)	Ctrl	Ctrl	Strg	Ctrl
Del (Delete)	Suppr	Canc	Entf	Supr
End	Fin	Fine	Ende	Fin
Enter	Entrée	Invio	Eingabetaste	Entrar
Esc (Escape)	Echap	Esc	Esc	Esc
Home	Orig	Home	Pos1	Inicio
Ins (Insert)	Inser	Ins	Einfg	Ins
Num Lock	Verr num	Bloc Num	Num	Bloq Num
Pause	Pause	Pausa	Pause	Pausa
PgDn	Pg suiv	Pggiù	Bild-ab	Av Pág
PgUp	Pg préc	Pgsu	Bild-auf	Re Pág
Print Screen	Impr écran	Stamp	Druck	Impr pant
Scroll Lock	Arrêt défil	Bloc scorr	Rollen	Bloq Despl
Shift	Maj	Maiusc	Umschalt	Mayús
Spacebar	Barre espace	Barra spaziatrice	Leertaste	Barra espaciadora
Tab	Tabulation	Tab	Tab	Tab

5.2 Readme File Names

	MS-DOS	Windows	Macintosh
English	README.TXT	Readme.wri	ReadMe
French	LISEZMOI.TXT	Lisezmoi.wri	Ouvrez-moi
Italian	LEGGIMI.TXT	Leggimi.wri	Leggimi
German	LIESMICH.TXT	Info.wri	Bitte lesen
Spanish	LEAME.TXT	Leame.wri	Léame

Appendix B:
Localization Resources

In this chapter, you will find information about localization resources that are available today, both online and printed.

T he Internet has become an invaluable source of information for translators and localizers. In the following sections, you will find address information of Web sites that could provide you with useful information about localization, Internet newsgroups and mailing lists that focus on translation and localization, and a list of currently available publications.

Finally, the end of this appendix contains a list of some of the companies that are currently dedicated to translation and localization services.

1 Web Sites

1.1.1 The Localisation Resources Center

The LRC site can be found at lrc.ucd.ie. The Localisation Resources Centre is the focus point and the research and support center for the localization industry in Ireland.

The LRC site contains the latest news from the localization world, viewable versions of presentations given at LRC/SLIG meetings, and a Tools Library.

1.1.2 The Software Localisation Interest Group

The SLIG site can be found at lrc.ucd.ie/SLIG/SLIGmainFR.html. SLIG is an Irish Interest Group for all parties involved in software localization.

The SLIG site contains information about the SLIG Working Groups for Tools, Terminology, Training and Education, and Multimedia.

1.1.3   The Localisation Industry Standards Association

The LISA site can be found at www.lisa.org. LISA cooperates with industry partners to provide professional support for the development of localization production standards.

The LISA site contains information about LISA members and membership application, LISA forums and workshops, the LISA newsletter, and several links to other localization-related Web sites.

1.1.4   The Silicon Valley Localization Forum

The SVL Forum can be found at www.tgpconsulting.com. The localization forum is maintained by Tiziana Perinotti's TGP Consulting. The site aims to provide information about multilingual software development and testing, international documentation and marketing issues.

The site contains the latest news about localization technology and tools, conferences and seminars, and links to numerous articles and books about software localization and translation.

1.1.5   The Translator's Home Companion

The Translator's Home Companion is a source of information for translators, interpreters, and localizers. It contains links to international news services, information resources for trans7lators on the Internet, translation organizations, online dictionaries and glossaries, and much more. The Translator's Home Companion can be found at www.lai.com/companion.html.

The site is sponsored and maintained by Language Automation, Inc (www.lai.com) and The Northern California Translator's Association (www.ncta.org).

1.1.6   Translation, Theory and Technology

Translation, Theory and Technology (TTT.org) is a Web site maintained by the Translation Research Group of Brigham Young University's Department of Linguistics. The site provides information about language theory and technology, particularly relating to translation. The Translation, Theory and Technology home page can be found at www.ttt.org.

1.1.7   International Webmasters Association Language Center

The Language Center was established by IWA to promote the internationality of the World Wide Web. The IWA Language Center site contains a lot of information about multilingual Web site creation and links to related sites.

The IWA Language Center Web site can be found at www.iwanet.org/languagecentre.

2   Newsgroups

A newsgroup is a posted discussion group on Usenet, a worldwide network of newsgroups.

Newsgroups are organized into subject hierarchies, with the first few letters of the newsgroup name indicating the major subject category and sub-categories represented by a subtopic name. Many subjects have multiple levels of subtopics.

Users can post to existing newsgroups, respond to previous posts, and create new newsgroups. Newsgroups can be accessed using newsgroup readers, which are included with most web browsers.

2.1.1   sci.lang.translation

Sci.lang.translation is a newsgroup that has existed since December 1994. It is a meeting place for translators and interpreters, and for all those who need their services or are just curious about anything to do with these professions. The group provides a forum for those interested in the problems, issues and concerns of translators/interpreters.

Examples of topics appropriate to this group are automated translation software; translation methods; membership of professional bodies; accreditation of professional translators/interpreters; international standards for translators/interpreters; discussion of dictionaries for a given language pair; software for displaying foreign character sets; translation requests for a given language pair; reviews of translated works; and training and education of translators/interpreters.

2.1.2 sci.lang.translation.marketplace

This newsgroup is meant for advertisements from translators and translation companies offering their services and from individuals and firms looking for translators.

2.1.3 comp.os.ms-windows.programmer.winhelp

In this newsgroup, items related to developing Windows Help, HTML Help and Multimedia Viewer files and applications are discussed.

2.1.4 comp.software.international

This newsgroup discusses the development, use and localization of multilingual software.

2.1.5 microsoft.public.win32.programmer.international

This is one of Microsoft's newsgroups, that focusses on international issues in 32-bit programming for Windows.

3 Mailing Lists

Mailing lists are a way of discussing some specific subject using e-mail. You can broadcast your own message to all members of a mailing list by sending it to the computer known as the list server. There are thousands of mailing lists devoted to subjects of entertainment, academia, business, and more.

3.1.1 www-international@w3.org

This is a mailing list about developing, internationalization, localization and multilingualism for the Web.

To subscribe, send the line SUBSCRIBE in the body of an e-mail message to www-international-request@w3.org. To unsubscribe, send the line UNSUBSCRIBE to the same e-mail address.

3.1.2 lantra-l: Interpreting and translation

This is a mailing list for translators and interpreters, and other people interested in languages. It also contains useful information for localizers.

To subscribe, send the line SUB LANTRA-L *your name* in the body of an e-mail message to listserv@segate.sunet.se. Please note that there are many messages every day. If you do not want to download numerous mail messages, it is also possible to view and search the message archives at segate.sunet.se/archives/LANTRA-L.html. To unsubscribe, send the line UNSUB LANTRA-L *Your Name* to the same e-mail address.

3.1.3   insoft-l: Software Internationalisation

Topics discussed on this list include techniques for developing new software; techniques for converting existing software; internationalization tools; announcements of internationalized public domain software; announcements of foreign-language versions of commercial software; calls for papers; conference announcements; and references to documentation-related to the internationalization of software.

To subscribe, send the line SUBSCRIBE INSOFT-L *your e-mail address* in the body of an e-mail message to insoft-l@magellan.iquest.com.

3.1.4   catmt: Computer Aided Translation and Machine Translation

The CATMT list hosts discussions regarding Computer Aided Translation and Machine Translation software. It is provided by Atril to the translator community.

To subscribe, send the line SUBSCRIBE CATMT in the body of an e-mail message to majordomo@atril.com.

3.1.5   LanguageTech News

LanguageTech News features the latest news for language technology and multilingual computing. It is prepared from materials compiled by Seth Thomas Schneider for the Language Technology Research Center and Multilingual Computing & Technology.

To subscribe, send the line SUB NEWS-L *your name & organization* in the body of an e-mail message to listserv@multilingual.com.

4 Magazines and Newsletters

The following section contains some general info on magazines and newsletters that cover localization subjects. Most magazines are printed publications, but some of them are also available in online format on the Internet.

4.1.1   Multilingual Communications & Computing

Multilingual is a magazine that focusses on translation localization services and technologies. Topics include internationalization, localization, global software development, and distribution.

Multilingual Computing, Inc.
319 North First Avenue
Sandpoint, Idaho 83864 USA
Tel: +1 208 263-8178
Fax: +1 208 263-6310

For more information about Multilingual, please visit www.multilingual.com or send an e-mail to info@multilingual.com.

4.1.2   Language International

Language International is a bimonthly "magazine for the language professions". It contains business and general news from the language industry, and sections on localization and language technology, language management, tools and resources, and language training.

John Benjamins Publishing Company
P.O. Box 75577
1070 AN Amsterdam, The Netherlands

For more information about Language International, visit www.language-international.com or send an e-mail to language.international@benjamins.nl.

4.1.3   Localisation Ireland

Localisation Ireland is a publication of the Localisation Resources Centre in Ireland. It is freely distributed in printed form to everybody on the LRC/SLIG mailing list.

Each issue of this regular publication is sponsored by a leading localisation vendor and freelance journalists write feature articles. Localisation Ireland features a special theme per issue and standard columns such as feature article and interview with sponsor; industry news (company mergers, new arrivals); people and job profiles; tools and automation

To subscribe to this list, visit the LRC Web site at lrc.ucd.ie. From this site, electronic versions of the newsletter in PDF format can be downloaded.

4.1.4   LISA Newsletter

The LISA Newsletter is published four times a year and includes general information about the localization industry, special projects initiated by LISA, and announcements.

For more information, visit the LISA Web site at www.lisa.org.

4.1.5   Language Today

Language Today is a magazine which is available both in printed and online format. It contains information on a range of language-related topics, and is aimed at translators, interpreters, terminologists, lexicographers, and technical writers.

Praetorius Limited
128 Derby Road, Long Eaton
Nottingham, NG10 4ER, United Kingdom

The online edition of Language Today can be found at www.logos.it/language_today.

4.1.6   The DevILE Gazette

The DevILE Gazette is an online newsletter by International Language Engineering (ILE). It focusses on new tools and technologies in the localization industry.

The DevILE Gazette van be found at www.ile.com/tools/news.htm.

5 Books

As mentioned in the preface, there are many publications about software internationalization. These books are mainly aimed at software developers in the United States that want to enable their software for use in other countries.

The books that are listed below contain information that is not only interesting for people involved in *internationalization*, but also for those in *localization*.

5.1.1   Software Internationalization and Localization

Authors: E.Uren, R.Howard, T.Perinotti
Publisher: Van Nostrand Reinhold, New York, N.Y, 1993
ISBN: 0-442-01498-8

5.1.2   Internationalization: Developing Software for Global Markets

Authors: T. Luong, J. Lok, D. Taylor, K. Driscoll
Publisher: John Wiley & Sons, New York, N.Y, 1995
ISBN: 0-471-07661-9

5.1.3   Developing International Software – For Windows 95 and NT

Author: Nadine Kano
Publisher: Microsoft Press, Redmond, WA, 1995
ISBN: 0-55615-840-8

5.1.4   Guide to Macintosh Software Localization

Author: Apple Computer Inc.
Publisher: Addison-Wesley Publishing Company, Reading, MA, 1992
ISBN: 0-20-160856-1

5.1.5   The GUI Guide: International Terminology for Windows

Author: Microsoft Corporation
Publisher: Microsoft Press, Redmond, WA, 1993
ISBN: 1-55615-538-7

5.1.6   Writing Localizable Software for the Macintosh

Author: D.R.Carter
Publisher: Addison-Wesley Publishing Company, Reading, MA, 1991
ISBN: 0-201-57013-0

6 Companies

6.1 Localization Service Providers

The following list of localization service providers is far from complete. Only international organizations with worldwide offices and offices with a special reputation in the localization industry are listed. The addresses listed are main offices or headquarters. For a more complete listing of localization vendors, refer to the TGP Consulting home page or the LISA Web site.

6.1.1   Alpnet

4460 South Highland Drive, Suite 100
Salt Lake City, UT 84124
United States
Tel: +1 801 273-6600
Fax: +1 801 273-6610
Web site: www.alpnet.com

6.1.2   Berlitz

15/16 Georges Place
Dun Laoghaire Co. Dublin
Ireland
Tel: +353 1 202 1200
Fax: +353 1 202 1209
Web site: www.berlitz.com

6.1.3   Bowne Global Solutions

10474 Santa Monica Blvd. Suite 404
Los Angeles, CA 90025
United States
Tel: +1 310 446-4666
Fax: +1 310 446-4661
Web site: www.bowneglobal.com

6.1.4   ILE (International Language Engineering)

1600 Range Street
Boulder, CO 80301
United States
Phone: +1 303 447 2363
Fax: +1 303 449 2897
Web site: www.ile.com

6.1.5   ITP (International Translation & Publishing)

The Boulevard
Quinsboro Road
Bray, Co. Wicklow
Ireland
Phone: +353 1 205 0200
Fax: +353 1 276 1062
Web site: www.itp.ie

6.1.6   Lernout & Hauspie

Sint-Krispijnstraat 7
B-8900 Ieper
Belgium
Phone: +32 57 21 9500
Fax: +32 57 20 8489
Web site: www.lhs.com

6.1.7   L10nBridge

950 Winter Street
Waltham, MA 02154
United States
Tel: +1 781 890 6612
Fax: +1 781 890 3122
Web site: www.lionbridge.com

6.1.8   SDL International

Butler House, Market Street
Maidenhead
Berkshire SL6 8AA
United Kingdom
Tel: +44 0 1628 410100
Fax: +44 0 1628 410505
Web site: www.sdlintl.com

6.2 Translation Tools Developers

6.2.1 Software Localization Tools

6.2.1.1 ACCENT SOFTWARE INTERNATIONAL – LOC@LE/GDK

28 Pierre Koening Street
POB 53063
Jerusalem 91530
Israel
Tel: +7 19 576 2503
Fax: +719 576 2604
Web site: www.accentsoft.com

6.2.1.2 MDR TELEMANAGEMENT LIMITED – JARGON

2381 Bristol Circle, Suite B103
Oakville
Ontario L6H 5S9
Canada
Tel: +1 905 829-3461
Fax: +1 905 829-5606
Web site: www.alda.com or www.mdr.com

6.2.1.3 COREL CORP. – CATALYST

Europa House
Harcourt Street
Dublin 2
Ireland
Tel: +353 1 478 2879
Fax: +353 1 478 5965
Web site: catalyst.corel.ie

6.2.1.4 KT INTERNATIONAL, INC – SUPERLINGUIST

20 Westbrook Street
East Hartford, CT 06108
United States
Tel: +1 860 289-0728
Fax: +1 860 289-0379
Web site: www.ktintl.com

6.2.1.5 MATHEMAESTHETICS, INC. – RESORCERER

PO Box 298
Boulder
CO 80306
United States
Tel: +1 303 440 0707
Fax: +1 303 440 0504
Web site: www.mathemaesthetics.com

6.2.1.6 SOFTWARE BUILDERS – APPLOCALIZE

14 Rue JB Clement
93200 Saint-Denis
France
Tel: +33 1 4940 0999
Fax: +33 1 4940 0998
Web site: www.sbuilders.com

6.2.2 Translation Memory Tools

6.2.2.1 ATRIL – DÉJÀ VU

Alonso Saavedra, 3
28033 Madrid
Spain
Tel: +34 1 383 5285
Fax: +34 1 383 5286
Web site: www.atril.com

6.2.2.2 IBM – TRANSLATIONMANAGER

1133 Westchester Avenue
White Plains NY 10604
United States
Tel: +1 770-863-1234
Fax: +1 770-863-3030
Web site: www.ibm.com

6.2.2.3 TRADOS – TRANSLATOR'S WORKBENCH

Hackländerstraße 17
70184 Stuttgart
Germany
Tel: +49 711-168 77-0
Fax: +49 711-168 77-50
Web site: www.trados.com

6.2.3   Machine Translation Tools

6.2.3.1   LANT - LANT@MARK

Research Park Haasrode
Interleuvenlaan 21
B-3001 Leuven
Belgium
Tel : +32 (0)16 40 51 40
Fax : +32 (0)16 40 49 61
Web site: www.lant.com

6.2.3.2   LOGOS

Techmart Building, Suite 238
5201 Great America Parkway
Santa Clara, CA 95054
United States
Tel: +1 408 987 5900
Fax: +1 408 987 6150
Web site: www.logos-ca.com

6.2.3.3   SYSTRAN

7855 Fay Avenue, Suite 300
La Jolla, CA 92037
United States
Tel: +1 619 459 6700
Fax: +1 619 459 8487
Web site: www.systransoft.com

Index

Accelerator Keys 18
Accent GDK 40
Accent Software International 300
Adobe Acrobat 129
    Distiller 131
    PDF Writer 130
Alpnet 152, 298
Amptran 47, 150, 280
Analyzing Received Material 260
Animated GIF 213
App Studio .... *See* Microsoft App Studio
Apple Developer Connection 229, 237, 284
Apple Glossaries 283
Apple Guide 242
    Compiling 244
    Guide Maker 95, 244
    Image Resources 99
    Introduction 93
    Testing 245
    Translatable Resources 97
    Translation 94
AppleGlot 50, 65, 230, 281
    Extracting Text 230
    Updating Software 233
AppLocalize 38, 47, 301
Atril 301
Atril Déjà Vu 47, 147
    Documentation 149
    Help 149
    Software 147
Atril TermWatch 147, 288
Avalon Glossary Assistant 287
BBEdit 66
Berlitz 219, 298
Bitmap Editing 170, 223
Books 297
Borland 248

Borland Resource Workshop .14, 27, 34, 156, 169
Bowne Global Solutions 298
Browse Sequence 79, 196
Bug Reports 181
Build Environment 34, 96, 155, 260
Captivate 241
Capture Professional 186
Catalyst .... *See* Corel Catalyst
Checking Hot Keys 169
Client Glossaries 278
Client Validation 269
CNT Files 73, 75, 84, 189, 190, 199, 206, 211
Collage Complete 185
Collateral Material 5, 122
    PageMaker 125
    QuarkXPress 122
Comment Delimiters 26
Communication 273
Companies 298
Compatibility Test 175, 180
Compiling
    Apple Guide 244
    HTML Help 221
    Software 161
    Windows Help 191
Components
    Documentation 4
    Online Help 4
    Software 4
Computer-aided translation tools 133
Concatenated Strings 24
Control Codes 22
Control Keys 19
Corel Catalyst 47, 156, 158, 160, 169
    170, 256, 280
Corel Corp. 300

Cross-references
    FrameMaker 113
    Word 118
Definition
    Globalization 3
    Internationalization 1
    Localization 2
    Translation 3
Déjà Vu .... See Atril Déjà Vu
Delivery Test 174, 180
Delphi 248
DevILE Gazette 296
Dialog boxes 10
Display Configuration
    Macintosh 239
    Windows 183, 186
Doc-To-Help 193
Documentation
    Collateral Material .... See Collateral Material
    Content 106
    Deliverables 104
    Fonts 105
    General Instructions 107
    Graphics 106
    Introduction 103
    Manuals .... See Manuals
    One-to-one Page Translation 106
    Platform and Version 104
    Preparation 104
    Printer Driver 105
    Proofreading 127
    Screen Captures 105
    Style Sheet 104
    Table Of Contents and Index 106
    Testing Source Files 106
    Translation Memory Tools 107
DTP 259, 271
Dynamic Localization Tools
    Jargon 47
    Super Linguist 49
Editing 268
Enablement 2
Engineering

Delphi 248
HTML Files 211
Java 249
Macintosh Help 242
Macintosh Software 223
Visual Basic 247
Windows Help 188
Windows Software 156
ETP 274
Eurolang Optimizer 153
Exposure Pro 241
External Repetitions 135
FIGS 6
File Management 12, 13
Fixed Names 23
Flash-it 240
FrameMaker
    Book Files 116
    Cross-references 113
    File Setup 109
    Headers and Footers 110
    Index Markers 111
    Opening Files 109
    Spell Checking Translations 115
    Translating Files 110, 117, 122, 125
Functionality Test 174, 179, 238, 270
Fuzzy Matching 134
Gantt charts 263
GIF Files 93, 184, 213
    Animated 213
Globalink Power Translator 135
Glossaries
    Tools 285
    Translation 259, 264
    Types 277
Gold Master 180
Graphics
    Editing 186, 241
    Transparency 213
Guide Maker 95, 244
Headers and Footers
    FrameMaker 110
    Word 117

Helicon Translator 249

Help .... *See* Online Help

HelpQA 189, 207, 256

Hijaak Pro 186

Hot Keys 18, 23, 169, 207, 279

HPJ Files 80, 190

    Button Names 82

    Copyright Info 83

    Titles 80

HTML Files 211

    File Format Overview 87

    Introduction 86

    Language Identification 214

    Language Tags 214

    Testing 219

    Translation 88

HTML Help 220

    Compiling 221

    Testing 222

HtmlQA 215

IBM 301

IBM TranslationManager46, 77, 90, 142, 173, 301

    Documentation 146

    Help 146

    Software 142

ILE 155, 214, 250, 296, 298

Index Markers

    FrameMaker 111

    PageMaker 126

    QuarkXPress 123

    Translation 120

    Word 118

Innoview Multilizer Suite 248, 249

Inprise 248

Installer VISE 69, 225

Installers

    Creating 171

    Installer VISE 225

    InstallShield 171

    Macintosh 69, 225

InstallShield 171

ITP 299

IWA 293

Jargon 47

Java 249

    Applets 249

    JDK 249

    Resource Bundles 250

Joust 152

Keyboard Key Names 290

KT International, Inc 300

L10nBridge 299

Language International 296

Language Today 296

LANT 302

LANT@MARK 135

Layered Graphics 93, 157, 213, 255

Length Restrictions 23

Lernout & Hauspie 299

Lingo Translator's Assistant 285

Lingscape MultLang 249

Linguistic Test 174, 178

LinkBot 214

LISA 292

LISA Newsletter 296

Loc@le 41

Locale Codes and IDs 165

Localisation Industry Standards Association ... 292

Localisation Ireland 296

Localisation Resources Center 291

Localization

    Future 6

    History 6

    Service Providers 7

Localization Kit 265

Localization Process 258

Localization Resources 291

Logos 302

Logos Translation System 135

Lotus Glossaries 284

LRC 291

Machine Translation 134

Macintosh

    Apple Guide 93

    AppleGlot 65

    Help 100, 242

Installers 69
Localization Tools 50
PowerGlot 67
ResEdit 52
Resorcerer 59
Software 50, 223
Software Preparation 52
Software Resource Types 50
Translating Software 52
Macintosh Help Files 100
Macintosh Programmer's Workshop ..... *See* MPW
Magazines 295
Mailing Lists 294
Manuals
FrameMaker 109
Software References 108
Style 108
Word 117
Market Developments 6
Mathemaesthetics, Inc 65, 301
MDR Telemanagement Limited 300
Menus 11, 17, 30, 54, 60
MFC Components 166
Microsoft App Studio 27
Dialog Boxes 28
Menus 30
Other Resource Types 32
Strings 31
Microsoft Developer Network .... *See* MSDN
Microsoft Developer Studio 14, 32, 156, 160
163, 165
Microsoft Glossaries 283
Microsoft GUI Guide 19, 277
Microsoft Help Compiler 75, 190, 191
Microsoft Hotspot Editor (SHED.EXE) 195
Microsoft Visual Studio 27
MLV 7
Mnemonic Keys 18
MPW 50, 229
MSDN 19, 155, 176, 191, 200, 283
MSG Browser 283
Multilingual 295
Multilingual Glossaries 283

Multilingual Localization Vendor 7
Multiple Language Versions
MacOS 237
Windows 3.1 175
Windows 95 175
MultiTerm .... *See* Trados MultiTerm
Nadine Kano 155, 297
NetGlos 284
Newsgroups 293
Newsletters 295
Novell Glossaries 284
Online Documentation 129
Adobe Acrobat PDF 129
Online Help
HTML Files 86
Macintosh Apple Guide 93
Macintosh Help Files 100
Windows 72
Operating Environment Glossary 277
OVUM 7
PageMaker
File Setup 125
Index Markers 126
Opening Files 125
Spell Checking Translations 127
Translating Files 125
Paint Shop Pro 32, 170, 184, 185
PDF File Format 129
Post-mortem 259, 272
PowerGlot 50, 67, 235
Preparation 11
Localization Kit 259, 265
Problem Reports 181
Program Files 4, 14, 27
Project Glossaries 278
Project Management
Analysis of Received Material 260
Project Specifications 252
Request for Proposal 252
Request for Quotation 252
Scheduling and Budgeting 261
Project Managers 6, 251
Proofreading Documentation 127

Accuracy and Consistency 128

Cross-references 129

Examples and Screen Captures 128

General Page Layout 128

QA and Delivery 259, 271

QuarkXPress

    File Setup 122

    Index Markers 123

    Opening Files 122

    Spell Checking Translations 124

    Translating Files 123

QuickHelp Compiler 100

Quotations 252

    Components 253

    Documentation 257

    Help 256

    Profile Information 257

    Software 255

    Unit Prices 254

RC Files 157

    Bitmaps 170

    Language Settings 163

    Locale Codes and IDs 165

    MFC Components 166

    Updating 173

    Verstion Stamp 164

RC-WinTrans 46

Readme File Names 290

Readme Files 101

Reference Material 12

ResEdit 52

    Balloon Help 58

    Controls 57

    Dialog Boxes 54

    Images 57

    Menus 54

    Strings 57

    Templates 59

    Version 58

Resizing

    Software 167, 223

Resorcerer 50, 59

    Balloon Help 64

Controls 63

Dialog Boxes 60

Images 63

Menus 60

Strings 62

Version 65

Resource Files 14, 15

    Comment 26

    Dialog Boxes 16

    Extensions 15

    File Contents 15

    File Format 15

    Menus 17

    Strings 21

    Version Info 24

Resource Localization Tools 37

    Accent GDK 40

    AppLocalize 38

    Comparison Table 47

    Corel Catalyst 37

    Microsoft RLToolset 45

    RC-WinTrans 46

Resource-only DLL 8, 14

Revision 268

RFP 252

RFQ 252

RLToolset 45

Robohelp 193

RTF Files 76, 190, 194

    Footnotes 78

    Formatting 197

    Graphics 80

    Jumps And Popups 77

RTFMod 197

Satellite DLL 14

Scheduling and Budgeting 261

Screen Captures 183

    Cursors 184

    Display Configuration 183

    Editing 241

    File Format 184

    File Formats 240

    Macintosh 239

Preparation...183, 239
Testing 186, 241
Utilities...185, 240
SDL International...299
Service Providers 7
SHED.EXE 195
Shortcut Keys 19
Show Dialog Boxes 238
Silicon Valley Localization Forum...................292
Simship...261
Single worldwide binary....................................8
SiteBoss 214
SLIG 291
SnagIt 186
Snapz 241
Software
    Resizing 223
    Testing 238
    Windows...14
Software Builders 301
Software Consistency Check............................269
Software Glossaries 279
    Macintosh..281
    Windows..279
Software Localisation Interest Group 291
Software Localization Tools 37
Space Restrictions..27
Spell Checking Translations
    FrameMaker...115
    Word..119
S-Tagger 141
STAR TermStar...288
STAR Transit..151
Status Report 264
STF File Format 141
Strings 11, 21
    Concatenated Strings...................................24
    Control codes 22
    Fixed Names 23
    Hot Keys..23
    Length Restrictions 23
    variables..21
Structured Project Management.....................274

Super Linguist 49
System Commander.......................................178
System Picker 237
Systran 135, 302
Technology...8
Terminology..277
Terminology Management...............................284
    Multiterm 136
    TermStar 151
    Termwatch 147
Terminology Resources 282
Terminology Setup 264
TermStar 151
Test-Compiling
    Help..188
    Software..156
Testing
    Apple Guide 245
    Delivery Test 174, 180
    Functionality Test................................174, 179
    Help..........................199, 209, 259, 271
    HTML Help...222
    Linguistic Test.....................................174, 178
    Macintosh Software....................................236
    Preparation..174, 236
    Software..........................173, 238, 259, 270
TMX..136
Tracking Sheet 264
Trados 301
Trados MultiTerm 285
Trados Translator's Workbench 46, 134, 136
    160, 173, 286
    Documentation...141
    Help..140
    Software..137
    S-Tagger 141
Trans Web Express..217
Translating Indexes 120
Translation...268
Translation Assistant.....................................289
Translation Memory
    Alignment 134
    Exchange 136

Fuzzy Matching.. 134
In Localization.. 135
Introduction... 134
vs. Machine Translation............................... 134
Translation Memory tools................................ 133
Amptran... 150
Atril Déjà Vu.. 147
Eurolang Optimizer...................................... 153
IBM TranslationManager............................. 142
STAR Transit... 151
Trados Translator's Workbench.................. 136
TSS/Joust.. 152
Winalign... 136
XL8 TransPro... 153
TranslationManager See IBM TranslationManager
Translator's Home Companion....................... 292
Transparency.. 213
TSS/Joust.. 152
TTT.org.. 293
Unicode.. 8, 165, 214
Updates.. 270
Updating
Program Files.. 173
RC Files... 173
Software.. 173, 233
Variables.. 21
Verifier... 238
Version Info... 24
Version Stamp... 25
Visual Basic............................... 18, 156, 247
Visual C++.. 168
Web Sites.. 211
Folder Structure.. 211
Images... 213
Localization.. 212
Testing Localized... 214
What's This? Help... 206
WhippleWare.. 247
WinBoot.. 176
Windows Help.. 72, 188
Bitmaps... 194
Browse Sequence.. 196

Character Set.. 198
CNT Files..................................... 84, 85, 206
Compilation... 75
Compiling... 191
Context-sensitive help.................................. 205
Custom Buttons or Menus............................ 207
Engineering.. 188
Formatting.. 197
General Page Layout..................................... 201
Graphics... 194
HelpQA... 207
Hotspots... 194
HPJ Files.. 80
Hypergraphics.. 194
Introduction.. 73
Jumps... 204
Navigation.. 73
Preparing.. 188
Project Statistics.. 200
Search Keyword List...................................... 205
Sort Order... 198
Test-Compiling... 188
Testing.. 199
Translation... 75
Window Titles... 204
Word
Cross-references... 118
Generating TOC and Index.......................... 120
Headers and Footers.................................... 117
Index Markers... 118
Opening Files.. 117
Spell Checking Translations........................ 119
Translating Files... 117
Word Counts
CNT Files... 190
Documentation.. 257
Help.. 256
PDF Files.. 257
Software.. 158, 255
Windows Help... 189
Wordwork Glossary Maker............................ 286
XL8 TransPro... 153